Contents

KU-481-580

Abbreviations

ACC	Assistant Chief Constable
ASU	Active Service Unit
ATO	Ammunitions Technical Officer
BRC	Belfast Regional Control
C6	Station Occurrences, Reports and Complaints Book
CID	Criminal Investigation Department
CID50	Intelligence input document
CIS	Criminal Intelligence Section
CT	Converted Terrorist
CVI	Central Vehicle Index
DMP	District Mobile Patrol
DPP	Director of Public Prosecutions
DRU	Divisional Research Unit
HMSUS	Headquarters Mobile Support Units
IPLO	Irish People's Liberation Organisation
IRA	Irish Republican Army
LVF	Loyalist Volunteer Force
MSU	Mobile Support Unit
PIRA	Provisional IRA
RIU	Regional Intelligence Unit
RMP	Royal Military Police
RUC	Royal Ulster Constabulary
SB50S	Intelligence input forms
SDC	Sub Divisional Commander
SDO	Station Duty Officer
SMG	Submachine-gun
SOCO	Scenes of Crime Officers
SSU	Special Support Unit
TCG	Tactical Co-ordination Group
TSU	Technical Support Unit
UDA	Ulster Defence Association
UDR	Ulster Defence Regiment
UFF	Ulster Freedom Fighters
UVF	Ulster Volunteer Force
UWC	Ulster Workers' Council
VCPS	Vehicle Checkpoints
VRM	Vehicle Registration Mark
WDA	Woodvale Defence Association
WPC	Woman Police Constable
YCV	Young Citizens Volunteers

Acknowledgements

I salute John Stalker and Sir John Stevens for their tireless determination in the pursuit of the truth. It is a measure of their professionalism that both were able to enter a very sinister arena and, despite extreme obstruction, uncover an unpalatable truth.

Within weeks of my retirement in 2001, I found myself pursued by investigative journalists. I will be forever grateful for the platform afforded to me by Ulster Television's "Insight" programme, broadcast in May 2001. Thanks go to the producer Justin O'Brien and his presenter Chris Moore, who was later to become a personal friend. Thanks are also due to Trevor Birney, Stephen Riley, Darwin Templeton and Ruth O'Reilly of UTV for their encouragement and support.

Special thanks must go to the groundbreaking author Martin Dillon, who led the charge and broke through the seemingly impenetrable armour of the Special Branch with his book, *The Dirty War*. He has also been on hand to lend his support and to afford me invaluable advice on this project.

Thanks are also due to Hugh Jordan, Donna Carton, and Jim and Lindy McDowell, all of whom listened tirelessly to me.

I would also like to thank John Ware of the BBC's "Panorama" programme. I was impressed at how he sought corroboration for every allegation I made. His contribution to uncovering the sinister hand of the Special Branch that guided Loyalist and, arguably, Republican murder squads in the controversial programme "A Licence to Kill" was invaluable. My thanks also go to the BBC's "Spotlight" programme's Kevin Magee, who also gave me advice.

I would also like to express my deepest gratitude to John Swift, a newfound friend. He led me out of the darkness and into the light. He made no judgements and made no criticism of anything that I had to say. John was also a member of the RUC. He spent a lot of his service in the Special Branch. He identified with me, in that he too has no time for the men he so eloquently called the "turkeys" of the RUC

Special Branch. John epitomises all that was good and decent about the majority of men and women who served honourably in the RUC Special Branch.

My thanks to the many others who have helped and encouraged me to write this book, including Ken and Valerie Hayes, Ian and Carrie Forbes, Margaret Dunne, Bobbie Hanvey, Johnnie and Charlotte Walker, Oliver and Pat Phillips, Liam Clarke, Kathy Johnston, my sister Louise Cooper and her husband John.

I would like to thank Andrew and Peggy Sweeney for typing up and checking my long narrative. Nothing was too much trouble for Peggy and I valued her contribution.

To everyone at Gill & Macmillan in Dublin for all their help, including their Publishing Director Fergal Tobin, and Susan Dalzell, my editor and teacher, for her help and encouragement.

Finally, I would like to express my sincere appreciation to all those persons, men and women alike, who came forward voluntarily and gave the crucial information to the Police that allowed us to save life after life. The citizens of this province owe these unsung heros a great debt. I can publicly reassure them that I will maintain their anonymity. I have no wish, however, to protect the anonymity of murderers who continue to hide behind a Police protection that should never have been afforded to them in the first place.

JOHNSTON BROWN
BELFAST SEPTEMBER 2005

Chapter 1
Introduction

The attack was so sudden, so unexpected and so brutal that I was not able to do anything about it. I had walked into it. I had failed to anticipate the danger signs. I would now pay the price for my lack of awareness.

Stationed in Newtownabbey, I had just under three years' service in the Royal Ulster Constabulary, Northern Ireland's former Police Service, and less than eight months in the Criminal Investigation Department (CID). Such sudden attacks upon us were commonplace: they were one of the many pitfalls of policing our violent society.

It was just before midnight when the attack occurred. In a split second, my assailant had lifted me clear off the ground and thrown me against the wall with all the strength he could muster. The blow to my head as I hit the wall was so violent that I was momentarily stunned. It also caused me to experience what happened next as if in slow motion. The pain was searing, almost unbearable, as blow after blow rained down upon me from my attacker's fists and feet. He was a tall, well-built man some twenty years my senior. I attempted to ward off the blows, but to little or no effect.

I can recall exactly what happened as if it were yesterday. I would physically revisit the scene from time to time during my service in the Police. I also have a tendency, even today, to revisit it mentally, to dwell on it in spite of myself. The sudden and treacherous nature of the assault is something I will never forget.

Even though the room was dark, I was able to look into my assailant's hate-filled eyes. I was so close to him that I could smell his foul breath and the stench of alcohol. I was aware of blood flowing from my nose. My mouth was filling with blood from internal cuts as my flesh was smashed against my teeth. I had bitten my tongue. I was terrified of losing consciousness as I felt myself slipping towards the floor.

My personal issue firearm, a Walther 9 mm pistol, was nestled snugly in my black serge shoulder holster, tucked into my left armpit. I had considered trying to get to my gun to use it in self-defence. That was exactly why I had been issued with the handgun in the first place: so that I would be able to produce it and use it as a means to extricate myself from such life-threatening situations as this.

I hung onto every word as my assailant screamed profanities at me. There was no mistaking the absolute venom in his speech. I then caught sight too of his accomplice, standing nearby keeping watch in case any other Police officer should come upon the scene. They were taking no chances: there were to be no witnesses to this assault. I was surprised to see my attacker's accomplice panic and do all he could to bring the assault to an end.

"He has had enough," he shouted to my assailant repeatedly.

Then it was over as suddenly as it had begun. They departed from the scene, leaving me sore and bloodied. I tried to stand but I couldn't. I had virtually no feeling in my legs due to the constant kicking and pummelling to which I had been subjected. I lay there on the ground and watched the perpetrators' hasty retreat. Then the door slammed shut behind them.

After a short time, I was able to get to my feet. I walked unsteadily to the men's toilets next door. I had been lucky. As attacks go, it was not the worst that I would suffer in my 30 years as a Police officer in the RUC.

But this was different. This was bizarre. My assailant and his accomplice were not thugs from some street corner, they were Police officers. They were members of the Royal Ulster Constabulary, just as I was. Worse still, my assailant was a colleague of mine working alongside me in the CID at Newtownabbey RUC Station. (He has since died.) The scene of the attack was the parade room of the station itself. As for the date, it is indelibly printed in my brain. It was Friday, 13 December 1974.

Earlier that night I had arrested five suspected members of the outlawed Ulster Volunteer Force (UVF). They had been found to be in possession of two illegally-held loaded handguns. In any other Police Force in the United Kingdom, all right-thinking people would have viewed my actions as commendable.

But this was Northern Ireland at the height of a terrorist campaign and not all things were considered equal. In my naivety, I was to get a rude wake-up call. Soon after the arrests, I had witnessed blatant collusion between certain CID officers and the Monkstown UVF. I had told these officers what I thought of it: they had seen me move to redress the wrongs.

What did I expect, they were to ask me later. Well, I didn't expect to be criminally assaulted by fellow Police officers. After the attack, I expected some support from my authorities. None was forthcoming.

I had not endeared myself to the UVF. The punishment I received was meted out by members of the RUC on behalf of the local Monkstown UVF. I stood there in that toilet area next door to the cells, examining my face and the inside of my mouth in a small wooden-framed mirror on the wall. I watched with pain and sadness as the blood flowed from my injuries into the white washhand basin and mingled with the running water. My head was still spinning. I leaned over to splash cold, revitalising water over my face.

I will resign tomorrow, I thought.

Still unsteady on my feet, I held onto both sides of the washhand basin. The blood was flowing freely. I pulled some green paper towels from the dispenser on the wall to try to stem the flow. I felt alone, isolated, no longer knowing whom I could trust.

Slumped over the washhand basin, I couldn't help feeling sorry for myself. Wondering exactly what sort of Police Force I had joined. This was my first encounter with such people in the CID. I had already unintentionally made enemies within the RUC Special Branch, that I knew. But I had not expected to find men of this kind in the ranks of our CID.

As I stood there in the darkness in that little corner of Newtownabbey RUC Station, wondering where to go from there, I could not have known that I was merely scratching the surface of some very sinister elements within the RUC. I could never have imagined then anyway the extent and nature of the depths I was to discover during the years that followed. No-one could have imagined such things. For many, even today, they may defy belief. But everything I am about to relate actually happened to me.

Chapter 2

Into Care

Throughout my life, people have often asked me why I chose a career in the Police. What, they wondered, kept me going in the face of all the dangers and the difficulties I faced, particularly towards the end of my service in the RUC? To understand my outlook on life and what motivated me to join the Royal Ulster Constabulary in the first place, it is helpful perhaps to look back to my formative years and some of the key experiences of my childhood and youth. Apart from one uncle on my mother's side, there was no history of Police service in my family. For reasons that will very quickly become clear, I was driven by a burning desire to deal with the bullies in our society. To put the bad men in jail. It all seemed to me such a simple and straightforward thing to achieve. The very last thing I ever expected was to be obstructed by members of the institution to which I devoted almost 30 years of my life. I did not anticipate that some of the worst difficulties and dangers I would face were to come from within the very organisation of which I was part . . .

I was born on 17 April 1950, in Holywood, Co. Down, the sixth child of Christina and William Brown. My parents had six more children. I have three brothers and eight sisters. The family home was at the top of the Downshire Road in Holywood, Co. Down. My friends in the district were both Protestant and Catholic: my mother had taught us to respect both religions equally. Our family was deprived in relation to material things, but we were certainly not poverty-stricken.

Violence in my home was commonplace. My father was a tyrant, a bully, and at 5'9" and 26 stone in weight, he towered above us. He seemed to actually get some sort of enjoyment from beating us frequently with his leather belt. Hardly a day would pass without a violent outburst from him. He would beat my mother senseless at least two or three times a week. There was always a good reason, it seemed. Even if there weren't one, he would find one. He worked as a chauffeur or as a store man but he was much happier during his long periods of unemployment. Prone to mood swings, his day-to-day temperament was completely unpredictable. He could at times be the nicest guy in the world, but more often than not he would erupt into a frenzy of unprovoked violence. We were terrorised by this bully.

At 5'1" and very slim and lightly built, my mother Christina was no match for my father. He would throw her about like a rag doll. She was a decent, kind and hardworking woman, and our rock in the stormy environment that was our home life. Her maiden name was Johnston. I was the first child to be born with her dark hair and piercing dark eyes, and so it was that I was named Johnston after her.

Growing up in this violent environment was never easy. It was like walking on egg shells. We strove at all times not to do or say anything that would provoke my father. It only took some alleged misdemeanour or misconduct and he would launch a frenzied attack on us. My mother would always intervene, throwing herself between him and the child he was beating. It would make no difference: he would just beat both. "He's just a bully," my mother would repeat over and over again, as she tried to comfort the victim.

Each day was filled with fear and trepidation. Terrified of our father, we children could never be sure that a moment of peace and tranquillity would not be broken by a sudden and unexpected outburst of mindless violence. I felt sorry for my sisters, who would find themselves suddenly being pummelled by his fists or feet, without the slightest warning. The cruelty of the violence was doubly so, perhaps, because it was impossible to predict.

I had to sit quietly as my father beat my mother and sisters, again and again. I wanted to do more but, as a young boy, I was of course physically no match for him. I so much wanted to stop him. I wished my life away. We could do nothing for our poor mother, who would have to wear sunglasses even in winter to hide her bruised and blackened eyes. She would never strike back or press charges for assault against him.

I could do nothing then, but I was determined that some day, I would be able to confront my father and put an end to the constant suffering of my mother and the smaller children.

Some of my earliest childhood memories were of evenings when my parents would be quarrelling, my father screaming at the top of his voice. This was a frequent occurrence. My mother would rush upstairs and get us out of our beds (my younger brothers and I would sleep three to a bed). She would gather us all together in the master bedroom, and we would help her barricade the bedroom door with wardrobes and chests of drawers. Sometimes the bed itself would be used to barricade the door. My father would be outside, swearing and hammering the door with his fists, attempting to force his way in.

On more than one occasion, we would be forced to jump from that first-floor bedroom window onto the lawn in the front garden below. The screaming and the turmoil of the whole situation were absolutely terrifying. So bad that the jump from that window seemed almost inviting at times. Thank God for our good, decent neighbours. Ours was a semi-detached council house and the family next door would be alerted by our screams. Knowing we had no telephone, they would ring the Police on our behalf. On some occasions, we would take refuge in our neighbours' house: they would always take us in and make us welcome. Sometimes we would make our way to my Grandma Johnston's on University Road, Belfast. Again, we would be greeted warmly there, and be able to stay for a day or two enjoying the relative peace and quiet. However, my mother would return home on every occasion, bringing us with her. Father always promised to change, but he never did.

Visits by the local Constabulary to our home were frequent. The flashing blue light on top of the Police car would announce their arrival. They knew exactly how to deal with a bully and they took no nonsense from my father. They would quickly restore calm to the household. We knew the sergeants and constables by name. The local station sergeant, a Sergeant Campbell, terrified my father in particular. Sergeant Campbell was tall and well built, and not in the least afraid of confronting such a bully. But my hero was Constable Vincent McCormick, who would talk to me about his experiences in the Police and, when I was older, would often encourage me to join the Force.

We knew that the arrival of these men would end our suffering. From a very early age, I learned to respect and be grateful for these keepers of the peace, the rank-and-file of the Royal Ulster Constabulary. Their words of encouragement sowed the seeds which would later inspire me to join their number. Throughout my child-hood, with its incessant cycle of violence followed by calm and then the inevitable return of turmoil, the local Police were always there to support us, and never once did they lose their patience. I was deter-mined that when I became a Police officer — and this was one of my very early ambitions — I would treat all people with the same respect and compassion as those officers had shown to us. I was determined too that I would help to keep the peace as they had, and do my best to put society's bully boys back in their place.

One of my earliest memories of unexpected upheaval was in 1956, when I was six years old. My mother had not been well and she was to go into hospital. The first I was aware that there was any problem was when the welfare authorities arrived at our home. We didn't know why they were there, but we knew that it was not a routine visit. We were accustomed to frequent, regular visits from the welfare. They usually called in a little dark van and brought us second-hand clothes or shoes. My favourite welfare visitor was a lady called Miss Lister. She would always help us. We welcomed her visits. I can still see her smiling face in my mind's eye. In later years I made many attempts to trace her within the welfare system to thank her. I only had her maiden name, however, and I was never able to contact her.

On this occasion the welfare officers were in the living room, dis-cussing us openly in our presence. They spoke about where each of us would be going. As if we weren't there. As if we were simply parcels to be despatched elsewhere. We were all listening to what was being said. I think their principal worry was for our welfare during my mother's stay in hospital, when we would otherwise be left alone with our father. There were tears as my mother tried to reassure us. I looked at my younger brothers and sisters, with fear written all over their faces. The scene was horribly upsetting. The younger children were taken away first. I watched as the welfare people, with stern faces, dressed in long coats, escorted them outside to waiting cars. We didn't know when we would see each other again.

Unless you have lived through something like this as a child, it is difficult to describe exactly what effect it has on you. For the first time in my life, I didn't believe my mother. I felt I couldn't trust her. For the first time I had become aware that my parents had no real control over what happened to us once the welfare authorities stepped in. All I knew was that I was destined for a bad boys' home. Yet I had not done anything wrong. It all seemed so unfair.

The two welfare officers came back into the house. The lady called out my name and the names of three of my sisters, who would be with me. My mother hugged us. Her eyes were streaming tears but she knew there was nothing she could do except hug us and try to reassure us that all would be well. I will never forget the walk in the dark from our hallway to the waiting car of the welfare officers. It was that journey into the unknown which filled me with so much dread. I really believed that I would never see my mother or my younger siblings again. I was so glad that Louise and my other two sisters were with me.

The welfare people told us that we were going to a foster home in Ballygowan, Co. Down, to a family called Gibson. We were as quiet as mice as we were taken out to a big black car and driven out of Holywood towards Belfast. The smell of the dark-maroon leather upholstery was overwhelming as I buried my head into the back seat of the car.

When we arrived at our foster home, the welfare man went inside to speak to our new foster parents. The house was sizeable, set back off the road and there was an old horseshoe-shaped gypsy caravan in the side garden. It didn't look like a bad boys' home! As I was taking in my new surroundings, the man returned to the car and ushered us inside the house.

Our new foster mother greeted us and brought us inside. She was a small, plumpish woman with a warm smile. There were two girls around my own age sitting on the floor of the living room in front of a glowing fire. They were watching a black-and-white television. We didn't have a television at home! As I went over and sat down beside them, the programme changed and "Champion the Wonder Horse" came on the screen. I was so enthralled that I didn't even notice the departure of the welfare officers. I was sitting in a strange house with two girls I didn't know and yet I felt strangely at ease.

My foster mother was cooking dinner for us. I sat glued to that screen, eating my dinner from a plate on my knee. There was an atmosphere of peace and calm in this house and I embraced it. It was a welcome respite.

Life in Ballygowan was wonderful. Even though we had to use an outside toilet and walk what seemed like miles to Ballykeagle Primary School each day, we had a great time. We collected eggs from the chicken coops and in the mornings Louise and I would volunteer to run across the fields to the spring and bring back a stainless-steel bucket filled with water.

Our departure from Ballygowan was as sudden and abrupt as our arrival had been. I remember my foster mother's face as we left. The tears were flowing freely down her face and mine as she hugged and kissed me goodbye. She had listened to our horror stories: she knew exactly what type of environment we were returning to. As we left in the same black car we had arrived in, I turned to wave again but the car had already turned the corner and she was out of sight. I never saw my foster mother again but I never forgot her kindness.

Then, when I was eight years old, our family was split up again. Unknown to me, my mother was to go into hospital for some months with her latest pregnancy. Complications meant that her life was in danger. I was to be placed in a welfare home with some of my older sisters. Once again, the move came completely out of the blue. Once more, I was convinced that I must have done something very wrong.

Marmion House was a local authority-managed children's home on the Church Road in Holywood, only a mile from our home. It was a large mansion of a house set in acres of well-maintained gardens. To a small child, it looked like a very forbidding house that first evening as we travelled up the driveway in the car with the welfare officers. By the next day, however, I was beginning to realise that my new temporary abode was not such a bad place after all. We were given a copious breakfast with generous portions of cereal, fried eggs and bacon, the like of which I had never seen at home. They kitted us out in brand new school uniforms, complete with new shoes to replace the old, worn-out ones we had been making do with for so long. There was a large sitting room full of huge settees and easy chairs. The floors of the entire house were covered in carpets. I had only ever seen carpet in my friends' houses—this was unashamed luxury!

Later that morning, we left Marmion House to walk down the Church Road to Holywood Primary School. There were five or six of us. This was exciting, like an adventure. I was enjoying every minute of it so far. I could nearly see my face in my new shoes. My stomach was full. I had a new pullover, new socks, and a new shirt. I was on top of the world. We arrived very quickly at the Church Road entrance to the primary school. It was only a short walk up the leafy, tree-lined avenue at 75 Church Road to the back gate of the school.

My teacher at that time was a dreaded man. We were all frightened of him. He would grab a child by his ear or the locks of his hair and virtually drag him up to the front of the class. It was very painful and humiliating. He would then make a fool of the child in question in front of the rest of the class. He seemed to delight in doing this. I had fallen victim to this man's bullying on a number of occasions. He knew that my parents could not afford a new school uniform every year, and so he habitually made fun of my old clothes. He would refer to them as rags and spin me round and round, encouraging the other children to laugh at me. I was as afraid of this man as I was of my father.

The morning after my first night at Marmion House, I wasn't in class any more than a few minutes when I caught the teacher's eye. I tried to avoid eye contact, hoping he would pick on someone else. Too late! I watched in horror as he rose to his feet and walked to my desk. After a brief pause, he walked around behind me. I knew exactly what was coming next. I couldn't understand what had provoked him. We had not even started the lesson and my homework was in order.

He lifted me to my feet. He took me to the front of the class. He spun me round and round as he addressed the class. He said he was impressed with my new uniform. Such a neat turn-out. Had my parents robbed a bank? The other children were laughing as this man ritually humiliated me. I told him the new clothes were mine. I was proud of them. I told him that they had been given to me by the staff at the home.

"What home?" he asked sharply.

"Marmion House Children's Home," I replied.

He studied me. "You are in Marmion?" he asked.

"Yes, Sir," I replied.

The teacher was non-plussed. For once, he didn't know what to say. This bully who was never usually lost for words. He turned to me and told me abruptly to return to my seat.

During the morning's lessons, I noticed that the teacher was study-ing me. He kept staring and staring at me. I averted my eyes. I did not need another trip to the front of the class. The bell rang, signalling the start of break-time. It was heaven-sent. I got up from my seat and went to leave the classroom.

"Brown, come here," the teacher shouted. He was sitting on the edge of his desk. I walked over to him. "Why are you in Marmion, son?" he asked.

I explained the reasons to him. He asked about my sisters. I explained that two of them were also in the home. He put his hand on my shoulder and looked into my eyes. There were only the two of us in the classroom. Petrified, I waited for the insults to flow.

"Look, I'm sorry about earlier on," he said.

Just at that moment the classroom door swung open, as some of the pupils returned to the classroom. I didn't know what to say.

"Run along now and get your break, Johnston," he said.

I turned and left the room. I was happy as a sandboy. I knew I would have no more trouble with him. I was right. He never bothered me again. In fact, he was always pleasant after that. It was sad, though, to see him turn his bullying attention to another classmate. He was never happier than when he had a pupil out in front of the class in tears, terrorised and humiliated. This was, I suppose, his way of keeping those large, post-war primary school classes in order. The other children behaved well in his class. No-one wanted to be next one up at the front.

When we arrived back at Marmion House after school that day, the staff ensured that we changed and did our homework. Then we were allowed to play outside in the grounds of the home. Those first summer months were wonderful. Five or six of us would run down the huge staircase, rush out the front door and clamber as fast as we could down the massive stone steps onto the driveway and then the grass. The front lawns were stepped in three or four grassy banks that led down to a flat, luxuriant expanse of grass, which was well laid and immaculately maintained. The perimeter of the lawn was set in dense shrubbery. The smell of the freshly-cut grass was wonderful. It sweetened every breath I took.

I settled down to life in the children's home at Marmion House very quickly, thanks in no small measure to the kindness of the staff. Life at Marmion was disciplined, but apparently not excessively so. At eight years old, I was a junior and would not normally have been allowed to stay up until 10 pm to watch television with my sisters and the other seniors. But the older children would sneak me downstairs to the lounge and hide me so that I could watch television with them. Television was a real experience for us all of course, since we didn't have a set at home. Many of the younger members of staff were well aware of what was happening, but few of them would move to intervene.

I prayed that my mother would be all right. I thought about my younger brothers and sisters in their new surroundings in Glendhu Children's Home. I hoped that they were as happy as I was at that time in Marmion. The greatest benefit to me as an eight-year-old was the peace and quietness of my new surroundings. I loved the Home. I ran from school to get back to it. There was no monster of a father. No bullies. It seemed like a normal, happy environment. I had never had so long a respite from the trauma and mayhem that until then I had viewed as a normal part of daily life. My early days at Marmion House were filled with fun and joy and excitement. The other children spoke of their dread of never being allowed to go home. They would often speak fondly of one of their parents. Almost always just one. One parent had deserted them and the other could not cope alone. All of us who had been placed into care had suffered a similar plight.

However, one day in the late afternoon, something happened to threaten my new-found sense of security. I was out in the grounds playing with some of the other children. We were interrupted by the sudden exodus of a large number of staff and older children from the front door of the home. It was obvious to us that something was wrong. They ran past us and on down the banks to the shrubbery below. We ran as fast as we could to catch up with them. When I reached the shrubbery I was amazed to see members of the staff teaching the older children how to pull stinging nettles out from the ground in big bunches. They were plucking them like flowers!

"Grab some and take them inside," we were told. I tried to, but I was stung on my bare arms and legs. I jumped back quickly in pain.

"No, no, not like that, Johnston!" one of the staff exclaimed. "Hold them as tight as you can at the bottom of their stems," she explained, grabbing a bunch to show us how to do it.

"Don't let the leaves brush against you. Hold the bunch in front of you," she added.

We all followed her lead, and then, holding our bunches of nettles, went back with her into the house. Then along the hallway and up those stairs which were wide enough to accommodate two people going up and two people coming down. I could hear the unmistakable sound of a girl screaming at the top of her voice. We followed the direction of her screams. What on earth was happening? The commotion was incredible. Some members of staff and other children were running downstairs towards us. They were laughing and excited. It seemed like a game.

I was intrigued. I was also very apprehensive. From my limited experience of such screaming I knew that whatever was happening to that girl, she was terrified. When we got to the area of the bathrooms, we were stopped abruptly by a queue of staff and other children outside one of the bathrooms. The queue moved quickly. Meanwhile the poor girl's screams were so close and so piercing that I closed my eyes. I squinted up at my friends' faces. I could see that they were afraid too. Before I knew it, I was standing in the bathroom. The floor was soaked with water spilling from the bath. I couldn't believe what I was seeing. Spent nettles were strewn all over the bathroom floor.

There was a girl in the bath—a senior girl aged about twelve or thirteen. Her name was Patricia. She was struggling as hard as she could to get out, but two female members of staff were forcibly pushing her to make her sit down in the bath. The cold tap was running as hard as it could. Other members of staff wearing rubber gloves were taking the nettles from us. I watched as they beat that poor girl relentlessly with the nettles. I will never forget that terrible scene. Patricia was naked and seated bolt upright in the bath. She had her back to us. She was being beaten with the nettles on her back, her front, her face, and her head. Her body was covered in nettle stings. Nettle leaves were floating on top of the clear water. Her screams were pitiful and increasingly desperate.

I was glad to run from that bathroom. I wondered why Patricia was being punished in that most cruel and degrading way. In front of us all! If it was intended to show us what would happen to us if we were bad, then it had the desired effect on me. What on earth had she done? What sort of bad behaviour merited such abuse? How could the staff, usually so good and so caring, be so cruel to Patricia?

I ran downstairs to join some of my young friends. I was asking everyone what Patricia had done. One of the girls, just a little older than myself, pointed to a large ornamental flowerpot lying on the floor in the front hall. It was broken into pieces. The soil was everywhere. I couldn't believe it! Was that all? An accident like that didn't merit such abuse! I was shocked. I thought perhaps Patricia had tried to run away. Some of the other children had run away once, but they had been brought back pretty quickly by the Police.

"It wasn't an accident, Johnston, she did that deliberately in one of her usual tantrums," the girl said. "Come on, we have to get more nettles," she added.

For the rest of the day I inquired after the welfare of that poor girl. There was an air of despondency over the whole place. My friends had no desire to play outside any more. I understood exactly why: any one of us could be next. I decided to seek out my big sister Louise. I found her a short time later in the television lounge with some of her friends. I snuggled up close to her. We talked about what had happened to Patricia. Everyone was talking about it. Louise and I agreed that we would be on our best behaviour. There was no way we wanted to be the next child into that bath of nettles. I would rather run away first.

That night in bed, I found once again that I couldn't sleep. I lay there in the darkness listening to the sounds of the other children sleeping. I reflected on the sights that I had witnessed earlier in the day. Louise and a member of staff I particularly liked had promised me that such a thing would never happen to me. But I couldn't get those scenes out of my head. When I finally did doze off, it was a fitful and disturbed sleep. The nightmares that I had left behind me in Downshire Road returned. I dreamed of sudden and unprovoked beatings by members of the staff as my father looked on, laughing at me. I awoke in a panic, trying to catch my breath. I rushed out to the toilets and sat there, forcing myself to stay awake. The incident with Patricia in the bath had upset me terribly. I no longer felt safe. My perception of the staff as caring and fun had gone. They were now an ever-present threat. It dawned upon me that I had just swapped one home of abuse for another. This one was just cleaner and better stocked. My previous feelings of well-being and security were gone. That one terrifying incident had taken them away from me. I would have to be very careful not to upset these people. Here I was again, back walking on egg shells . . .

———

I started my first year in Holywood Secondary Intermediate School (now called Priory College) in September 1961. When I arrived at the school on my first day, I was overawed by the size of it. Where should I go? Which class was mine? Louise showed me the notice board which would tell me where I was to go.

"Oh God," she exclaimed. "You're in 1D, Johnston."

I knew by the pained expression on her face that it wasn't good news. I was about to ask her why when she was called away by her classmates.

I ended up going to our classroom with a friend from primary school, who was also to be in 1D. When we got there, the teacher, a fat, balding man, was standing at the front of the class. He urged us to be seated quickly. I chose a seat at the front of the class near the windows.

"These next few years are the most important years of your life," the teacher started. "What you boys and girls learn here will be what you need to know before you all go out into that big, bad world. It doesn't matter to me what you choose to do. I have a nice, big house just around the corner, on My Lady's Mile. I have a good job and I will receive a very good pension, thank you very much."

I took the view that this man was talking down to us, smug in the knowledge that he was going to be alright anyway—unlike us, the implication seemed to be. Remembering Louise's reaction on learning which class I was to be in, I decided to ask what 1D meant. I will never forget the answer.

"Mean, son? Let me just tell you what it means. The 'A' stream is excellent. The children there will become teachers, professionals, Police officers, the pillars of our community. 'B' stream is above average—these children will do well in whatever profession they choose. 'C' stream is for those of average intelligence, son. They are not expected to excel. They will hold down mundane jobs. They will go through life as shop assistants, factory workers. They will be the grey, unnoticeable people."

"And 'D', Sir, what about us in 1D?" I asked.

This man was obviously enjoying himself now. He leaned over towards me.

"'D', son?" he said with a smirk. "'D' stands for the dregs of humanity. That is exactly what you are. So far you have chosen not to work. You have settled for putting the hours in. You are destined for menial jobs."

"Nothing too mentally taxing," he added. "That is of course unless you decide not to lie back. If you decide to do a little work or to try harder, you could even reach the dizzy heights of 'C' stream. Is that clear enough for you, son?"

I understood very well. Someone in authority had written me off. At eleven years old, I was destined for the human scrap heap! I hung on to every word. I will never forget that teacher's flippant attitude. As far as he was concerned, my fate was sealed. Worse, he was obviously talking from experience. I decided right there and then that I would change the course that this teacher obviously believed I was destined for.

Meanwhile, the situation at home had not improved. Minor misdemeanours on my part would continue to trigger ever more violent outbursts from my father. The beatings continued. There were times when I was black and blue. Bruises covered my entire body: my back, my arms and my legs.

All my brothers and seven of my eight sisters were blonde-haired and blue-eyed. The fact that I was the first child to be born into the family with my mother's dark hair and penetrating dark eyes meant that I was to be selected for special attention. I would receive even more severe beatings than the others . . .

The fact that I would always be covered in bruises meant that I could not undress at school. Sports and physical exercise (PE) were always followed by a shower with the rest of the boys. A PE instructor would wander about the changing rooms.

This had not been a problem in primary school because my mother would give me a note for the teachers to say I had some ailment. This meant I was never made to undress in front of the other children.

Secondary school with its stricter regime was a different kettle of fish. I remember an incident in the gymnasium that was particularly traumatic for me. I had changed with the rest of the children. I was enjoying the exercise.

We were laughing and carrying on. I wasn't too concerned because it had been a period of little trauma or abuse and the many bruises I did have were fading. I was trying to climb up a rope, but I couldn't quite manage it. The PE teacher came over to explain in a good-natured way what had to be done. Even today I can still recall clearly what happened next.

After several futile attempts on my part to master the footwork that would help to propel me upwards, the teacher came over to me, laughing and in very good humour. He was wearing navy-blue tracksuit bottoms, white socks and black gym slippers. He had on a bright white T-shirt. A silver whistle dangled around his neck from a green silk ribbon. Before I knew what was happening, he put his arms around me and lifted me off my feet. His idea must have been to take my body weight while I manoeuvred my feet into position. He did not expect what happened next.

As soon as he lifted me off my feet and took my weight gently, as he thought, I let out a scream of agony which got the attention of all my classmates. The teacher let me down immediately. He was extremely surprised. I fell to my knees and gasped for breath.

"What is the matter?" he enquired, genuinely concerned.

"I'm sore there, Sir," I said.

He lifted my T-shirt to expose the bruises briefly and I pulled it down again quickly so that my classmates wouldn't see. I was so, so ashamed.

"What happened to you, son?" he asked.

"Nothing," I replied.

"Right, boys," he turned to the class.

He nominated one boy to ensure that the others got on quietly with their exercises on the wall bars, the ropes, the horse, and with the heavy medicine balls. Then he turned to me.

"Come with me, son," he said.

We walked into the changing room. He sat me down on the small wooden slats. There was the heavy stench of dirty socks and body odour mixed with dissipating steam from the adjacent shower room. The dark red-tiled floor was wet here and there. I looked at it. I couldn't look at him. I was eleven and a half years old, but I knew what discovery would mean. Our family had been split up before. I knew that the separation had had a devastating effect upon my mother. If abuse were unearthed now, it would mean the welfare getting involved again. Separation again, God knows what else. We might never be together again.

"Take your T-shirt off, son," the PE teacher ordered.

I didn't want to. I shook my head.

"We can do it here or in the headmaster's office," he said. "What is your name?"

"Johnston," I replied. "Johnston Brown."

He lifted my chin with his hand.

"Well, take it off, son."

I did. I watched the expression on his face as his eyes went from area to area, and he put his hands on my chest and my back, gently prodding the larger areas of bruising. I winced in pain.

"How did this happen, Johnston?" he asked. There was no longer any hint of authority in his voice.

"My father beats me, Sir," I replied.

"What for?" he asked.

"Mainly for nothing, Sir," I told him.

I was shaking like a leaf. Uncontrollably. I could see that he was aware of this.

"Why are you shaking, Johnston?" he asked.

"I'm afraid, Sir."

"Why would you be afraid of me, son?"

"I'm afraid of what you will do."

"I must report this," he said. "You will get help," he added. "They will stop this."

"My father will kill me, Sir, you have no idea. They will split us up. It's happened before. Please, Sir," I pleaded with him.

"But you need a doctor, treatment, they will see you are OK." It was more of a question than a statement.

With dry eyes and pleading, I told my PE teacher what would happen to me and my brothers and sisters. He listened intently.

"Sam," he said, referring to the headmaster. "I have to let Sam know. I don't want to do this, Johnston, but I don't have a choice."

He took me to his office where he went to a first aid cupboard and handed me two tablets.

"Painkillers," he said, smiling broadly. "Go and wash them down at the drinks fountain."

I did as he told me and I was back in his office in two minutes. He put his arm around me gently. He was crying. He was embarrassed. Something inside me told me to pretend not to notice. He began to busy himself with paperwork on his desk and from time to time he would sniff or clear his throat.

"Sit there, Johnston, I'll be back in a minute," he said. He left the room. Moments later I heard his whistle and barked commands to my classmates in the gymnasium. Then there was the thunder of their feet on the wooden floor as they rushed from the gym to the changing room. Then the bell sounded to mark the end of that period.

My PE instructor came back to his office.

"Go and get changed, Johnston," he said.

I joined my classmates in the changing room. I did not shower. I put my school uniform on over my gym shorts and white T-shirt. I had learned to come to school dressed like that on gym days so that my classmates would not see me strip. A few minutes later I was back in the PE instructor's office. He was surprised. He looked at me quizzically.

"Did you not shower, son?" he asked.

I bowed my head. I shook it. I couldn't look at him.

"It's OK, son, I understand," he said. "Go along and join your class."

Each period lasted approximately 40 minutes. We were halfway through that period. My stomach was doing somersaults when I saw my PE teacher, Sam Christie the headmaster and a small, very stern-looking woman I had not seen before arrive outside our classroom door. They summoned our teacher from the room. All eyes were on me.

"What have you done?" was coming from the rear of the class.

I did not care. All I could think about was that woman! Was she from the welfare? Would I now be taken like before and put into care again? Was I to be removed from this new-found happy environment, Holywood Secondary School? Would I be sent to God knows where, for God only knows how long? I feared that the little stability that I enjoyed in my turbulent life was about to be taken from me. So much for the PE instructor's caring attitude. He was going to keep himself right and damn the cost to me.

Sam Christie summoned me outside. I contemplated flight. As I stood in the corridor listening to those people talk seemingly unintelligibly about me, I stared at the fire exit to my right at the end of the corridor some 30 yards away. It opened when one pushed the bars and led outside to the front gates in Downshire Place and to temporary freedom. Left led to left again and down a few steps to the principal's office. I was shaking. It was the fear of the unknown. Of having absolutely no control over what would happen next. The teachers were so engrossed in what they were talking about that they did not appear to even notice me. I couldn't take my eyes of that fire exit. Sam Christie broke my trance.

"Go to my office, Johnston, and wait for me there," he said in his usual polite and gentle manner. There was something in his tone, something in his demeanour that reassured me that nothing bad was going to happen. All thoughts of flight left me. I stood obediently outside the headmaster's office. I saw all three appear at the top of the small flight of stairs as they walked towards me. The only one I was concerned about was the small, stern-faced woman whom I did not know. As they reached me, Sam went into his office alone. The PE instructor patted me on the head as he turned to leave the building with that stern-faced woman.

I stopped momentarily and watched the pair, as they looked proudly at the cups and shields in our display cabinets in the front hallway of the school.

"Johnston!" Sam called me into his office.

"Sit down," he said.

I did. At this time I had only been at the school for a few months. I did not have the benefit of knowing this man as I later would do. To me he was a person in authority. A person whose decisions in the next few minutes would mean the difference between handing the case over to the welfare or allowing the status quo to continue. He too was quick to notice me shaking. He immediately reassured me.

"Johnston," he began. "I am fully aware of your family background. I have no intention of informing the welfare authorities."

"But, Sir, that welfare woman with the PE instructor?" I blurted out.

"Welfare woman?" he said. "That is not a welfare woman. That is a teacher, who may come to work here. We have not informed the welfare," he said.

"We should be informing the Police," he added.

"The Police, Sir?" I asked with obvious concern.

"Yes, son, according to my PE instructor you are covered in bruises. Open your shirt and let me see the nature and extent of the bruising," he said.

I did as I was instructed. I waited as Sam Christie studied the mass of bruising that covered my body. He shook his head in disbelief as he turned me round and round in order to examine me. He returned to his seat and studied me.

"What did you do, son, to deserve such a beating?" he asked.

"Nothing, Sir," I replied quite honestly.

"Nothing? Why would your father beat you for nothing?" he asked.

"I don't know, Sir, he just does," I replied.

"And your mother, Johnston, what does she do about it?" he asked.

"She tries to stop it, Sir, she stands between us and our father, but he just hammers her as well," I replied.

Sam Christie continued to question me, trying to find a logical reason for a father to beat his children in this manner. He couldn't.

"Fix yourself up, Johnston. I will have to speak to your father," he said.

I begged him not to, because to do so would only make things worse.

"No, son, I have to, but he will never know that you have spoken to me or anyone else. I shall tell him that one of my more astute teachers saw those bruises when you were changing for PE. He will never know that you have told me, but he must be made aware that I will not tolerate abuse of this nature. If it continues, I will inform the appropriate authorities. Have you any problem with that?" he asked.

"No, Sir, but if my father gets as much as an inkling that something I did started this, God only knows what he will do," I replied.

Sam Christie stood there towering above me, holding the lapels of his gown. He was looking at me but he was obviously deep in thought.

"Hmmmm," he kept repeating. "I will have to be very careful," he said. I was sent back to my class.

It was the next day or the day after that. I was standing with a few classmates at the side of the school building. Some of our number were enjoying a sly smoke.

One of our friends who was supposed to be watching for teachers came rushing around the corner causing panic. He stopped beside me. He could hardly get a breath.

"Your Da is away into Sam Christie's office," he said.

My heart leapt. I felt physically ill. I could feel the panic welling up inside me. It was hard to breathe. However, my dread was not for that particular moment. I feared having to go home. My father would be seated in his usual place, at the window in his chair at the table in the living room. This meant that he could watch us approach the house. He would also have had all afternoon to brood about his visit to the headmaster's office. Would he suspect me? Would he punish me anyway? My fear was indescribable. I had told no-one of the incident in the gymnasium, not even my mother. I was too afraid of her panicking.

As I got to the front gate, I saw my father seated in his usual position. I tried to smile, tried to act as if I hadn't a care in the world. I deliberately avoided eye contact. I could feel his eyes burning into me. I ran to the front door. There was a routine and I knew that I had to keep strictly to it. I would throw my schoolbag up the hallway at the side of the stairs. There would already be three or four bags there: my younger sisters and brothers were at the primary school around the corner at the top of Hill Street, and they were always home first. I would then hang my blazer on a coat hook in the hallway, and go upstairs to change out of my school uniform. I was halfway up the stairs when my father summoned me back down.

"Coming," I replied. I knew better than to delay or to disobey. I walked into the living room and stared him straight in the eye. He looked away. He always did. He could never look you straight in the eye. I didn't know what to expect. I looked for signs that he was about to attack me. I didn't see any.

"Would you fill that coal bucket, son, the fire is dying out," he asked almost politely.

"Yes, Dad," I replied.

I leaned forward into the fireplace and grabbed the heavy, metal coal bucket. I went outside to the coalhouse and filled it as full as I could. I then returned to the living room and put coal on the fire. At all times, I kept my back to him, praying that he would not notice me shaking.

Mother was busy in the kitchen preparing the evening tea for us, she and my siblings unaware of the drama unfolding in this game of cat-and-mouse between me and my father. I prepared myself for a hammering. When he did speak, my father's voice was soft and enquiring. Not as I had expected.

"Were you speaking to the headmaster?" he enquired.

"Yes, Dad, I was."

"What was that about?" he asked.

I could see his attitude change immediately. He was now looking at me with malice as he waited for my answer.

"About me becoming a monitor," I lied.

He asked me what a monitor was and I explained we helped the teacher with their tasks and got a yellow badge with Monitor written on it.

Father studied me carefully. I knew he was looking for telltale signs that I was aware of his visit to the headmaster's office. He found none. I turned back to the fire and replaced the fireguard before leaving the room to go and do my homework. He remained sombre and subdued. We had a very quiet night at home that night. For me it was restless, but quiet.

The next day following assembly, Mr Christie took me to the side.

"How did it go last night, Johnston?" he asked.

"Fine, Sir," I replied.

"Do you think he fell for it?"

"Yes, Sir, I think he did," I said.

"I left your father in no doubt, Johnston, that if I find any further indications of physical abuse on you or any of the other children, I will personally call in the authorities," he said. "Please tell me if he ever beats you in that manner again."

I nodded.

"Run to your class now, Johnston, and keep me informed."

"Yes, Sir," I replied.

Tell him?! There was not the slightest chance of me telling him. I had been very lucky. There would be a day or two of calm but I knew it couldn't last long.

It didn't. After a few days of respite, the abuse continued unabated. My father had no self-control when he went in to one of his rages. Our problem was that it took very, very little to provoke him. The least annoyance was enough to set him off. Then the cycle would start again.

The Royal Ulster Constabulary visits to our home ceased when I was about fifteen years old. I arrived home one day to find my father beating my mother. Without thinking, I grabbed a heavy bronze ornament from the mantlepiece and stood between them. I raised the ornament in the air and told my father that if he ever lifted his hand to her again, I would kill him. He glared at me. It was a moment of intense madness. I thought he was going to disarm me and beat me. I raised my arm higher in an act of defiance. It worked. He turned and left the room without saying another word. He never again threatened me. He never again beat my mother. Thank God that bullies cow down in the face of courage. I am only sorry I didn't challenge him like this a year or two earlier.

I mention this incident because in many senses it was a crossroads in my life. If I had brought that heavy ornament down on my father's head, it might well have killed him. It most certainly would have injured him greviously. I would have been arrested and charged. There would have been no chance of a Police career. Looking back, I am intensely aware that my life could so easily have taken a very different course, that I could just as quickly have found myself on the other side of the law, launched in spite of myself on a career of a very different kind . . .

Throughout the incessant cycle of mayhem to calm and then the return to violence that was my childhood, the local Police never lost their patience, always intervening whenever called upon to restore calm and order. My encounters with the officers of the RUC who came into our home to restore the peace left a lasting impression on a child who never forgot their kindness, compassion and words of encouragement.

Chapter 3
Into the Royal Ulster Constabulary

I t was snowing and bitterly cold outside the car. As evening drew in, the temperature had plummeted. We had already made one unscheduled stop to change a flat tyre just a few miles south of the Lisburn intersection on the M1. Despite the fact that we had travelled for nearly an hour since the puncture, I was still very cold. We had left Holywood, Co. Down, my home town, at around 6 pm in order to be in good time. The heavy drone of the car engine behind me reminded me that we were travelling in a Volkswagen Beetle. It had snowed intermittently throughout the journey. Every time I travel in falling snow like that, it reminds me of the journey to Enniskillen that day.

The date was Sunday, 30 January 1972. Now known to everyone as Bloody Sunday. It was the date that I joined the Royal Ulster Constabulary (RUC), Northern Ireland's former Police Force. I was three months away from my 22nd birthday and by that time was a fully qualified electrician. Yet I still hankered after a career in the Constabulary. My motives had little to do with financial reward. As an electrician, I was earning £48 per week, while the RUC were offering a mere £80 a month. I had decided to become personally involved in helping my troubled community in the only way that I legally and honourably could. Some of my friends had joined the vigilante groups of the day, only to find themselves drawn into various para-military organisations.

The road signs for the villages of Augher, Clogher, and Fivemiletown which would later become so familiar to me were flashing past in a blur as we made steady progress towards Enniskillen. We were unaware as yet of the events which had occurred earlier in the day in Londonderry: events which would have such a profound effect on our future and on political stability in the Province.

The journey from Holywood to Enniskillen took around two hours. We were ready to enjoy some refreshments by the time we arrived at the RUC Training Centre. We approached the checkpoint at the front gates of the Depot cautiously. Several vehicles filled with recruits stopped in front of us. We waited in line as the heavily-armed and stern-faced RUC men checked our documentation. This guard squad was responsible for the security of the entire Depot.

We entered the gates through the substantial security barrier. My colleague produced his warrant card as proof of his identity and we were waved through. He had joined the RUC only six weeks before me. Once we were inside, I looked around at the different buildings which formed the huge complex. I noted that just above the door on the outside of one of the building there was a decorative plinth which stood out. The plinth had a royal crown at the top with the initials GR (George Rex) and the year 1930 embossed into it. It struck me that many members of the RUC must have passed this way during the 42 years since the building had been built. We went inside for refreshments, joining the other recruits already assembled there.

Thirty-eight of us had joined the Police on that day. Men from all walks of life had congregated to report for training. My colleague was well used to the routine of returning to the Depot. I followed his lead. We dropped my suitcases off in the doorway to the lounge/bar.

There was talk of tragedy in Londonderry. There were rumours that a large number of protesters had been shot dead by the Army. A number of men were watching a colour television in the corner of the lounge. They were demanding silence. I had not heard any news up to that time, so I made my way over to the group. Reporters were recounting the events that had occurred in Londonderry that afternoon. A civil rights march had clashed with soldiers of the Parachute Regiment with disastrous consequences. The graphic scenes were being shown in full, living colour. Everyone's eyes were glued to the television screen.

Thirteen civilians had been killed in that one afternoon of violence. I was stunned. I looked around that dimly-lit room at the faces of the RUC men assembled there. They were obviously as shocked as I was by those horrific scenes. Who would not have been? No-one was laughing or smiling. There were no signs of the joy or triumph that Republicans at the time might have expected.

Later I joined some of the others in a heated discussion about what those events would mean for us all as Policemen. This was the greatest loss of life in a single day since the beginning of the Troubles in 1969. That a rioter could be shot dead in such an incident was tragic and sometimes inevitable. But thirteen civilians? There must have been legitimate reasons! Surely there would be an inquiry to establish who was responsible and any wrongdoers from within the ranks of the Security Forces would be made amenable and brought to justice? We all firmly believed that this is what would happen. Northern Ireland was already into the third year of serious civil unrest. We were very much aware that we would be called upon to police any future marches of that nature. There was silence as we all took in the enormity of what had occurred in Derry.

Peace seemed more and more like a distant dream. An elusive and unattainable goal. And yet, at 21 years of age, I could remember peace. I could remember a time not so long before when Protestant and Catholic alike could travel anywhere in the Province without fear of attack from anyone. Perhaps we had taken it all too much for granted. What on earth had happened to cause this descent into near-anarchy?

Within a couple of hours of my arrival at the Depot, I got talking to one of the other recruits, a man of around my own age. He was shocked, as we all were, by the images on the television. He said he was a Catholic from Cookstown, Co. Tyrone, and asked me if I was Catholic. That age-old question which has led to such division in our community. I told him that I was Protestant, from Holywood in Co. Down. This did not appear to concern him in the least. We discussed the television coverage of the events in Londonderry. He was deeply concerned and unnerved by the footage of several Roman Catholic clergymen speaking from a mobile platform, referring to the Security Forces as "murderers". I brought it to his attention that we were all shocked at those images.

"It is all right for you, you're a Protestant," he said.

"Why, what difference does my religion make?" I asked.

It was a genuine if very naïve question. I had had many encounters with officers of the RUC and I never heard anyone question another's religious persuasion. Why on earth should they? Personally speaking, I could not understand why religion should make any difference.

"I'll tell you exactly why it matters," he said. "If you are a Catholic and you live in Cookstown, Republicans who live in our community don't like you to join the Police. It was hard enough to convince my friends and family that I have always wanted to be a Policeman. But after what has happened in Derry today? No way! I'm out of here."

Sitting in that dimly-lit lounge, he and I talked about exactly what had motivated us to become Police officers. It certainly had nothing to do with politics or religion. We spoke of our admiration for those brave men of the RUC who had gone before us. We recalled instances of having seen RUC men in action. Men who had unknowingly inspired us to join their number. Like me, this man had always wanted to be a Police officer. I was able to identify with so much of what he was saying. Yet I had had the full support of my family and friends in my sudden change of career. I had never really given any thought as to how difficult it would be for my Catholic neighbour to join the RUC. I argued the point that as a member of the Force, he could make a difference. That was exactly what he had intended, he said, but now, with what had happened in Derry, he felt it would be ill-advised to remain in the Constabulary, that he could no longer serve in or support the RUC. I tried to talk him out of leaving the Training Centre, but it was no use. He had made up his mind. I thought that he might end up joining an English force or perhaps waiting until the political climate here would change.

I have often wondered what route his life took once he made that decision to drive out of the Training Centre that night. That Sunday was to be a watershed in thousands of lives in Northern Ireland, with many young men and women feeling compelled to join Republican groupings. Decisions which would have disastrous consequences not only for themselves and their families but also for the entire Province. It is a sad fact that as a consequence of the tragic events of Bloody Sunday, hundreds of young and impressionable new volunteers flooded into the Irish Republican Army (IRA).

Nineteen-seventy-two was to prove to be one of the bloodiest years of the Troubles. Even in those early days of my initial training with the Police, I was very aware of the grave dangers that I would face. We knew that to join the RUC and to go out on duty in that black uniform would mean that we would be viewed by one side of the community as their enemy. Republicans regarded us as the armed wing of Unionism. The Loyalist community on the whole saw us as their Police, the protectors of Unionism.

During our RUC training, however, we were taught differently. It was made clear to us that we were above all public servants. The insignia of the harp and crown in plain view on our lapels and on our forage caps were potent symbols of both our British and Irish identities, and as a Police Service, we were expected to embrace both traditions. We could be as proud of our Irish identity as we were of our British identity. The same symbols of the harp and the crown were visible on each of the buttons of our tunics. Shamrocks were woven into the sergeants' gold stripes and the other insignia of the senior ranks.

These badges were inherited from the former Royal Irish Constabulary (RIC), disbanded in 1922 following the partition of Ireland. The Police officers who had been members of the old RIC had rejected the proposal to adopt a badge for the new Constabulary, which depicted the red hand of Ulster on a white background. They saw it as too blatantly sectarian. This alone speaks volumes for the attitude of the Police officers of the period. They had no wish to be identified as a Police Force serving only one section of the community, and so they favoured the badge of the former RIC which so plainly embraced both traditions.

We were reminded that a bullet fired by a Protestant thug had murdered the first RUC man to die in these recent Troubles. It was made clear that sympathy or support for Loyalists from within the ranks would not be tolerated by the RUC. Terrorism was the scourge of our society, and our Police Force would deal effectively with all of the perpetrators, no matter what their religious or political persuasion. RUC officers would always be the meat in the sandwich. We were the "piggy-in-the-middle", so to speak, at the mercy of every trigger-happy terrorist no matter which camp they came from.

We were encouraged to be proud of our impartial role in the policing of our divided society. "By our actions we will be judged," they had said. I often thought of my squad mate who left the Depot on our first night. Here was a classical example of a young man robbed of a career in the Police on his first day of service because of fear of reprisal by Republicans. He was not afraid for himself personally or he would not have been in the Depot in the first place. His fear was for the safety of his family. I was beginning to understand just how divided our society had become.

The IRA had already shown that they would attack and kill any member of the RUC where the opportunity arose. But they went out of their way to target our Catholic members and murder them in the most cowardly manner. Their intention was of course to discourage any other Catholics who may have been contemplating joining the RUC. The IRA knew that if significant numbers of Catholics were to join the RUC, it would not augur well for the Republican propaganda machine, which was busy expounding the fact that the RUC was 95 per cent Protestant and 100 per cent Loyalist. The truth was that Catholics were not excluded by the RUC: their numbers in our ranks were small due to their very real fear of Republican retribution.

This did not, however, stop the many brave Catholics who came forward to join our number. Young men who had the same desire as their Protestant counterparts and who would not be intimidated by the ruthless activities of the IRA.

We met our training sergeants that first evening. One was a Scotsman known as Jock. He took us to our dormitory and showed us how to make our beds, hospital-style. We were given little pieces of cloth which we had to walk on. These "skids" were issued to us to ensure that we did not ruin the high gloss on the polished vinyl floors. By just standing on them and moving along the floor, we were in effect helping to maintain the highly-polished surface already on the floor. We would be responsible for the cleanliness of our uniform and equipment, and were expected to press our own uniforms and polish our boots to perfection.

The next morning, Monday, 31 January 1972, was a beautiful day. The sun was shining even though it was bitterly cold. We were taken to the .22 firing range. It was there in that sandbagged backdrop that we were sworn in to the Royal Ulster Constabulary by an elderly Justice of the Peace. We were handed New Testaments and were asked to share one between two. We were called upon to stand in alphabetical order. Bailey, Baillie, Bell, Boal, Brown . . . the next name called was that of the young man who had decided to leave the Depot the night before. He would have shared the New Testament with me. The sergeant kept calling his name. I brought it to his attention that one of the recruits had departed and explained why. He shrugged his shoulders. He asked me to hold the New Testament with the next officer in line, whom I had never seen before. His name was Joseph Cusack, a Catholic. We were to become inseparable during our initial three months' training in the Depot. The rest of the men dubbed us "Pixie and Dixie". At the end of six weeks' training all recruits would be given a room of their own. Joe and I were the only two senior recruits asked to share a room for the last six weeks of training. Throughout our time together, our different religious persuasions were never an issue. I know that Joe would say the same thing. We held the New Testament and took our oath to serve the community without fear or favour.

After the solemn swearing-in ceremony which took only a few minutes, we set off to class for our welcome lecture. Then we were issued with our training uniform, which consisted of a pair of black heavy serge trousers, a bottle-green serge combat jacket of the type used by the British Army during the Second World War, and four green Police shirts complete with detachable collars and black ties. We had to buy a pair of Skerry boots from the Depot shop at our own expense. In this attire we looked more like a squad of borstal boys than we did Police officers. Due to the size of our "T" squad intake, we were split into two groups, "T1" and "T2". I was in "T1". Our youngest officer, just over eighteen years of age, was baby-faced and full of life. Our oldest man was in his mid-forties. There was a good mix of all types of people drawn from all walks of life. We all had a common sense of purpose: to make a contribution towards a more peaceful environment in Northern Ireland.

Those initial three months of training were supposed to prepare us for what we were to face out on the streets of the troubled Province. Every one of us knew exactly what we were getting ourselves into. The daily newspapers were full of examples of just how determined the terrorists were to murder us without warning. Life inside the Training Centre in those days was one of a strictly disciplined routine. First thing in the morning, we would have inspection out on the parade ground. The commandant who held the rank of superintendent and a duty officer of the rank of chief inspector would come to inspect us, accompanied by one of our training sergeants. Failure to maintain a first-class presentation of one's uniform or boots would result in a punishment known as "show parade". This meant that the offender would face a further inspection at lunchtime while all the other recruits would enjoy a period of relaxation. This ensured a high standard of turnout: no-one wanted to be put on "show parade".

Drill, or marching around the parade ground in time to recorded military music, was the order of the day. Not long into our training, we were joined on the parade ground by a drill sergeant, a man in his late forties or early fifties, who was to be our drill instructor. He walked towards us with a military bearing. Despite his age he carried the uniform well. He looked like something straight out of an RUC recruitment poster. He stood before us and introduced himself. His address was faltering at times and his voice was full of emotion. I was standing in the front rank, very close to this man. I could see tears flowing down his cheeks unchecked. He was obviously terribly upset, yet he was trying hard not to let us see this.

It was a crisp, clear, freezing February morning. I was non-plussed. Why was this man crying? What on earth had caused him to well up with such emotion? His next words are etched indelibly onto my soul. He shouted loudly:

"If you believe that you are here to prop up some Unionist regime—get out the gate! If you believe that you are here to get at Catholics—get out the gate! If you think you are here to join some sort of Hitler Youth—get out the gate! I am here to teach you that you are public servants and that you are here to serve both sides of this community impartially." He added, "You have no idea of the perils that you will face when you leave this Training Centre, no idea at all."

He paced up and down in front of us, appearing to study us closely. He told us that for the next three months it would be his duty to make our lives a misery on that parade ground. He said he wanted us to know and never to forget the fact that none of what he would put us through was to be taken personally.

"I am proud of each and every one of you. You are very brave men indeed!" he concluded.

He stood there silently for a moment with his head bowed. We waited patiently for his next command. He came to attention and reverted to his instructor mode. He put us through our paces on the parade ground, barking his commands in a forceful manner as he marched us up and down. I was fortunate. My earlier drill training in the sea cadets and in the Royal Naval Reserve stood me in good stead, meaning that I was familiar with most of the tough manoeuvres that we were to encounter on that parade ground.

That drill sergeant did indeed test our patience and resolve to the limit. One of the recruits in our intake left during our initial training. A member of our "T1" squad, after one particularly gruelling session, actually walked off that parade ground and out of the Depot gates, never to return. He was a Protestant lad from Ballymena in Co. Antrim.

As soon as I got off the parade ground that first day, I made enquiries about the new sergeant. I soon got the answers to my questions. This officer, Jack McCarroll, was a devout Christian. His 21-year-old son had also been an RUC man, and had made the supreme sacrifice when a cowardly Provisional IRA (PIRA) unit had brutally murdered him in Belfast, just days earlier, on 28 January 1972. I remembered reading of the spineless attack on the off-duty RUC man, Constable Raymond McCarroll, just before I started my training: I had been filled with disgust. The young man had been gunned down at a time when he least expected it by a Republican terrorist who hated him because of the uniform he wore, and who had a twisted view of what it represented. All of us knew that it could happen to any one of us. It was a fact of life. It did not deter us. Our new drill sergeant had just returned to duty after a short period of compassionate leave. As he stood before us, he must have seen his son's face in every one of us. He had said that he was proud of us. Well, I was equally as proud of him. If the RUC was made up of men of his calibre, I was proud to be one of them. Despite the intensity of the drill training, I always enjoyed being in the presence of that sergeant.

Drill on the parade ground was interspersed with lectures on law, practice and procedure in the classrooms. It was during these sessions that our lecturers, sergeants and inspectors alike, spoke of how the post-Hunt Report RUC was free from any political interference, and as such could afford a Police service to both sides of our divided community. Our role was first and foremost one of public service.

We were the new face of a totally reformed Constabulary. Seasoned officers spoke of how they felt tainted by allegations that they had been less than impartial. I saw this as an acknowledgement that such abuses had occurred in the past and that there was now a genuine desire to ensure that there would be no further cause for such complaint in the future. There was a clear wish to send out new recruits who would be impartial, not trained to be loyal to one particular section of the community or another. As far as I was concerned, it was exactly what I wanted to hear.

It was extremely gratifying to know that we would all work together with a common goal: to enforce the laws of the Province in a fair and equal manner. We did not make the laws: we were responsible only for enforcing them. Coming from Holywood in Co. Down, where even until very recently relationships between the two religious persuasions have been harmonious, I knew the value and the long-term benefits of respecting your neighbour, Catholic or Protestant.

Our routine included physical training in the gymnasium, and three- and six-mile road runs around Enniskillen. The sergeant instructors were the mainstay of the whole setting. At least three of them were "born-again" Christians. They invited us to attend gospel meetings in Ballynamallard Gospel Hall and some of us travelled with them in several cars to the Gospel Hall, not far from the border with the Republic of Ireland. None of us were armed. No one was worried about the possibility of being attacked. On each of those occasions we all returned safely to the Depot.

I found the class work interesting. My preferred time to study was from 1 am until around 4 am—by torchlight. This worked well for me academically because I excelled in the examinations, but it left me very tired the next morning! I found topics such as fraud boring and if I lost interest I had a tendency to nod off in the classroom. Frequently I would find myself being awakened by the sergeant instructor, whispering into my ear and apologising for "keeping me up". I would then be sent to run several laps of the racetrack on my next break whilst my colleagues were able to relax. My classmates dubbed me "Rip van Winkle". In fact, I would retain this tendency to lapse into a near-coma at the drop of a hat throughout my entire Police service. Especially whilst attending the courts, where my colleagues would know to keep a sharp eye on me in case I would nod off. Luckily though, many of the topics covered in our training syllabus were fascinating and held my attention easily.

The principles of Police work were hammered home to us. Our main goal was the "Protection of Life". This was the primary duty we were sworn to. It was our chief raison d'être, the primary purpose of our existence. Further, it was our duty to protect the lives of all of our citizens without distinction. All life was sacred: no life was worth less or more than any other. To really bring this home to us, our instructor would remind us that no group of subversives was any better than any other. He spoke of the three main groups we would come up against as Police officers in Northern Ireland.

"Republicanism is a legitimate aspiration," he said. "Nationalism is a legitimate aspiration. Unionism is a legitimate aspiration. It is only when these people take up arms to promote their ideals by subversion that we become involved. When this happens, it is our duty to step in and to enforce the law and prevent this small country of ours from descending into anarchy," he said.

He did not advocate hatred of Republicans, nor attempt to lay blame for our troubles at any particular door. He did not talk of the politics of the situation. Nor did he wish to hear any of us expounding our own political views.

"Politics are no concern of ours. Leave politics to the politicians," he would say.

I found myself thinking again of the colleague who had walked out of those Depot gates on his first night. I wished that he could have stayed to hear that lecture. In my three months in the RUC Training Centre, I would hear those same principles time and again. The instructors frequently stopped me on my way to class or in the corridors of the Depot. They would ask me a very simple question.

"What are you, Brown?"

"A Police officer," I would reply.

They would look at each other and shake their heads.

"An RUC officer," I tried again.

"Wrong." A pace stick would be shoved into my midriff gently but firmly enough to emphasise their point.

"You are a public servant, Constable," they said. "What are you?"

I did not need to be told twice: "A public servant, Sir," I would reply.

There was no doubt that these men wanted to turn out a whole new breed of recruit. Gone was the drilling with rifles and the wearing of gaiters. We would not be turned out as a paramilitary Police Force. There was talk of disarming the RUC again. It had not worked the last time. These instructors were sure that a political solution was just around the corner that would allow us to police a Province free from the threat of terrorism. In the meantime, they said, we would be charged with keeping the very fragile peace. Yet in reality, politicians here in Northern Ireland in 1972 were poles apart. To suggest that things would suddenly get better was no more than a pipe-dream at that time.

We learned the core skills of everyday Police work — the protection of property and the preservation of the peace. Our powers of arrest and the procedures involved in the detention of criminal suspects were explained to us fully. We heard of how we should deal with road traffic accidents and how to perform random Vehicle Checkpoints (VCPs). We also learned what was expected of us as we patrolled on the beat or in the car. I enjoyed this learning process immensely.

We were also trained in key policing attitudes such as courtesy and exercising our powers of discretion. We would not be expected to prosecute offenders every time and in every instance. We also had the power to caution, warn or advise them in relation to minor infringements of the law. These could be better options in suitable cases. Such freedom to use one's own discretion was invaluable to a constable out on the streets attempting to enforce legislation with tact and diplomacy. It would also endear us to those citizens who would jump at the chance to heed our advice rather than face prosecution.

The political scene in Northern Ireland during those first three months of 1972 became increasingly volatile. Widespread civil unrest led to violence which quickly spilled out onto the streets. Things were bad, but they were to get worse. On Tuesday, 28 March 1972 the Prime Minister Edward Heath suspended the Stormont Government and set in place direct rule. William Whitelaw became the first Secretary of State for Northern Ireland.

In the classroom, one of our sergeants made us aware of these developments and of all the possible political ramifications. He said that each of us should consider applying to the *Guinness Book of Records* as the holders of possibly the shortest Police careers ever! It was rumoured that the RUC was to be disbanded immediately.

There was also talk of new RUC uniforms arriving at our central stores at Sprucefield which no longer bore the Royal Ulster Constabulary label, but instead "Northern Ireland Police Service". It was a time of confusion and grave concern for us all. In those early days of my service in the RUC, the threat to disband our Constabulary, or at the very least to rename and reform it, was very real.

At the end of our three months' training, we were told which Division and which RUC station we would be posted to. As a single man, I was entitled to no concessions. I had stated clearly at my interview for the Police that I would be prepared to serve anywhere in Northern Ireland. I was therefore pleasantly surprised when I received my posting to Glenravel Street RUC Station in Belfast. This was only a short distance from my family home in Holywood, Co. Down. It was also at that time the Divisional Headquarters of the RUC "D" Division. Some of my colleagues, however, had not been so lucky. Joe found that he was to stay in Enniskillen—a very long way from his family home in Downpatrick in Co. Down.

Our passing out parade took place on Thursday, 27 April 1972. The "T" squad numbered 38 men in total. Two of our intake were from the Airport Constabulary and they would serve in that capacity. Our training officer, Chief Superintendent J. C. (Jack) Hermon, was present.

Our friends and relatives were there in large numbers to support us. It was a joyous occasion. No-one dwelt on the daunting task that lay ahead. We were just glad to have passed that first hurdle on our way to becoming fully-fledged Police officers. The next day, we left the Depot for the last time.

The next step in our training was to undergo firearms training at the old Ropeworks complex near Connswater. In less than two weeks, we were trained and approved as proficient in the handling of the .38 Webley revolver which we would carry routinely as a sidearm for purposes of self-defence. Each of us was issued with a service revolver and 30 rounds of ammunition.

We were also trained in the handling of the Sterling submachine-gun and the awesome Browning pump-action shotgun. Each of us was warned that any use at all of our firearms would be the subject of both criminal and disciplinary investigations. The firearms we traditionally carried were solely for the purpose of defending ourselves from attack and protecting the general public from armed terrorists or criminals.

I had passed a Police driving examination whilst in the Training Centre, so after the firearms training I was allowed to report to my station as a qualified Police driver. The rest of my colleagues who held driving licences but had not passed the driving test in the Depot went on to the RUC Driving School at Castlereagh to be trained to drive Police cars before reporting to their stations. (Castlereagh Police Office was the terrorist holding and interrogation centre in East Belfast.)

As far as the RUC authorities of the day were concerned, we were now ready to join our stations and start our two-year probationary period. It was during the next two years that we were expected to prove that we had what it takes to become fully-fledged Police officers.

I knew it was going to be a very challenging time, but I had absolutely no idea exactly just how demanding it would prove to be. I was about to be propelled into a roller-coaster lifestyle which would test me to the limit. As a member of the RUC, I would look death in the face on an almost daily basis. Each day could be your last.

Many colleagues took the view that it could not happen to them. I decided to err on the side of caution. I took one day at a time. I tried to be always alert. I was cautious but never despondent. I had joined the Police to deal with the bullies in our society. From the experiences of my childhood, I was already painfully aware of the dangers inherent in that. Yet I intended to do my best. I could do no more than that.

Chapter 4

Newtownabbey RUC Station, May 1972–August 1976

I had reported for my first day of duty as an RUC officer to Glenravel Street RUC Station in Belfast in May 1972, only to find myself a short time later on my way to the Newtownabbey barracks: due to an administrative error, it seemed that I had been wrongly posted to the inner-city station.

It was a beautiful spring day. The hot sun was splitting the rocks. As I made my way through Whiteabbey, I recalled how I had made that first telephone call to the RUC recruitment branch from a pub there, the Halfway House, in 1971. The coincidence was not lost on me.

Twenty minutes later I was standing in the station sergeant's office in Newtownabbey before the station sergeant. He had been expecting me. In sharp contrast to the scene at the Glenravel barracks from which I had just come, there was no mad rush of telephone calls or queues of personnel waiting for orders from the station sergeant here. I had his undivided attention. He took me onto the roof of the barracks and delineated the boundaries of our subdivision.

Rathcoole Estate was in our patch, and as the second biggest housing estate in the United Kingdom, it presented major challenges for us from a policing perspective. There were other estates in the area that would give us trouble too, such as Rathfern, Fernagh and Monkstown, but nothing we couldn't handle, the station sergeant assured me.

"We have Police officers and their families living in all of those estates," he added.

As I listened to my new station sergeant, I found my gaze constantly drawn back to the front garden of the Police station. It was well landscaped, laid in a lawn with well-positioned flowerbeds where shrubs and roses were in abundance. I complimented the sergeant on the presentation of the front of the barracks. I then made the mistake of mentioning my avid interest in gardening. He was impressed. He stood there in his shirt-sleeves puffing on his pipe, waxing lyrical about the station garden, obviously a great source of pride to him. It was immaculate. The lawn was cut short and mown in stripes. A low, red-brick wall surrounded it. A new twelve-foot tall chain link fence stood solidly around the entire perimeter, spoiling the otherwise tranquil impression of the scene. Nonetheless, this was a far cry from the bedlam of the heavily-guarded and fortified old city barracks in Belfast's Glenravel Street. We went down into the garden and the sergeant showed me his prized rose bushes and shrubs one by one, reciting the names of each. We stood there for what seemed like an age before he was called inside to deal with some firearms query.

Had it not been for the presence of a crude sandbagged Sanger, an eyesore of a structure built by the military and positioned at the large, solid sheetmetal front gates of the barracks, there was little evidence of the reality of the Troubles in that scented, flower-filled environment. The strong May sunshine shone down upon me, adding to the general sense of peace and tranquillity. Yet it was a scene that belied the real state of affairs in that area.

The truth was that Newtownabbey and the surrounding area at that time was a seething cauldron of potentially serious civil unrest. One which would in the very near future boil over and threaten to engulf us. Our district, like many others in the Province, was soon to collapse into near-anarchy.

The station sergeant was an RUC man of the old school variety. He gave out instructions with an air of authority more befitting a superintendent. How could I have known that this man could be just as powerful as any very senior Police officer? In those days the office of station sergeant was in fact the hub of the whole barracks. Everything revolved around him. I would soon learn that you should never cross or offend the station sergeant.

I was detailed to be what in those days was called assistant guard, which meant that I was to assist the Police officer who was on duty in the guardroom of the barracks. This guardroom was later to be renamed the Enquiry Office, to dispense with the obvious military connotations. I was to alternate on an hourly basis between assistant guard duty and armed security duty outside in the Sanger with a Sterling submachine-gun.

I recall my first conversation on duty with a "real" Police constable. He was in the guardroom and was responsible for dealing with queries from any member of the public who called at the barracks. Today he would be referred to as the Station Duty Officer (SDO). I entered the guardroom with more than a little apprehension. The constable who greeted me was middle-aged. A small, round man with a broad smile and a cheery disposition, he had ruddy red cheeks and blonde, curly hair streaked with grey. Although he was busy, he stopped what he was doing and greeted me.

"Just out of the factory, are we, son?" he asked with a huge grin, staring at my shiny boots and laughing to himself. This was obviously a derogatory term for the Training Centre in Enniskillen.

"Well, take my advice and forget everything them boys told you. Welcome to the real world: you won't be able to apply any of that crap here," he said. "What age are you, son?"

"Me?" I asked stupidly, because apart from him I was the only other person in the guardroom.

His eyes rose to the ceiling as if to say, "I've a live one here."

"I am 22," I replied, half-apologetically.

"Me Tommy," he said, pointing to his head and giggling. "What's your name, son?"

"Brown, Johnston Brown," I replied.

"Right, Jonathan, grab that roll of paper and pull it off the telex machine," he said.

"Johnston," I repeated.

"Johnston what?" he enquired with a quizzical stare.

"My name is *Johnston* Brown, not Jonathan," I insisted.

"Well, what's your first name, then?" he asked, now deadly serious.

"Johnston *is* my first name," I reiterated. He stared at me for a moment.

"That's far too long, son. Far too much to get my tongue around," he said. He appeared to think for a moment. "That's it, we'll call you *Jonty*," he said after a while. "Hand me that black ruler over there, would you, Jonty?"

And so from that day on and for the rest of my 30-year career in the Police, I would be known as "Jonty" Brown. My mother would have had a fit if she'd known: I had never been allowed to abbreviate my name before. I, however, couldn't have cared less. I was keen to fit into this new environment: if these guys wanted to call me "Jonty", that was fine by me. I was taking my first tentative steps in a new career, and wanted nothing more than to be accepted by my colleagues. Little did I realise it at the time, but the path I would find myself on would bring me into conflict with some of those who by rights should have been my greatest source of support . . .

The station sergeant had not missed my admiration of his expansive front garden. I had told him that I loved gardening. One day, only a month or two into my new posting, I arrived at the barracks to find my duties clearly marked on the duty sheet: "Fatigues".

"What does that mean?" I asked a smirking colleague.

"That means that you are his slave for today. You report to him and he will tell you what your "fatigues" will be," he said. "Could be anything from cleaning the barracks, washing the cars, brushing the yard, or clearing out the garage. Whatever the Sarge decides."

I found him in the garage at the rear of the barracks. He was wearing a pair of brown overalls and he handed me a pair of blue ones. We cleaned and stored three Police roof signs that had been removed from our local Police cars for security reasons. At the time of my arrival at Newtownabbey, the RUC was patrolling in unmarked cars so that they blended more easily into the other civilian traffic. They deliberately did not wear their forage caps on mobile patrol, so as to make it harder for those who might mean them harm to pick them out. Being easily identifiable as an RUC patrol responding to what might be bogus calls, or "come-ons", as we called them, could mean sudden death. Travelling more or less incognito could afford us those vital few additional seconds which might literally mean the difference between life and death.

The sergeant explained to me that a Republican terrorist had ambushed one of our RUC patrols on 10 February 1972. The RUC patrol was fortunate because the terrorist's weapon had jammed, giving our officers the edge. The terrorist, a 26-year-old Catholic lad, had not been so lucky. He was shot by the RUC in the incident, and fatally wounded. This was the point to which things had escalated. Any measures that we could adopt to protect ourselves were being considered.

The sergeant and I cleaned the gardening tools and equipment. We soon had the two station garages sitting pretty. The Sarge was well pleased. He asked me to cut the front lawn and attend to the flowerbeds. I loved—and still love—to tend to a garden. Within a very short space of time, I had the front lawn and the flowerbeds in fine shape. My problem was that the sergeant was so pleased with my performance that he detailed me for "fatigues" on a regular basis. To the extent that I was beginning to feel more like the station gardener than one of the local policing team! How could I break this mould?

The answer came from an unexpected quarter. An old hand called Alec, dubbed by the rest of the lads as a "hate-the-world", heard me complaining. He came up with a master plan:

"Cut the heads of his favourite roses just outside the station sergeant's window and place them on his window sill. That'll sicken him, son. He will never let you near his precious garden again," he said. "I mean to say, son, you've two years to make an impression and believe me, in this job two years flies in. What are you going to say? 'I'm sorry I wasn't able to catch anybody because the Sarge wouldn't let me out of his garden?' That'll not wash, son," he added, before going back to his duties in the guardroom.

I stood there looking out of the window onto his beautiful garden. Even the pedestrians walking along the Shore Road outside the barracks were stopping every so often to admire the garden in all its splendour. With the July sunshine on my back, I set about my work, spending the guts of an hour mowing the lawn and tidying the flowerbeds. Then I finally plucked up the courage and started to cut off the heads of the sergeant's prize blooms and place them one after another on his windowsill.

One, two, three, four, five, . . . ten, eleven, twelve. Why was he not shouting? Hadn't he noticed the cut roses lying on his windowsill? I was starting to panic at the devastation I had wrought upon those rose bushes. Where was he anyway? I decided to find out. I walked to the open window. Joyce, his typist, explained that he was away for lunch, but was due to return in a few minutes. I looked wistfully at those roses already starting to wilt in the hot summer sunshine. I started to feel a deep sense of regret and guilt as I stood there at the window ledge.

"Hey!" I was jolted out of my daydreaming state by the loud guldering and raving of the station sergeant. His face was red with rage. He was dumbfounded. He tried to call me names but his mouth couldn't keep up with his brain and his words flowed incoherently. I did make out that he was questioning my sanity and my parentage.

"Stop it, put those secateurs down and get out of my garden!" he shouted. He was incensed, his face flushed. The air was blue with his expletives: he couldn't think of names bad enough to call me.

It was about an hour later before I had plucked up sufficient courage to enter his office. He didn't even look up at me. He seemed to be writing a report of some kind and I was hoping that it wasn't for my transfer! He didn't speak to me, but simply pointed to the duty roster hanging on the wall to his right. I lifted it down to study it. The air was thick with the tension between us.

The "Fatigues" entry which had been marked for that day was crossed out. So were the "Fatigues" entries for the next three days, leading up to my long weekend off. In their place was clearly marked "Ex OBS 10". This meant that I would now be the third member of the crew in the District Mobile Patrol car (DMP), Delta November one zero. This was the result I'd wanted! Within minutes I was out of overalls and back into full uniform complete with the green military flak jacket which was compulsory garb at the time.

It was nearly two months before the station sergeant spoke to me again with anything more than a grunt. He never forgave me for what he believed was an act of gross stupidity. As far as I know, he never suspected that it had been merely a ploy to escape from what might otherwise have been my inescapable fate: that of being permanent station gardener.

The station crew was divided into four Sections: A, B, C, and D. I was attached to B Section. We had no sergeant of our own, only six regular constables. Had it not been for the existence of our part-time RUC Reserve colleagues, we could not have afforded the Newtownabbey public the level of policing that we did. These men, all volunteers, turned out with enthusiasm and commitment. Nothing was too much to ask of them. They patrolled with us until 4 or 5 am. Then, while we slept, they would get up the next morning and go to their regular places of work. This left them in some senses at even greater risk than we regular Police. Many of our part-time reservists were gunned down at their workplaces. The cowardly terrorists who carried out such murders knew that it was there that they were most vulnerable to attack. When you consider that it took a man each to cover guard and station security and a further two to crew our district car, very little regular manpower was left to spread over the remainder of the duties. The part-time Reserve Force was always a welcome extra resource. In those days of the early seventies, we leaned very heavily upon them. I have often wondered what became of the brave reservists I was lucky enough to work with during my time at Newtownabbey.

Our relief sergeant Arthur Scott (not his real name) would debrief us at the end of our shift when he was coming on duty. He would also remain on duty to brief us as we arrived at the beginning of our shift and before we went out on patrol.

I found patrolling our subdivision from May 1972 onwards to be especially rewarding. I quickly built up a good local knowledge, as the older Policemen introduced me to the business community: doctors at the local Health Centre, shopkeepers, the Justice of the Peace and many others with whom we would come regularly into contact. We even enjoyed breakfast in the canteen of Whiteabbey Hospital at greatly subsidised rates. It was a time of intense comradeship. Our morale was always very high.

I loved my job as a uniformed "copper". The challenges it provided on a daily basis were tremendously rewarding. You were very seldom dealing with the same thing twice. The "old guard", as we called our senior colleagues, were always on hand to teach us the basics. Alec, the canny constable who had come up with the cunning plan to behead those roses, was my favourite. He told me that I should always try to "positively interact" with the general public and the criminal element in our area.

"Criminals are our bread-and-butter work, son. Never look down your nose at a criminal. Treat each one with the same dignity and respect which you would hope for yourself," he said.

Respect criminals? I couldn't believe what I was hearing! I thought Alec was going soft in his old age. Little did I know it, but those words of wisdom, which seemed so contrary to me at that time, would pay dividends for me in later years. Beat patrol with men of the "old guard" like Alec was a real treat.

Yet these were the men who were allegedly hated by Catholics and Nationalists. The men who were so brutally murdered by

Republicans. I studied them, searching for some failing, some reason which would make sense of why they were so reviled. Yes, there was the odd bigot, but in the main these were men that any Police Force would be proud of, and most of the old hands like Alec hated the bigots in our midst as much as we younger men did.

I remember the first time I drove our patrol car into Merville Garden Village, just off the Shore Road opposite the old Merville Inn. The cherry trees were in full bloom, the profusion of bright pink and white flower petals dazzling to the eye. Abbots Cross Shopping Centre on the Doagh Road was exactly the same. It was hard to believe that our district was in such political turmoil. We also called frequently at the Alpha Cinema to ensure that the staff were able to cope with any unruly elements. This duty was especially welcome during the winter months, as it gave us the excuse to call in and warm ourselves by standing inside at the rear of the cinema watching the films. The cinema closed down shortly after my arrival into the district. It later re-opened as a Community Centre and UDA Club.

I recall my first tour of night duty at Newtownabbey RUC Station. I was detailed on the duty sheet as the observer in the DMP car. A colleague was detailed to drive. As observer and front-seat passenger in the Police car, I would be personally responsible for dealing with all incidents and investigating all offences which might come to light during our night shift. I would also be required to write up all calls in the "Station Occurrences, Reports and Complaints Book" (otherwise known as the C6). This is the large book which sits on the enquiry room table. The SDO would enter all calls he received from whatever quarter into the C6, noting the names and call signs of the officers responsible for dealing with the call. This C6 was perhaps the most important and certainly the most referred to record of events in any barracks. Our relief sergeant Arthur Scott had impressed upon me the absolute necessity of full and factually accurate entries into this book.

I checked my equipment. I had my brand new Police torch, complete with a red dome which fitted neatly onto the front, so that the white beam could be changed to a red one. This would be used to stop cars at Vehicle Checkpoints (VCPs). I also had my new gloves. I grabbed a green army flak jacket from a colleague who was going off duty. I went to the armoury to sign out a submachine-gun (SMG). I also signed out a portable radio. In those days, it was called a Pye Bantam set and came in a cumbersome denim bag and was carried across the shoulder. This radio rarely worked more than a mile or so from the barracks. I also carried a clipboard with all the necessary statement forms and Road Traffic report forms. With all of this very necessary equipment, it was always a relief to be able to get into the Police car and unburden yourself.

My old friend Alec stayed on duty from the late shift to boost our numbers and we found ourselves out on mobile patrol. We received a call to attend a domestic disturbance in Rathmore Drive in the sprawling Rathcoole Estate. Alec warned me that this couple were notorious. He expected trouble. He also said that we would probably be called back to this house several times during the night. I asked Alec to let me deal with it. He nodded in agreement, but got out of the car and stayed close to me. He knew it was my first "domestic" and he was aware of just how volatile these situations could become.

As we approached the scene, memories of how the local Police in Holywood had handled my own parents came flooding back to me, along with words of wisdom from the "old guard" on how it was important not to take sides. I knew I had to make sure that our presence did not add to the upset by frightening the children. I was also aware how important it was that the husband was left in no doubt that we would have to arrest him if we were called back again. As we approached the door, I hoped I was up to the task.

I entered the house. I separated the parents into different rooms, and politely and courteously listened to each one individually. I smiled at and tried to settle the children who were obviously upset about the fighting between their parents. We left the house around fifteen minutes later with both the husband and wife thanking us for calling. I just knew there would be no more trouble with them, at least not for the rest of that particular night.

Alec and I returned to the Reserve constable we had left waiting in the car. Alec himself had had so little to do that he had lit his pipe and was enjoying a smoke. He looked at me. "You handled that like a professional, son," he said, patting me heartily on the back. He was shaking his head in awe. "That Depot training is definitely getting better," he added, as he struggled to get back into the driver's seat of the Police car.

If only he knew, I thought!

Using some tact and a little time, I had done my best to make the same impression upon those children as the local Holywood Police had made upon me all those years before. In fact, my courteous hand-ling of the situation had also endeared me to the parents. I was often called to that same house again, but always only needed a few minutes each time to settle things down.

Several months into my time at Newtownabbey, I decided to move closer to the barracks: Holywood was too far away. I soon obtained the tenancy of a Housing Executive flat at 5a Abbotscoole House, Rathcoole. There were quite a large number of Police officers living in the Rathcoole Estate at that time. What we did not realise was that we were there under licence. A licence which the local UDA were about to remove. Many Police families were to be intimidated out of Rathcoole and the neighbouring Loyalist estates by threats, bomb and gun attacks on their homes.

While the Province had been relatively peaceful, RUC officers could and did patrol alone on the beat or in the car. Patrolling solo in cars was not really encouraged, but it was still acceptable on the beat. Charlie Herdman was the Rathcoole beat and community cop. He patrolled the Rathcoole Estate alone and was widely respected by all of the locals. He policed in a fair but firm manner. As he mingled with the general public while out on his beat, he was the epitome of all that was good in a community cop.

I had now been in the RUC for just under a year and as a proba-tioner constable I was invariably accompanied by a constable senior to me. My duties were standard beat and patrol. We had some very good old coppers who showed us the ropes. There was a great deal of on-the-job training. We also had some good young lads who took their duties seriously and tried to make a difference. Yes, unfortunately there were also the bigoted coppers. In this respect, things were no different in the RUC than they would have been in "Civvy Street". I learned very quickly whom I could trust. I was frustrated at the lack of acknowl-edgement from our authorities that bigots existed at all. In fact, some of our very senior officers were suspected of such attitudes and con-duct themselves. There were not many of them, but it was easy enough for them to ruin a Police operation by tipping off Loyalists or Republicans of pending house searches or arrests. It was also very hard to gain any evidence of such conduct. We were all supposed to pretend that such things did not happen. Needless to say, this fostered a great deal of frustration amongst those RUC men like myself who would become directly affected by it.

I learned very quickly to keep my intentions to move against any criminal or terrorist to myself, rather than risk compromise, or worse. Yet out there on the streets of Northern Ireland, especially in those early years of the Troubles, your very life depended upon the trust you could place in your colleagues. I quickly acquired a healthy disregard for authority or regulations if I saw that they were obstructing me in getting the job done. This attitude allowed me to stay one step ahead of colleagues—no matter what their rank—who were hell-bent on frustrating my policing efforts. But it did not make me popular with those officers who would rather that I did nothing. Those who did not want me to "rock the boat", so to speak.

The political climate at that time was highly unstable. Many of our law-abiding locals were deeply unhappy with the status quo. Catholics saw their rights threatened and they mistrusted Protestants. Protestants saw their Catholic neighbours as potential IRA men and they too felt threatened. The local paramilitaries saw their chance and used this political vacuum to bolster their numbers and to instil the fear in their respective communities that the "other side" would soon attack. All we as a Police Service could do was watch with alarm as our community sank into an atmosphere of almost tangible fear. People stayed indoors as bomb and gun attacks escalated. No-one was safe.

We did our best to stand between the two warring factions. In reality there was little that we could do. Our numbers were insufficient; we were being spread too thinly on the ground. Other duties, such as policing riots elsewhere in the Province or operating anti-bomb patrols out of Belfast City Centre, ate into our resources. In 1972, around the time that I started my service in Newtownabbey, there was an exodus of decent Catholic families from the notorious Rathcoole Estate due to blatant intimidation by unruly thugs. Local vigilante and UDA patrols were in evidence on the street corners as rumours of civil war circulated. Many of the vigilantes were ex-servicemen and very decent men too. Our standing orders were to interact with them with tact: our approaches to them were usually met with a polite and courteous reception. There were of course exceptions. Vicious, hard-core criminal elements were targeting local Catholics for intimidation. They would always be there in the background, ready to take advantage of any reason for civil unrest. We had had our fill of it. We worked tirelessly to get to grips with the problem. Military patrols from the British Army worked with us.

On occasion, however, we would find ourselves with only three RUC men in a car reacting to a complaint of a disturbance and would arrive to be confronted by a hostile mob of some 30 or 40 UDA men. Only eye contact with their leader and a great deal of tact could prevent the situation from escalating out of control. It was terrifying enough for me as an RUC man to be confronted by a horde of these thugs. How on earth must a civilian have felt when confronted by them? Generally speaking, when we arrived, the bulk of a UDA gang would disperse, leaving only a few genuine vigilantes, men who had more sense than to get sucked into the local Loyalist paramilitaries. These men would try to help us and tell us who the ringleaders of the unruly element were. I was always grateful for their assistance.

We had to stand back and watch the Ulster Defence Association (UDA) and the outlawed Ulster Volunteer Force (UVF) develop rapidly. Sinister hooded and uniformed men openly carrying wooden cudgels of all descriptions replaced the law-abiding vigilantes who had been only too ready to co-operate with us. Some of these menacing individuals had even taken it upon themselves to stop cars and question the occupants. We now needed to take firmer action if we were to ensure that they did not usurp our RUC function.

My problem was that I was short on tact when it came to dealing with thugs of any kind or persuasion. The fact that they claimed allegiance to one Loyalist faction or another was neither here nor there to me. I tried to imagine how I would feel if I was a decent Catholic trying to live in these estates like Rathcoole. Would I feel intimidated by the presence of these hooded men wandering about the estate in the dark in groups of six or more, openly armed with cudgels? Would I expect the Police to take a strong line with them? The answer was always a resounding "YES".

Our instructions at that time were to monitor the activities of these paramilitaries and intervene only if we came upon a breach of the peace. However, I, like many others, found the very presence of masked men offensive. If they were masked I would stop and challenge them, ordering them to remove their masks and identify themselves. It was no surprise to me that the majority of the masked men were from the local criminal contingent. The fact that I dared to challenge them did not endear me to them.

Not all of my colleagues shared my enthusiasm to show these thugs that we would not tolerate such behaviour. They stood back in support of me but voiced their opinion that such confrontation could start a riot. In fact, it never did. What the hoodlums behind those masks did not know was that we often acted from information supplied by their decent counterparts who were unmasked and who were not involved in unlawful activity. The decent Loyalist vigilantes were as afraid of the criminal element in the UDA as their Catholic neighbours.

The hardliners objected to my stops and searches, complained to my authorities and threatened to barricade the estates and keep us out. This would be in no-one's interest. We had to agree to strike a balance. The hoods were taken off and we received instructions to leave the UDA alone except in so far as was necessary to keep the very fragile peace. Our local Police commanders were trying hard to meet these people halfway. This compromise lasted for only a short time before masked UDA men were once again on patrol and stopping cars. Once again, I started to challenge them and to identify the masked men. The UDA men threatened to get me transferred: they had, they said, friends in very high places. I would be "seen" to. I treated these threats with the contempt they deserved.

However, following a number of complaints of Police harassment, an instruction appeared on the notice board in the guardroom in the form of a written report. I read it with some dismay before going out on night duty. Its content shocked me. The local vigilantes were "working with the RUC and in support of us". Some "over-zealous officers were harassing the vigilantes." That "the actions of these few officers were alienating the vigilantes and their goodwill." That "in future, officers on patrol were not to stop or harass them." That "assurances had been given to the vigilantes that such harassment would stop." No distinction was made between the good or bad vigilantes. There was no mention of the masked UDA thugs who roamed the estates at night for the sole purpose of intimidating Catholics. The bullies, it seemed, were to have a licence to continue their activities unhindered by the RUC. I thought not.

This was at the time of the mass exodus of Catholic families from these mainly Loyalist estates. Intimidation was at fever pitch. The flee-ing families often left in daylight to go God knows where, parents clutching their bewildered children in their grasp, their belongings hastily bundled into open-backed lorries. Protestant families fleeing Nationalist estates in a similar fashion were taking occupation of the empty houses as quickly as they were being vacated. No-one referred to the Housing Executive who was responsible for the allocation of the houses. Normal protocol was breaking down. We could only look on, feeling powerless to do anything about the situation. Wholesale intimidation of this kind was rife all across the Province. Some residents were actually destroying their homes by fire as they fled in terror, so that they left nothing of value for the "other side". The scenes reminded me of movie footage of refugees during the Second World War.

With all of this in mind, I knew even as I read that notice that for me at least, ignoring its instructions was the only option. We could not police the district effectively without putting a check on the activities of those hooded thugs. It was our duty to stand between them and our law-abiding citizens and a chance to prove our impartiality. And so on each occasion I encountered masked men armed with wooden clubs, I challenged them, removed their masks and identified them. My attitude towards them was always measured and professional. I certainly did not accept that they were acting in collaboration with us, the Constabulary. The thugs hated me for this, again threatening to "get me seen to" by Police officers they knew in high places. "Just you wait," they would shout.

I did not have long to wait. I was at home at around 10 am on a morning following night shift. I was due to start duty that day on the late turn at 3 pm. I received a telephone call from the barracks, telling me to report to the office of a senior RUC man at 2 pm. I was told that the senior officer was none too pleased with complaints from the UDA about harassment, in total contravention of his written instruction. This senior officer had no love for the UDA but he was under intense pressure from local community leaders and councillors.

As I arrived at the barracks at 1 pm, I bumped into Arthur, my relief sergeant. I explained why I was there so early—the UDA men had said they would get me fixed. Arthur listened intently to my side of the story, as I reminded him that even the decent UDA men had asked us to help them to control the criminal element that was causing so much unnecessary grief in the area. I was worried that the senior officer would want the names of the decent men who had helped us to locate and identify the troublemakers. If the malicious UDA element got as much as a hint of such betrayal, there could be dire consequences for those who had tried to assist us.

"I'm going in there with you," was Arthur's response, once I'd finished my analysis of the situation. "You are entitled to have a friend with you. It's in the regulations," he added, smiling at me.

I felt better already. I was glad of Arthur's unexpected support. His character and integrity were without question. If you had the support of this man, there were few Police officers that would dare to tackle you. If I had been wrong, Arthur would have been the first to tell me so, the first to chastise me. I was no longer dreading my fast approaching appointment with the senior officer.

At 2 pm I was summoned to his office. I knocked the door and entered, as was the custom. The man had a face like thunder. Arthur followed me in and stood beside me.

"I am here as the constable's friend. He is entitled to have a friend in accordance with the regulations," he said.

The senior officer was none too pleased, but there was nothing he could do. He became flustered and made as if to examine papers on his desk. He ignored Arthur and addressed me sternly:

"Tell me why you continue to harass the vigilantes in Rathcoole in clear contravention of my written instruction?" he asked.

All of the legitimate arguments that I had intended to use in my defence left me. My mind went blank. I mumbled and stuttered in my attempts to try to explain how I was trying to balance my duty as a Police officer and my wish to comply as far as possible with his written instruction. I could tell by the twisted expression on his face that he was not happy with my answers, that it would not have mattered how eloquently I argued my case. He was having none of it and he flew into a rage. His utterances were even more incoherent than my own.

Suddenly the flow of abuse from the senior officer stopped abruptly. He was looking at Arthur. I turned around to see what on earth had caused this sudden change. He was watching in disbelief as Arthur produced his notebook: he was starting to take notes. The senior Police officer deflated suddenly like a balloon. I can see it all as vividly as if it happened yesterday . . .

"*I* told the constable to stop and to identify the criminal or rogue element, Sir," Arthur lied. "It was me who told him to remove the masks and properly identify those men roaming the estates. There could after all be anyone behind those masks. If what they are doing or what they are intending to do is legal, then they wouldn't need masks," he added. "Furthermore, Sir, your instruction is at odds with RUC policy at Headquarters," Arthur concluded.

He started to write in his official notebook. I could see the senior officer panic. He looked up at me and waved his hand towards the door to indicate that I must leave at once. I didn't need to be told twice. As I was closing the door behind me, I caught a glimpse of a very stern-faced Arthur. He was dealing with this tricky situation in the straight and authoritative manner he knew best. He did not fear any senior-ranking officer. If only there were a thousand men just like Arthur. As I closed the door behind me, I heard a very subdued senior officer say,

"Now, Arthur, there's no call for . . ."

I didn't wait for the rest. The senior officer had fallen at the first hurdle.

I knew that there was still work to be done. We would have to teach these thugs that we would not tolerate their attempts to dictate what the RUC did or did not do, no matter how many complaints they made about us to our authorities, no matter how much pressure they put upon our local commanders, politically or otherwise. I knew by the mass exodus of Catholic families from our area that we had lost their confidence. A confidence which would take years and years to win back. I was determined, however, to try. Again I reflected on the words of those Depot instructors during our training: "We will be judged by our actions!"

I could see that there were a number of RUC officers serving alongside me who should have been sent back to the Depot to listen to those words of wisdom. The theory was that the RUC did not tolerate bigots. The practice was so very different. Well, I was going to try to change that in whatever way I could. There were to be times when I would be lucky to escape with my life in my attempts to make a difference. I knew it was not going to be easy to challenge my authorities when necessary. But that was not going to deter me from my endeavours to provide the public with a fair and impartial policing service as far as I personally could. In fact I had always enjoyed a challenge. However, in those early days, I seriously underestimated just how far some of my colleagues would go to frustrate my efforts. The nature and extent of the betrayal was something to witness and would later be something I had to suffer and endure without any support. I was never again to find another supervisor as strong as Arthur at any time during the rest of my service in the RUC.

———

One cold February morning in 1973, I was on security duty in uniform in the sandbagged Sanger at the gates of the barracks. I was armed with a submachine-gun (SMG), my favourite weapon in the Police armoury. I had enjoyed the training we had had in the use of the SMG, and had in fact excelled in my scores for accuracy on the range with it. I liked the fact too that there was very little recoil from this weapon. To pass the time that morning, I decided to practise handling the gun. Removing the magazine containing the bullets and releasing the safety catch, I went through the different firepower options. "Safety," I checked. "Single shot," I checked. "Repetition," I checked. And again, "Single shot" . . .

I was so engrossed in what I was doing that I had failed to notice a car arriving at the front gate. It was only when the car horn sounded that it caught my attention. As luck would have it, the driver was the same senior Police officer with whom Arthur and I had had the run-in about the vigilante patrols. I lifted the SMG magazine containing the 9 mm bullets and slammed it back into the magazine assembly before rushing to open the huge, steel front gate. Unfortunately in my haste I hadn't noticed that the SMG was cocked and ready to fire when I slammed that magazine home. The senior officer launched an attack on me. I was not his favourite constable, to say the least.

"Why did it take you so long to get to the front gate?" he asked. I didn't answer.

"Why is there a pen behind your ear?" he asked.

"I always carried a pencil there, Sir, when I was an electrician," I replied.

"You are no longer an electrician. Here we supply you with pockets for your pens. Use them!" he thundered. "And take those gloves off!" he said, adding, "You can't handle that firearm properly with those on."

He was certainly not in good humour that morning. He left his brand new car parked just outside the door and disappeared inside, glancing back at me with disdain. Several minutes later, as I walked up and down outside the barracks on duty, I noticed that the SMG in my hand was ready to fire. The cocking handle was pulled right back and was resting on the seer. The magazine was full of bullets. The safety catch was off! I realised that I would have to make the gun safe as quickly as possible, but I was panicking and not thinking straight. I tried to recall the instructor's advice on how exactly to make the weapon safe. I checked that it was on single shot only. It was. I did not remove the magazine. That was my big mistake. I knew that the SMG did not hold any bullets in the breech, so I decided to let the cocking handle slide forward slowly, holding it between my left finger and thumb.

Everything went well until the cocking handle passed the magazine. I did not remember that it would automatically extract a bullet on the way past and deliver it to the breech. Fortunately I was holding the weapon firmly and ensuring it was pointing in a safe direction. It discharged with a deafening roar. I felt a sharp pain in my left thumb. To say that I was shocked would be an understatement. The cocking handle slammed back with a reassuring click and came to rest against the seer again. The gun now smoking in my hand was ready to fire again. I was back to square one and had already considerably embarrassed myself. My thumb was throbbing and I feared that it was broken.

I set the gun down on the ground and was rushing to ask a colleague for advice when the same senior officer from earlier on shouted from his office window upstairs, "Did you hit my car?"

"No, Sir," I replied.

I knew that the round had gone upwards. It was a good job that the senior officer hadn't stuck his head out of that window a few seconds before because he would have lost it! I retrieved the spent bullet case. I was immediately summoned to the office of the senior Police officer. I believed that he had been waiting for just such an opportunity to get back at me. He now had a clear chance to discipline me: he, at any rate, was not about to miss me and hit the wall! I reflected upon my short Police career thus far as I walked up the stairs that led to his office. Only one year's service and this was to be the end for me. I already knew that the senior officer was in bad form that day. I was fully expecting a roasting or worse before being officially suspended from duty. Incidents of this nature with firearms were viewed very seriously by the RUC and I was still on probation. I certainly deserved to be disciplined, at the very least.

Much to my surprise, the officer was only concerned that I was not seriously injured. He ran downstairs and arranged for someone to get me a hot cup of tea before I followed him back up to his office. He could see that I was in shock. He was genuinely supportive, and keen to ensure that I had learned from my experience. I was aware that in fact I couldn't even handle the small telephone exchange in the guardroom: on at least two occasions that morning, I had cut him off when he had been in mid-conversation with senior Police at Headquarters! So what duties would he be able to give me where I would not cause havoc, I wondered? But he merely laughed at me: I was not to be "blocked". I was not even to be severely admonished. Apparently his chief concern was that I receive adequate additional training in the handling of the SMG before I killed someone.

"Look, go and join the car crew," he said. "I will arrange further training for you." As I turned to leave his office, he called me back. He handed me the spent bullet case that I had retrieved outside and told me to keep it in my baton pocket in my uniform trousers. I immediately did as he suggested.

The officer arranged further weapons training for me with a nod and a wink, not alluding to the accidental discharge in front of my colleagues, so as to save me the least embarrassment. It was, as he said, a cheap lesson: I could have killed someone. I was also very lucky that I had not fractured my thumb. Following that incident, I was always very cautious in handling firearms of any sort. I still have that spent cartridge case to this day.

———

My subdivision, or my "patch", became my new-found garden. I was soon able to distinguish the weeds from the flowers as I set about stopping and checking cars and pedestrians that appeared suspicious to me. I also became highly skilled at being able to identify new groups of individuals who had been drawn into the different paramilitary groups. This knowledge would stand me in good stead as I tried to decide whom I needed to stop and check on a regular basis.

Often before setting out on patrol, I would remark to my colleagues that I was going out to do a bit of "weeding", referring to terrorists or ordinary criminals alike as "weeds". It seemed to me to be a particularly fitting analogy, and one which I was to continue to use throughout my whole Police career. The truth was that these undesirables stood out from the crowd just as weeds do in a garden.

In those days of the early 1970s, for example, many UVF men wore black trousers, with black polo neck jumpers and black leather jackets. In fact, it was these trademark black polo neck jumpers which resulted in them being nicknamed "black necks" by their own communities. Their junior counterparts in the Young Citizens Volunteers (YCV) wore similar apparel, except for their beige parallel trousers. Those who dressed in this way were keen to be identified as belonging to such groups in their respective communities, proud as they were of their association with these organisations.

I was equally enthusiastic to see them wearing such "uniforms", for this meant that when on patrol we could easily see who was in which organisation. It was then only a short time before we were able to set about identifying those of their associates who were for some reason or other not so keen to be identified in this manner. I was starting to "positively interact" with the locals, just as my senior colleague Alec had advised me, in order to be able to build up what we called "local knowledge". I soon grasped the beauty of having such knowledge and would take any opportunity to consolidate it. This—my enthusiasm and aptitude for gathering such intelligence—was to be the reason that I would be invited to join the CID just two years into my time in the Force.

Unfortunately I was to receive only qualified support from some circles, and blatant obstruction from others. In those early days of my uniformed service I had little or no contact with the RUC Special Branch. Their absolute power over the rest of the Force was legendary. I had heard talk of this power: it seemed unreal, almost mythical. Little did I suspect that when I finally did get a glimpse into the sinister world which they inhabited, I would soon find myself locked in deadly conflict with them: a conflict which would very nearly destroy me completely.

Chapter 5

Dealing with the
Travelling Gunmen

It was 31 March 1973, Grand National Day, and less than a month since the incident with the accidental discharge of the Sterling submachine-gun outside the Newtownabbey barracks. I had completed my unofficial refresher course in the handling of the SMG only a couple of days before. I was on the early shift, which ran from 7 am until 3 pm. I was the observer in our District Patrol car, call sign Delta November one eight, with Constable John Newell as the driver. The day had started out just like any other. We were responsible for patrolling flashpoint areas such as the mainly Protestant and Loyalist Rathcoole Estate, where violence could flare up in an instant and without warning. We were going about our routine duties in a diligent manner.

Things had been relatively quiet in the early part of our shift. By the time our break came around we were ready to relax for the allocated three quarters of an hour. This time normally enabled us to get a bite to eat, but anything could happen and we would be required to respond immediately to whatever came up. The theory was that the Glengormley car would cover for us and we in turn would cover for them whilst they enjoyed a break, but in reality, their car would be often be too busy and we would have to attend ourselves.

At around 12.30 pm or so, while John and I were still on our break, a telephone call came in on the 999 system from a very distressed old lady at Doagh Road, Newtownabbey. She had, she said, recently had an argument with her elderly male neighbour, a Mr Ernest Mitchell, and had not seen or spoken to him for a few days. His milk was still on his doorstep and he usually brought it in early in the morning. She was concerned that he might have come to some harm.

The operator who took the 999 calls at Belfast Regional Control (BRC) was anxious that we attend as soon as possible. The elderly lady was inconsolable. John and I stopped eating and rushed out to our patrol car. A life could be in danger in a case like this. The elderly man could be lying injured, unable to move or to summon help for himself.

As we left the barracks hurriedly, I stopped briefly to pick up my tunic and an SMG, slamming a magazine with thirty rounds of ammunition into its housing. We were at the scene within minutes and informed Control of our arrival.

The elderly lady, a Miss Agnes Ryan, was waiting for us at her front door at 13 Doagh Road. She was in a severely distressed state. She was 80 years old and very small and frail. My first instinct was to comfort her, but our priority was her friend and neighbour at number 15. The two front doors faced each other and were only feet apart.

Although the address was Doagh Road, the little pensioners' bungalows were actually in the Rushpark Estate just off the Doagh Road and opposite the Rathcoole Filling Station. Rushpark itself was a small Housing Executive estate and a peaceful, tranquil area unlike some of the neighbouring estates. With large expanses of grass and mature trees, it was in a beautiful setting, in stark contrast to the sprawling Rathcoole Estate just across the Doagh Road. Rushpark was one of the few estates in the Newtownabbey area that threw up very few problems in policing terms. In the previous year, there had been some tragic incidences of the wholesale intimidation of Catholics from the estate by the UDA, but since then things had generally settled down. The RUC could come and go there with little fear of attack.

I discovered that Miss Ryan had a front-door key to her neighbour's house. I opened the front door, fearing the worst. As I entered the living room the nauseating smell of death was overwhelming. Mr Mitchell was lying on top of his bed still in his clothes. A little mongrel dog was lying across his stomach, growling at me and baring its teeth. It was none too pleased at our intrusion. The heating was on and turned up fully. All of the windows were closed too, only aggravating the problem of the smell.

It was obvious that there was nothing to be done for the poor man. He had been dead for some time. I went to break the news to his neighbour, but she had followed me inside and had unfortunately witnessed the heartbreaking scene. She broke down in tears. She had lost a dear friend. She declined the offer of a doctor.

I left her home and walked out to the Police car. I updated the control room in Castlereagh by radiotelephone that we had a sudden death on our hands. We would need a doctor to pronounce life extinct and an undertaker to remove the body to the morgue.

At times like this, one overcomes one's natural repugnance. There were standard procedures to follow, questions to be answered, forms to be filled relating to this man's demise which would enable the coroner to hold an inquest into the death if necessary. We had, however, left the barracks in such a hurry that we had forgotten to lift the forms in question. John volunteered to return to the barracks to get them and set off alone in the Police car.

I approached the bed. It was my intention to touch nothing at the scene, but I needed to take notes of any medication in evidence. As I neared the body, the little dog once again growled menacingly at me. It would not move from its master's side.

I set my machinegun down on a small table covered with a clean, white, linen tablecloth. I opened as many windows as possible to allow fresh air to circulate in the room. I also kept the front door open for the same reason. I could see right into Miss Ryan's living room. She was pacing up and down, wringing her hands and obviously very upset.

Doctor Brolly from the Whiteabbey Health Centre arrived at 1 pm and pronounced life extinct. He knew the deceased, had in fact recently examined him at his home and was able to inform me that Mr Mitchell had a known medical condition that had caused his death. The doctor made it clear that he would issue a death certificate.

There were no suspicious circumstances and there would be no need to hold an inquest. When Dr Brolly left, I again asked BRC to summon the undertakers to remove the remains to Wilton's Funeral Parlour on the Shore Road. At least the deceased would not have to suffer the added indignity of an autopsy. He would not be going to the morgue. The undertakers arrived very quickly and set about their grim task with an air of professional indifference.

It had been almost an hour since we had arrived at the scene. This was too long to be hanging about anywhere in those days of travelling gunman. There was the added difficulty that we had been drawing unwanted attention from passersby and from overly curious neighbours with the ghoulish interest in the proceedings which such incidents attract. This interest from onlookers was at its height just before John left to get the forms.

With the Police car no longer in evidence at the scene, people began to drift away. It dawned on me that in our haste to get to the scene I had also forgotten my gun belt and my revolver. My tunic was unbuttoned and lying open. I needed to remain at the scene, however, to await the arrival of the relatives of the deceased. In such cases, we were required to stay at the scene until we could hand the house and its contents over to a responsible relative. We had had some difficulty in contacting the family, who lived in East Belfast. Their estimated time of arrival was unknown.

My instinct was telling me again that I had already been there too long. I was hoping that the absence of our Police car from the Doagh Road would lead anyone wishing us harm to believe that we had completed our enquiries and had departed.

Nevertheless, I needed to take stock of my situation. These were troubled times. Usually we never stayed too long in one place, even if there was no obvious sign of trouble. Persons hostile to the Police could well have become aware that I was alone there. I was starting to feel vulnerable, especially without my gun belt and my revolver.

The Sterling SMG was still sitting on the table in the living room. I kept looking out the front window through the net curtains to see if there was anyone outside interested in my presence there. I was grateful for those net curtains which shielded me from prying eyes.

In the meantime, I tried to comfort Miss Ryan. Her front door remained open too. She was obviously not used to all this commotion. She was in shock. She wandered between her own home and the deceased's. Dr Brolly had given her some potent sedatives but they were still sitting on her telephone table where he had left them. The whole episode was more than she could bear. My heart went out to her. She went back to her home to make me a cup of tea.

John was taking an age to get back. I assumed that he must have been caught up in something else. I was in the middle of taking some notes when the old lady handed me a cup of strong tea and informed me that the relatives of the deceased had just arrived outside. She pointed to the pathway that led out of the estate onto the main Doagh Road. What happened next was totally unexpected. It was exactly the sort of incident that every Policeman dreads. The type of incident that tests a Police officer to the limit.

I glanced out the front window to see who was coming. It was extremely fortunate that I did. I had almost walked out of the house to greet what I thought were the deceased's "grieving relatives". There were three men outside and they were acting very suspiciously. It was obvious to me that their presence was not connected with the death of the old man. The more I observed them, the more suspicious I became. I was tempted to walk out and challenge them. My better judgment told me to wait until John got back.

The area outside the pensioners' bungalows was set in grass with mature, thinning fir trees. There was a little tarmac path that led from the bungalows to the Doagh Road, meandering through the grassy area to a hedgerow. It hasn't changed much, even to this day. The three men were crouching down behind the hedge and were engrossed in discussion with each other. They could not be seen from the Doagh Road, and were obviously up to no good.

I suddenly realised that John would arrive back very soon. He would be totally unaware of the potential threat from these three men. I decided that I could not wait for his return after all. I ushered Agnes into her own home, asking her to close her door and stay inside.

I had no Police radio and could not use Miss Ryan's telephone without exposing her to unnecessary danger. If those suspects saw me going into her home or leaving it, they might wrongly believe that she was knowingly helping the RUC. The penalty for that could well be a petrol bomb.

The first thing that had struck me about the men was their attire. Each of them was wearing a black leather jacket and a black polo neck jumper—the standard "uniform" of the day of members of the outlawed UVF.

Their ages ranged from early twenties to mid-thirties. One of them, obviously the eldest of the trio, was heavily built. He was giving instructions to the other two. He pulled his polo neck jumper up to cover the lower half of his face and pointed across the Doagh Road. I saw the heavy man reach down to the waistband of his trousers. He lifted his hand up again in a manner that imitated that he was holding a gun. All three of the men were so engrossed in what they were doing that they had failed to look behind them. I had no doubt that they were engaged in some criminal enterprise.

I knew that I would have to move quickly before John stopped on the roadway in front of the suspects. I grabbed the machinegun from the table and hurriedly left the deceased's home. As I passed her partially open front door, Agnes looked at me fearfully. I put my finger to my lips to indicate to her that she must be quiet. She understood.

"Bad men," I whispered.

She nodded, terror written all over her face. I winked at her in a bid to reassure her. She closed her front door silently as I moved out to deal with the trio. I did so as if on autopilot. I did not have time to plan anything. As I walked those few yards to approach the suspects, I wondered who they were and what they were doing. And most importantly at this moment, if they were armed.

My stomach was in knots. My mouth was dry. I was shaking. My feet felt as heavy as lead. I was hoping that this nervousness would not be evident to the men I was about to challenge.

The last time I had felt fear like this was in the previous year, 1972, when I came under fire from the UVF in Lord Street at the junction of Paxton Street whilst on patrol with the Royal Military Police as part of Willie Whitelaw's Task Force. I had felt the pressure of the .45 bullets from a Thompson submachine-gun as they sailed past my head. I had been lucky then. I had weathered that storm without firing a shot. I was determined to do the same here.

I only had time to don my RUC forage cap, and was still fastening a few buttons on my black RUC tunic as I walked the short distance to where the three men were standing. The belt of my tunic hung loosely by my side. I gripped the body of the submachine-gun. The cold steel frame was rough but reassuring.

I was standing only a few feet behind them when I cleared my throat.

"Police!" I shouted.

What happened next seemed to occur in slow motion. I was no longer shaking. No longer afraid. I had seized the initiative. I felt that I was now in complete control of the situation, and I intended to keep it that way. All three men swung around in my direction. Their facial expressions were a picture. They stared at me in utter disbelief. I saw them all scan the surrounding area for other RUC men. They quickly realised that I was alone.

I was holding my SMG in my right hand and lowered to the ground in a safe direction. I was trying to take as much tension out of this encounter as was possible.

I desperately needed to keep this situation in check until the arrival of reinforcements. I tried to be as courteous as was possible in the circumstances.

"What are you doing here?" I asked the men.

"We are Prods," said one.

"Waiting for a mate," said another.

"Catching a bus," said the third man.

All of them spoke at once. I questioned them for a time, as if I was trying to establish which of their accounts was true. I was merely playing for time. Yet I knew that John would be in no hurry to come back. After all, as far as he was aware, I was in a safe area inside a house and out of harm's way.

As I continued questioning the suspects, I looked for indications of worry, signs of panic. I was not disappointed. The eldest of the trio was red-faced and sweating. His hands were shaking.

I scrutinised all three, noting that two of the suspects in front of me had bulges in the waistbands of their trousers, which of course suggested that they were armed.

I also noticed the eldest man moving slowly to my right in an obvious bid to try to get behind me. They were exchanging furtive glances. I saw one nod. The other would shake his head. They were obviously considering not going quietly. The third man, the eldest of the trio, was now almost behind me!

Nothing in our training would have prepared me for a situation like this. You had to rely on your own initiative. You had to keep your wits about you. Any sign of weakness or hesitation could cost you your life. I realised this and decided to act assertively. Courtesy was going to have to take a back seat on this occasion.

I took two steps back and raised my SMG. I cocked it as hard as I could. The heavy metallic crack of the gunmetal broke the eerie silence as the cocking handle came to rest against the seer. Anyone who has made ready to fire an SMG will know exactly what I mean. I moved the safety catch off to the first notch, single shot. I felt my confidence soar.

This had the desired effect. Their reaction was one of pure fear. Seeing the gun was now ready to fire, they all raised their hands high in the air, obviously afraid that I would kill them. Certainly I had no wish to harm them. My handling of the SMG was not great and I told them so. I had once again grabbed the initiative that had so nearly slipped away from me.

I singled out the stouter, older man.

"Open your coat!" I commanded, pointing the SMG at him.

He was extremely ruddy-faced and looked as if he was about to cry. He opened his leather jacket. He was sweating profusely. He lifted his jumper and exposed the butt of a large revolver. I told him to remove the gun slowly and put it on the ground. He did so. He offered no resistance. The gun that he had put down on the grass before me was very familiar. It was a .38 Webley revolver, exactly the same make and calibre of revolver as was standard issue in the RUC, and traditionally carried in our side holster as part of our uniform.

"What is your name?" I asked.

"Redmond," he replied.

"Your full name?" I barked.

"William Erskine Redmond," he replied sheepishly.

"Pick a tree and put your arms around it," I commanded.

He did so immediately and without question. He nodded to the other two as if to indicate that they should co-operate. I turned to the next man.

"Put your gun on the ground and pick a tree," I ordered.

He was terrified. He removed his gun slowly and put it on the ground beside the first one. I was surprised to see that it too was a .38 Webley revolver.

"What is your full name?" I asked.

"Stanley Campbell," he replied.

He too walked to a fir tree near to his friend and put his arms around it. I turned to the third suspect. He was the youngest of the three. He was shaking visibly. Before I could say a word to him, he said,

"Jonty, it's me, Terry. Terry Nicholl. You remember me from the car accident on the Church Road, don't you?" he asked.

I studied the young man standing nervously before me. I didn't remember him, but I had dealt with a car accident there recently.

"Are you armed?" I asked him.

He nodded.

"Then do as you are told and place your firearm on the ground slowly," I commanded.

He nodded again but hesitated. He wanted to object. "Look," he said, "We are Prods . . ."

He appeared to honestly believe that this would make a difference. That somehow I was supposed to let them go on their way. He was very much mistaken.

"Put it down!" I barked. My tone left him in no doubt that his religious persuasion was of no interest to me. Nor would it help to extricate him from his present position. I saw him look left and right and I realised that he was contemplating flight. "Don't even think about it, Terry," I said.

I pointed the SMG directly at him. This rattled him. He couldn't take his eyes off it. He was staring straight down the barrel.

The truth was that even though I was aware that I had a firm legal right to use lethal force in such circumstances if necessary, I did not wish to harm any of them.

This young man's indecision meant that the third disarming was taking an absolute age.

Where the hell is John? I thought. If only he would come back.

Terry Nicholl reached very slowly for his gun. I believed that he was about to try to use it to resist arrest. If he did, I would be perfectly within my rights to shoot him. Our training on the range was to shoot to kill. There would be no question of trying to aim to wound a terrorist in these circumstances. I could feel the adrenalin rush. I was as frightened as he was but I knew better than to show it! Terry was studying me carefully. I knew instinctively that he was looking for any sign that I would allow him to flee. I gave him no such hope.

He slowly removed his gun from the waistband of his trousers. He dropped it down on the grass beside the other two. This young man was the most defiant of the three. I was so glad that he had not attempted to use his firearm to resist arrest. His gun, a semi-automatic pistol, was larger than the other two.

There were now three fully-loaded handguns lying on the grass at my feet. Terry walked to a pine tree beside his friends and put his arms around it. I had encountered three travelling gunmen and had successfully disarmed them. I had no handcuffs. We didn't carry them as a part of our equipment. I would have given anything for three pairs at that time.

I now addressed all three, telling them that they were under arrest for the illegal possession of firearms. I also told them I would shoot them if they made any attempt to escape. I was totally unaware that a woman who lived nearby had witnessed the entire episode from her upstairs window and had dialled 999 to get me some help.

John arrived back within two or three minutes of my disarming of the three terrorists. He parked the Police car exactly in front of where the gunmen had been hiding. He knew nothing of the drama that had unfolded until he arrived at the scene. He very quickly rushed to my aid. We could both hear the reassuring sound of Police sirens in the distance. Help was on its way. I breathed a sigh of relief. Other Police officers arrived in large numbers a short time later and assisted us in removing the prisoners to the barracks.

As John and I walked back to our car, without even thinking about it, I removed the magazine from the SMG. I let the cocking handle slide forward before inserting the magazine into its housing again. I put the safety catch to "safe". John was well impressed: despite the excitement I had remembered exactly how to make the weapon safe. This was a far cry from the inept handling of the same weapon only the month before that had caused me so much embarrassment.

It wasn't until an hour or so later when I was alone in the barracks waiting to be interviewed by the CID that the realisation of what could have happened to me set in. I found myself shaking uncontrollably. I was so embarrassed. What on earth was wrong with me? I thought.

I did not know it at that time, but this was a common effect of trauma. I tried my level best to hide how I felt. It was expected that I would cope. No-one had explained that in fact I would revisit these traumatic scenes in the form of terrifying flashbacks and disturbing nightmares throughout my service. This was something that you didn't talk about. You were expected to just get on with it.

Many sterling RUC men turned to the bottle in an effort to cope and were lost to us as they succumbed to alcoholism. They would fall foul of the rigid discipline regulations, regulations that failed to take into account the fact it was their occupation that had caused them to turn to drink in the first place. They were seen as weak-willed and pensioned off or drummed out of the Constabulary.

In the macho world of a Police service, any signs of nervousness or debility were viewed as weakness. I had become aware of this very early in my Police service. Colleagues who did speak of experiencing these things were privately ridiculed. They too were seen as weak and untrustworthy.

Yet a part of me had enjoyed the challenge that I had been confronted with. But I knew too that I had been very lucky. I could so easily have lost my life. The whole affair served to add to my already built-in instinct for self-preservation.

I also realised that if it did happen again I would be better prepared to deal with it. I would make sure that I came away from it safely. If I could do so without firing a shot or hurting anyone, then that was a bonus. The first principle of Police work was the protection of life. I resolved that I would never be involved as a Police officer in the taking of life. The RUC had taught us that in our initial training. I did not want to betray that principle. Not ever.

The euphoria that followed was incredible. The Sub Divisional Commander (SDC) praised us. The next day, John and I were also summoned to the offices of our Chief Constable Sir Graham Shillington at RUC Headquarters at Brooklyn, Knock in Belfast. He was well pleased at the recovery of those firearms from the suspected UVF terrorists.

"Brown, you are exactly the sort of Police officer I am looking for," he said. "Not long ago I had the authority to promote a man like you in the field," he added. "I don't have that authority any more or you would be a sergeant today," he said.

The Chief Constable's endorsement was very welcome. It was exactly the type of support I had expected and hoped for. As I stood there, I reflected upon the first time that I had stood before Sir Graham. The circumstances had been so very different. Twelve years earlier, in 1961, I had been caught raiding his orchard by RUC men who were hiding in his garden guarding him from IRA threats. I was eleven years old at that time.

I had been caddying that day at the Royal Belfast Golf Club with some other boys from Holywood. Our bus stop on the way home was outside a big house that had an orchard just inside the gateway in the lawns below the house. We had always gone in there to pick up windfalls in the garden. We had never had any problems before.

This occasion was different. At that time Graham Shillington was RUC Commissioner of Police for Belfast based at the Commissioner's Office in Castlereagh. His RUC guard squad had found me in the orchard and brought me before him. He had looked at me with disgust then and had ordered his men to summon the district car to take me home to my parents.

I was tempted to put my arm around the Chief Constable's shoulders and remind him of that first meeting in his orchard. I decided, however, to bite my lip. To keep it for another day. Somehow I feared that he might not see the funny side of it.

This was a time of a professional high. John and I were elated as we left RUC Headquarters in John's new Morris 1300 cc car. There were to be many of these high points throughout my service. There were also to be lows and I was just about to experience one of them . . .

Several days after the arrests of the three armed terrorists, I was on duty at Newtownabbey Barracks. It was mid-shift on the early turn and I was busy preparing to go back out on patrol. Congratulations were still flowing from the majority of my colleagues. I was still on a high. My two-year probationary period was beginning to appear secure. I had only fourteen months service in the RUC at that time, but I felt that I could do no wrong.

I was walking from the guardroom to the kitchen, in the corridor just below the stairs, when I felt a hand firmly on my chest, stopping me in my tracks.

My green military flak jacket was pushed up into my chin. I found myself staring into the blazing eyes of a well-dressed man in his early forties. He was clothed very casually, in slacks and a fine woollen jumper. He looked as if he was dressed to play golf.

"Excuse me, son," he said politely.

He had a broad smile on his face. He was glancing left and right, acknowledging everyone who passed us in the corridor or on the stairs. He grabbed me by the arm and ushered me roughly into the snooker room at the bottom of the stairs.

Still holding on to me, he pulled the door shut behind him. We were alone in there. I had no idea who this man was or what rank he held, but I assumed by his manner of dress that he was a detective.

"You have caused all sorts of shit," he began. His tone was aggressive.

"Pardon?" I replied.

"Look", he said. "Take your f****n' boot out of the Prods. Those guns that you recovered have started a whole f****n' storm. You have been causing too many waves, throwing your weight around like that. A real 'Proddy basher', aren't you, son? Well, you better pull your reins in or we'll put you in Londonderry, you wee bastard! You can throw your weight around there all you want. So don't have me to have to come back here to see you again. Do you understand?"

He spoke without pausing for a breath. Urgently. Excitedly. He leaned in to my face. He punctuated his threats by pointing at my face with his finger. He didn't enlighten me as to who he was or who had sent him to speak to me.

I was speechless, unable to make any sense of what he had said. This was the first time I had heard the term "Proddy basher", but it would certainly not be the last time it would be hurled as an accusation against me.

There were so many questions that I wanted to ask this man. There was no doubt that he was beside himself with anger, but I had no idea why. However, before either of us could say another word, the door of the snooker room flew open. My partner for that day, Constable Kenny Johns, was standing there with a beaming smile on his face. When he saw the man with me, his smile vanished and he became sombre.

"We have to go," he said.

The man with me acknowledged Kenny, and then he turned on his heels and was gone as quickly as he had appeared. The whole encounter had lasted minutes, no longer. The real reason for it was lost on me. I believed that I had just been subjected to the outburst of a Loyalist bigot, someone most likely acting on his own behalf. I followed him out of the room, making faces behind his back. I walked to our patrol car with Kenny.

"What did he want?" asked Kenny.

I answered him with a question: "Who is he, Kenny?"

"He's a Special Branch man," Kenny said. "What did he want?"

"Want?" I replied, "Oh, he just wants me to take my boot out of the Prods."

Kenny laughed for a short time. Then he grew serious.

"Watch him, Jonty," he warned, "He is a bad bastard."

I found the whole incident unsettling. I asked a trusted supervisor what I should do.

"Do what you do best, Jonty. Go out there and police without fear or favour. Never mind the Special Branch, son, they are working to their own agenda," was his reply.

I was pleased to hear this, which seemed to confirm that the man was probably acting alone. I felt I had nothing to fear, that I had the unqualified support of a senior supervisor at least. Let them do their worst, I thought. I had never had as much as a cross word with the two Special Branch officers attached to my own barracks. I had always found them pleasant. I decided to put the whole sordid episode behind me.

However, my earlier euphoria had left me in that instant, evaporated into thin air. The congratulations flowing from well-intentioned fellow officers now seemed to have a hollow ring to them.

I had long since realised that it was a sad matter of fact that not all of my colleagues shared my enthusiasm for taking down Loyalist terrorists. Yet I believed that this would be the end of the matter. How wrong I was.

A few days after my sinister encounter with that Special Branch man, I was called into the Station Sergeant's office to take a personal telephone call.

"Son, is that Brown?" the voice at the other end inquired.

"Yes, Johnston Brown, can I help you?" I asked.

"No, son, you can't help me. You have really f****d me up. I bet you think you did a real good job getting those guns, didn't you?" he asked.

"Yes, I did do a good job . . . But who is this, please?" I asked.

"Who is this, son?" his tone was sarcastic. "I'll tell you who I am, son," he continued. He said that he was an RUC sergeant based outside Belfast. "I am the fool that's been signing those three guns present and correct in my armoury since I got here. Now I am going to fall for the whole affair. I just want you to know that it is likely that I will lose my job and pension over this."

He slammed the telephone down.

I stood there for several minutes still holding the handset. I felt lost, saddened by this development. I wanted to ring him back. Tell him I was not to know that the guns were stolen from an RUC armoury. Tell him how sorry I was that he was in trouble.

Surely the internal enquiry which would necessarily follow would establish exactly who had stolen those three guns? I knew even from my limited experience at the time that very few Police officers had unsupervised access to an RUC armoury. Suspects could be narrowed down, he might be exonerated by the enquiry team.

I sat alone in that office, worrying about that officer's predicament. I wanted to ring him back and tell him that he should blame the people who had betrayed the Constabulary and their trust by stealing

those three guns. I decided not to ring him back. After all, I had done
no more than what was expected of me. I had nothing to apologise
for. Let the enquiry take its natural course. It would be vital of course
to establish as quickly as possible who had stolen those weapons and
how on earth they had fallen into the hands of the local UVF. But these
were matters best left to the enquiry team. This was of no concern
of mine. How on earth could I be criticised for recovering stolen
RUC weapons?

It wasn't until later that day, when I was recounting to a colleague
what the caller had said to me about the theft of the guns from the RUC
armoury, that my mind wandered back to the earlier encounter with
the Special Branch officer. Was this what he had meant by "a storm"?
It was all starting to make sense. Yet why would the Special Branch
officer fear such an enquiry?

This was my first foray "into the Dark", as we were later to call it. It
was "into the Dark" when you found that in the course of carrying out
good Policework to the best of your ability and in accordance with
procedure, you were inadvertently stepping on Special Branch toes.
The Special Branch trusted no-one other than themselves: no-one
else, even at the most senior level, would be party to their operations
or overall agenda. All the other branches of the RUC may as well have
been working blindfolded. The fact that your prosecution of a Special
Branch source or your stumbling upon an ongoing Special Branch
operation was inadvertent or unintentional was purely academic.
You had managed to get in their way. In their eyes you were guilty.
The Special Branch would exact a price. You would be transferred to
a different area. Or you would be the subject of a Special Branch
whispering campaign against you which would lead your superiors
and your colleagues to conclude that you were less than honourable,
less than competent. The power of the Special Branch in this regard
was formidable. It cannot be overstated.

Personally speaking, I knew that no-one in their right mind would
argue that my timely intervention in arresting those armed men in the
middle of some criminal enterprise was anything less than proper. So
why was I made to feel so guilty?

This was my first experience of how, when the waves went out,
their ripples could run on far beyond the point where I believed they
had stopped, far beyond my wildest imagining, into uncharted
depths. This was not a black-and-white world.

Yet even with the benefit of hindsight, I would not change any part of what I did on that Grand National day in 1973. My ability to confront and deal with such rogue terrorist elements was to earn me the respect of all my decent RUC colleagues. The rest of them could go to hell.

Chapter 6
The Enemy Within

Everyone around me was full of cheerful anticipation in the lead-up to Christmas 1974. The horror of the Ulster Workers Council (UWC) strike, which had almost brought the Province to the brink of civil war, was well behind us. I was proud of the manner in which the Constabulary had handled that threat. It had been a year of intense political activity. One initiative after another had failed as the British Government reached out to the different paramilitary groups in a bid to bring them closer to democratic politics. It had been a very turbulent and confusing time for the ordinary copper trying to keep the peace.

In May of 1974, I had been appointed a detective constable at Newtownabbey, just one week before the change from our black RUC uniforms to the new green ones. In fact, I had very much enjoyed my time as a uniformed copper, and in some ways would have far preferred to stay where I was, but various colleagues and a senior supervisor had actively encouraged me to apply for a post in the CID and I had decided to follow their advice. I was just one element in a policing team responsible for keeping the peace in that predominantly Loyalist area. I had looked on with interest and more than a little cynicism as the government of the day lifted the proscription from the formerly-outlawed UVF in April 1974.

UVF men appeared on our streets as if out of the woodwork, basking in their new-found lawful status. Many of them had stood proudly unmasked and in uniform at their barricades during the UWC strike. They professed to be guarding their respective districts from possible Republican attack. I got a few surprises at the identities of some of these men. I was about to meet some of them again sooner than I expected in a sinister encounter with an armed UVF unit on the move.

In fairness to the UVF, I personally never experienced any policing problems in relation to their conduct during the strike. On the contrary, many of their volunteers were keen to assist us in dealing with large unruly elements roaming the district. This was in stark contrast to the lawlessness that prevailed in the neighbouring housing estates, such as Rathcoole, which were under the absolute control of the UDA. The lawful status of the UVF was short-lived, however: the murderous activities of the Shankill butchers, and the Dublin and Monaghan bombings on 17 May 1974 put paid to all that.

All of this was fresh in my mind as I asked a CID colleague in Newtownabbey Barracks to go out on patrol with me to do what I had come to call a spot of "weeding". The date was Friday, 13 December 1974. It was to be a day that I would never forget. The peaceful atmosphere which prevailed at that time of year in our district was a welcome respite from what had preceded, and we intended to ensure in as far as was humanly possible that our area remained quiet.

An office party was in full swing in our CID office that evening. My choice of partner for the patrol was Detective Constable Derrick McCourt: neither of us drank alcohol and we were at a loose end. We left the barracks, intending to spend an hour or so on patrol. I was driving an unmarked CID car, a standard fleet unmarked Ford Escort. We were both in plain clothes. At 8.45 pm we drove into the Loyalist Monkstown Estate—from the Monkstown Road into Cashel Drive and then right into Cloyne Crescent. Our aim was to monitor any suspicious activity outside the local UVF club there.

My partner, Derrick, was a formidable detective. I admired him for a variety of reasons, not least for his proven ability to make a considerable impact on the criminal and terrorist element from his base in Glengormley RUC Station. Derrick was a former body builder and British soldier. A devout Christian, Derrick was an officer of great personal integrity and unusual tenacity. As Derrick was based in Glengormley, we seldom patrolled together, but we got on well and it made sense to take the opportunity to work together on this occasion.

As we entered Cloyne Crescent, Derrick brought my attention to a large, dark furniture van coming slowly towards us from the opposite direction. It was displaying no lights. It was also taking up more than half of the road. Derrick had been an RUC road safety officer and did not like what he saw. Like me, he had joined the CID in May 1974, and was still to some extent in uniformed copper mode.

"Pull in front of that van, Jonty. I want to speak to the driver," Derrick said.

I was looking at the van and its occupants in a different light: as possible evidence of UVF terrorist activity. The vehicle was coming from the direction of a notorious UVF club not 200 yards away. The place in question was a hotbed of UVF activity. I pulled our Police car across the road in front of the van, effectively stopping it in its tracks as Derrick had requested. The van shuddered to a halt, the driver obviously having difficulty controlling it.

We alighted from our car. As I approached the van, I noticed a young man standing at the half-open driver's door and clinging on to the inside of the van to steady himself. He jumped down onto the roadway and identified himself to me. His surname was Cooper (not his real name).

Neither the name nor the young man's face meant anything to me. I did, however, recognise the driver of the van immediately. In fact, I knew him well. Now here was a "weed" if ever there was one, and I was hoping to get the chance to pluck him from our midst. A despicable man by any standards, and also a suspected member of the UVF.

Cooper was in full view of our headlights. I made a mental note of his clothing as I looked for the telltale bulges which would suggest that he was armed. There was none. He was wearing parallel trousers and a very short jumper exposing his midriff as he held his hands high on the door panels. My observations were to prove crucial later. I did not at any time lose sight of this young man. I searched him and confirmed that he was unarmed. I told him to stand away from the van and against a nearby wall. He co-operated fully. I asked the driver of the van to step down. I searched him. He was unarmed too. He stood against the wall beside young Cooper.

Derrick and I became aware of the presence of several more men inside the van. The PSV disc was traceable to what was obviously a Catholic firm, judging by its name, at any rate. I leaned into the rear and asked for the owner of the van by name. There was no reply. Then the men inside started to chant a well-known refrain: "Why are we waiting?" Derrick walked to our CID car to summon uniformed assistance.

We knew that a large number of RUC patrols were out in the area with back-up from several high profile Royal Military Police (RMP) vehicles. Instinctively Derrick and I had realised that these men were up to no good. We worked as if on automatic pilot, each of us instinctively looking after the other's back, an ability which came naturally to any Police officer involved in dangerous duties of this nature. I could hear the welcome sound of several Police sirens in the distance, signalled the imminent arrival of our uniform support vehicles.

I glanced over at the two suspects detained at the wall beside the van. I was studying their faces in the light of the street lamps for those telltale signs of panic. I was not disappointed. The van driver appeared to be under a great deal of pressure for some unknown reason. He avoided eye contact. Cooper also appeared very nervous. There had to be a reason for their anxiety.

Our immediate problem was that locals passing us in cars had become aware of the Police activity. There was the added danger that any one of them could alert the local paramilitaries. I could hear the siren of one Police car getting closer.

It arrived very quickly. It was a Royal Military Police Austin 1800 vehicle, fully liveried. The three military Policemen on board dismounted from their car and gave us armed cover. They were a very welcome sight.

An "Amber serial call sign" also attended the scene: this is an RUC transit van which has been specially drafted in, with at least five or six officers in it. With this support we now felt able to approach the rear of the van. There were at least four men inside and they were banging repeatedly on the inside of the van. If these guys were of the same calibre as the van driver, we had stumbled onto a motley crew indeed.

I remarked that I was surprised that the men had not left the van from the rear. The van driver replied that the only door which could be opened was the driver's door and it just opened halfway. The men were in effect trapped inside the van.

We asked the uniformed Police to invite each of the men inside to come out one at a time. As each UVF suspect stepped outside, they were searched, and all were found to be unarmed. I noted their details and they joined the driver and young Cooper at the wall. This took only 10 minutes. We sent an officer inside the van to search it. I could see with the aid of a torch that the floor at the rear of the van was strewn with debris. This made the search even more difficult.

Two loaded handguns were found lying on top of the debris inside the van. There was a .45 revolver in a canvas holster. The second handgun was a 9 mm semi-automatic pistol. The weapons were brought out of the van and shown to each of the UVF suspects. They all denied any knowledge of the guns. I did not expect anything else.

We instructed the uniformed Police to separate the prisoners and convey them in different vehicles to the station. We stressed the point that they must be kept separate and not allowed to talk to each other. If we were to get to the bottom of what was happening, it was vital that there was no conferring by the suspects.

Our uniformed colleagues fully understood. A sergeant agreed that he would ensure that at least one of his officers would remain with each suspect at the Police station to enforce the No Talking rule. We were grateful for that. Derrick and I would have a lot to do simply to process the prisoners.

We were about to move out of the Monkstown Estate when a heavy-set man in his late thirties ran up to speak to me:

"What's happening?" he asked. "Where are my men?"

"Your men?" I asked

"Yes, the men from this van. Where are they?"

"They have been arrested, Sir," I replied. "We have found two illegally-held handguns in the van," I informed him.

"Yes, they were going out on guard duty," he replied in a matter-of-fact manner.

"These men, Sir? Tell me what you know."

"They are my men. The guns were for their protection," he volunteered.

I called another constable over.

"What is your name, Sir?" I asked him, "What is your full name?"

"Richard Moffet (not his real name)," he told me.

"You are under arrest, Mr Moffet, for possession of these guns," I informed him and then cautioned him. He made no reply. As he was being arrested I saw the look of surprise on his face. He was obviously not used to being treated in this manner. He walked to the Police car like a lamb. It was my first encounter with this man. I was to have many more.

Once the uniformed officers had already departed with the prisoners, we left the Monkstown Estate and returned to base. As we arrived on the roadway outside the station, I was surprised to see Richard Moffet, the man I had just arrested, walking out the gate of the barracks. He spotted me as I turned into the gate of the barracks. He walked briskly towards the Station Road.

This man's hasty departure was a mystery to me. What had happened? Who had he spoken to? What had he said which had prompted his immediate release? But I could find out the answer to all of those questions later. There was still the time-consuming form-filling process to be done in order to book all the other prisoners into custody.

Our duty inspector of the day was a new promotion into our station. He had already gained a reputation as a strict disciplinarian. Hard-working and conscientious, he expected the same from his men. Where he didn't find it, he had no qualms about using the threat of discipline. He was supervising the uniformed lads who were still helping us to process the prisoners.

Derrick and I walked into the CID office, which was housed in a large five-roomed Portakabin® in the rear yard of the Police station. The party we had left earlier was still in full swing. We held up the guns we had recovered less than half an hour before. We were greeted with roars of support.

"Where did you get those?" someone asked.

"Monkstown," I replied, "Outside the UVF club in Cloyne Crescent."

"We have arrests as well," I added.

Another roar of support went up but I noticed the immediate departure from the room of two of my more mature colleagues. They both made it clear by their facial expressions that they were none too pleased. I saw them disappear into the main building towards the cells. We only had two cells in the station. I did not pay any more attention to the departure of those two colleagues.

We called in our Scenes of Crime Officers (SOCO), Mapping, and Photography. I was busy in the CID office when I received a call from the uniformed duty inspector.

"What's happening, Jonty? I thought you wanted all the prisoners kept separate so they can't confer?" he asked.

"I do, Inspector," I replied.

"Well, you better get over there because Detective Constables John Duncan (not his real name) and Walter Jamieson (not his real name) have taken them from their jailers and they are with all the prisoners now in the parade room. Let me know why things have changed, please," he added tersely.

The truth was I didn't know why things had changed. None of those men had been interviewed as yet. None of them had admitted possession of the two guns except for their boss, Richard Moffet. Yet someone had thought it prudent to release him within minutes of his being brought in to the station under arrest and with a uniformed escort.

I left the CID office and went over to the main building. Sure enough, all of the prisoners who had been separated and held in different rooms and corridors since their arrival were now gathered together in the parade room. The two detectives had relieved the uniformed staff of their guard duty. I knocked on the door and heard a familiar voice shout loudly: "What?"

I opened the door of the parade room and peered around it in a bid to discover what was happening.

"Get out," shouted Detective Constable Duncan.

"What's happening, John?" I asked. "The Inspector wants to know…" I never got to finish what I was going to say.

"GET OUT!" he shouted again, more forcefully.

He was obviously none too pleased about something. I was extremely surprised at the sight of the prisoners standing around having open conversations with each other. The atmosphere in that parade room was more cordial than official. I peered around the door again.

"GET OUT OF HERE, JONTY," Detective Constable Duncan shouted, much to the delight of the suspected UVF prisoners, who were pointing and laughing at me.

"We're dealing with this now," he added.

With only seven months' service in the CID I was in no position to argue with seasoned CID officers such as these.

I contacted the duty inspector and explained the situation to him. None of us had any real reason to believe that anything untoward was happening. I returned to the CID office. The atmosphere was friendly and euphoric. Congratulations were still flowing to both Detective Constable McCourt and myself.

Due to our lack of prisoner cells, plans were in progress to transport all of the prisoners to the Police Office at Townhall Street, Belfast, where there would be adequate accommodation to house them. There would also be enough trained staff to look after them until the next morning. Time was passing very quickly as we processed the prisoners prior to their transfer.

It was much later, and everyone else had gone home. I was alone in the CID office when the guard rang me from the guardroom to tell me that the father of the youngest prisoner, Cooper, wanted to speak to someone in charge of his son. As he put the call through to my extension, the guard warned me that this man was in an extremely distressed and agitated state. I identified myself, preparing myself for a barrage of insults and complaints about the nature of the arrest of his son. It would not be long until Christmas, after all, which would no doubt add to this man's upset.

I wasn't, however, prepared for what he did say:

"Is that the Newtownabbey UVF?"

What on earth is he talking about, I wondered.

"Hello," I said, thinking I had misheard him.

"Could I speak to a senior UVF officer?" he asked.

"There will be no officer above the rank of sergeant on duty here until 9 am tomorrow morning, Sir," I explained, "Can I help you, Sir?"

"You can tell me why your detectives Duncan and Jamieson told my son tonight that the orders from the UVF in Monkstown were that he has to admit that he alone was in possession of both of those guns, because he is the youngest of the men you're holding. He is not married and has no children, so he has to make a statement tomorrow that will clear the others. He has been told to say that they had no knowledge of the guns. The truth is, Mr Brown, my son had nothing to do with them."

I was taken aback to say the least—where had the poor man heard this? Why would two RUC detectives pass on orders from the UVF and force the youth to take responsibility for those guns? But did they pass on orders? Was that the real reason for bringing all the prisoners together in the parade room?

It certainly did not make sense for any investigator seeking to get to the truth of their criminal intent to bring the prisoners all together to confer in that manner. I felt sick and ashamed as I listened to this distraught man question the integrity of my colleagues.

"Since when did members of the RUC carry orders from the UVF to their UVF men in custody, Mr Brown?"

"They don't," I replied half-heartedly.

"Oh, but indeed they do, and it happened tonight in your station. My son told me himself this evening. In fact, apparently whenever he refused to make such a statement, Duncan and Jamieson went down to that Police station in Belfast where he is being held tonight and told him that the UVF said his family would suffer if he didn't take full responsibility for the guns," he said.

What could I say? This man was certainly not ranting or raving. I told him that senior Police officers would be present in the morning long before his son would be returned to us for his first formal interviews. That would be a good time to broach the matter with them. I explained that as a junior member of the CID, I would be unable to do anything about his allegations tonight. Mr Cooper was not impressed. He assured me that if he didn't get any satisfaction from the Police he would go elsewhere. He did not elaborate on where that would be.

I put the telephone back on its cradle and sat back in my seat. It was late. I was tempted to ring a number of trusted colleagues. I decided against it. I would just put a note in the CID Occurrences Reports and Complaints book (C6) to the effect that Mr Cooper wished to see a senior Police officer to make a complaint about the alleged conduct of CID officers attached to this station. That would start the ball rolling in the morning. If there was found to be any substance to these allegations, then the two officers concerned could be disciplined and transferred out. That would be in the interests of both the public and the RUC.

Within minutes of the call from Mr Cooper and before I got a chance to put an entry in our C6, Duncan and another detective, Glen Hurst (not his real name) came storming into the CID office. Duncan was obviously the worse for drink. He opened the bottom drawer of his desk and produced a ten-glass bottle of Black Bush whiskey. He poured a stiff drink for Hurst and one for himself. Duncan was a bulky man of massive frame. He was carrying very little weight and was what was known in Police circles as a "tight fit". Hurst walked over to check the entries in the CID C6.

"Anything happening, Jonty?" he asked. He was about to move away from the desk with the C6 on it, when I told him about the sinister telephone call from the young prisoner's father.

"I have to put a small reference to his complaint in the book," I said.

I watched as he and Duncan exchanged furtive glances.

"Leave it until tomorrow morning, son," he said. "Leave it for the duty inspector in the morning, if Cooper rings in again or calls down to see us. Did he give you the names of the two detectives?" he asked.

"Yes," I replied. "He mentioned Duncan here and Jamieson."

He winked at me and shook his head as if to indicate that I should say no more. He was too late. Duncan lost it, and began to scream and swear at me like a man possessed. He got up on his feet and stumbled as he tried to rush at me. Before I could react or say anything in reply, Hurst ushered me quickly out of the CID office by the back door which led directly across to the kitchen of the main station.

"Stay over there out of the way until I can get Duncan out of here. Let's talk about this in the morning," he said.

To see Duncan in a drunken and dishevelled state like that was not uncommon: it was in fact becoming quite a frequent occurrence. I knew to stay well out of his way at such times. I decided to go over to the guardroom and speak to Police on duty there.

As I walked towards the main station, I wondered how even Duncan with all his contacts with senior officers could talk his way out of this one. Mr Cooper had raised some very disturbing issues. I believed that he was telling the truth. I knew I had been lucky. The presence of Hurst who was relatively sober had defused a very fraught situation. Surely he wouldn't be so stupid to as to get involved in such criminal and unseemly conduct!

Perhaps I was too agitated—or perhaps it was because I was so very disappointed in Duncan, but I had no intention of letting this go. I would wait until the pair left the station and then I would make that entry in the C6 in relation to Mr Cooper's complaint. I had to, because if I didn't this could all be swept under the carpet. I was extremely disappointed in my two CID colleagues, especially Duncan. He was a terrific guy when he was sober. He was affable, strong and extremely capable in his handling of all situations. He was basically a good detective and an artist in the interview room. It was this other, flawed side to the man, this alter ego, which he only exhibited when he was intoxicated and which caused him to explode without warning. I hated to see him like that. I hadn't, however, seen anything yet . . .

About ten minutes after I had been ushered quickly out of the CID office to escape Duncan's wrath, I was in the guardroom talking to some of the lads on night duty. Just prior to midnight, a colleague took a call from Hurst telling me to report to the parade room. I was not surprised to be summoned there: it made sense that he would want to speak to me, away from Detective Constable Duncan. He probably wanted the full details of the allegations made by Mr Cooper so that Duncan and Jamieson would be in a better position to answer any allegations in the morning. Calls of that nature did not come in often from the general public, so when they did it was imperative that they were vigorously investigated.

I made my way from the guardroom to the parade room. My notes of the conversation with Mr Cooper were still sitting on my desk in the CID office, but I couldn't retrieve them without encountering Duncan again. I decided I could wing it—that telephone conversation was still very fresh in my mind.

As I walked up the corridor towards the parade room, I passed other officers who were busy preparing for night duty. I received congratulations, smiles and pats on the back as I walked past them. Through the frosted glass of the upper half of the parade-room door, I could as I approached just about distinguish Hurst's outline.

Hurst opened the door of the parade room when I knocked. I will never forget what happened next. As I entered the room and walked past him, Duncan suddenly confronted me. In a split second he had lifted me clear of the ground and, with all the strength he could muster, he threw me against the wall. My head and my back struck the wall so violently that I was winded and momentarily stunned.

What happened next seemed to occur as if in slow motion. Duncan punched me on the side of my head. As my head flew back and hit the wall, I saw blue and white flashes. I thought I was going to pass out. Then he slapped me across the face, once, twice. It stung, yes, but it also brought me out of a near trance. In fact it was not just the shock and the blow to my head which had rendered me immobile and helpless. Suddenly, I was transported back to that nightmare world of my childhood and that all-too-familiar feeling as a small boy of being faced with the frenzied violence of a brutal bully. A violence inflicted on me without warning or provocation.

What on earth is happening? I thought.

I tried to push Duncan away, but he was too strong. He brought his face right up against mine. Even though the room was dark I was able to look into his hate-filled eyes. I was so close to him that I could smell his bad breath and the stench of alcohol. My mouth was filling with blood from internal cuts as my flesh was smashed against my teeth. I had bitten my tongue, and I was afraid of losing consciousness as I felt

myself slipping to the floor. I did not want to pass out: God knows
what would have happened then.

I considered reaching for my 9 mm Walther pistol to extricate
myself from what might be a virtual life-threatening situation. In a
split second I decided to err on the side of caution. To produce my
firearm would serve only to up the ante of this sinister encounter,
perhaps to a point of no return.

Duncan levelled a tirade of abuse at me: "You think you're smart,
don't you? You think *those* are guns you recovered? They aren't guns.
I could take you to a wee place just outside Ballyclare and show you
guns—a whole UVF arsenal."

"Those men you stopped were on their way to guard the
Cloughfern Arms from Republican attack," he said. "Decent men and
you have ruined their Christmas," he added.

Each utterance was punctuated with another thump or a dig with his
knee. Duncan was clearly identifying with the UVF, and making it plain
to me that he stood firmly on their side. He was insinuating that I was
the bad guy! This was incredible. These guys were dishing this out to
one of their own CID colleagues at the behest of the Monkstown UVF. I
will never forget the sudden and treacherous nature of that assault.

I hung onto every word as Duncan spat profanities at me. There
was no mistaking the absolute venom in his speech. Where on earth
was Hurst, I thought, as I fended off the blows. Had he deliberately left
the room, knowing what was going to happen next? Should I shout?
Would anyone hear me this far from the guardroom? I looked over
Duncan's shoulder and saw to my dismay that Hurst was standing at
the door of the parade room watching the corridor outside. He had
witnessed the entire assault. He was holding the parade room door
ajar, on the lookout in case any other Police officer should come upon
the scene. There were to be no witnesses to this assault. His right hand
was on the light switch.

The lights in the parade room were out! I hadn't even noticed that,
yet they had been on when I entered the room. Hurst continued
to glance over his shoulder, watching the corridor as Duncan pummelled me with his fists and his knee.

"There'll be no complaints from old Cooper, you can be sure about
that," Duncan said. "And there'd better be none from you either or I'll
see you're shot. Do you understand me? Take yourself down to
Bawnmore and stop Fenian cars there. No, you're not too keen on

that, are you?" Duncan said, without pausing for breath.

He started to walk off.

"We'll see," I replied indignantly.

It was the wrong answer. Duncan was back again in an instant. He lifted me off my feet again. He placed one large hand around my neck as if to throttle me. I started gasping for breath. My arms were flailing and I was pushing my feet against the wall. It didn't help. It seemed an unreal situation.

Hurst visibly panicked.

"That's enough, John," he kept repeating. He ran from the doorway and pulled Duncan off me. I felt that I was about to pass out when Duncan at last loosened his grip and walked away. I was lying there choking for breath. I'll never forget Duncan's words as they both stormed out of the room:

"Did you hear what he said: 'We'll see'?"

He ran back and levelled another kick at my right shoulder.

"You're right, we'll see. You'll see. Say one word about this or Cooper and I'll see you get it," he said.

He clearly meant that he would use his UVF contacts to kill me! Hurst stood at the door, eerily illuminated by the light flooding in from the corridor. He looked at me and shrugged. Then it was all over as suddenly as it had begun.

They departed the scene, leaving me sore and bloodied. I tried to stand but I couldn't. I had virtually no feeling in my legs due to the constant kicks and pummelling with my assailant's knee. I lay there on the ground, watching them leave.

After a short time I was able to get to my feet. I walked unsteadily to the men's toilet next door. I was lucky. As attacks go, it was not the worst that I would suffer in my 30 years as a Police officer in the RUC.

But this was different. My assailant and his accomplice were not thugs from some street corner. They were Police officers, colleagues of mine. Friday, 13 December 1974 is a date that would haunt me forever. It was to be a turning point in my career within the RUC.

I stood there in that little toilet area next door to the cells, examining my face and the inside of my mouth in a small, wooden-framed mirror fitted to the wall. I watched with pain and sadness as my blood flowed into the white washhand basin and mingled with the running water. I leaned over to splash cold, revitalising water over my face. My head was still spinning.

I will resign tomorrow, I thought.

I was still unsteady on my feet. I held onto both sides of the wash-hand basin. I pulled some green paper towels from the dispenser on the wall to stem the flow of blood. I had never felt so alone or isolated, no longer knowing whom I could trust.

I stood there wondering exactly what sort of Police Force I had joined. This was my first encounter with these people in the CID. I had already unintentionally made enemies within the RUC Special Branch. I had not expected to find such people in the ranks of our CID.

Little did I know it at that time, but this was to be just the beginning. I was to encounter many more such people during my Police service. I stood there in the darkness in that little corner of Newtownabbey RUC Station, wondering how had it all gone so terribly wrong.

I couldn't believe what had just happened. Yes, there had been previous snide remarks about me being a "Proddy Basher" more times than I cared to remember. But I was shocked to the core by Duncan's obvious hatred of me.

Everyone in the office knew who could be trusted to Police with impartiality and who couldn't. Suspicion of collusion was one thing. This was entirely different. Again, I contemplated resigning, leaving the RUC altogether. I was so very disappointed with my colleagues. But who would dare challenge these men, I wondered. Who could I go to? Who would grasp this nettle?

I composed myself as best as I could and made my way past the guardroom. The SDO was too busy to even notice me. I went out through the public area and into the car park outside. The cold, December night air was refreshing on my skin. I walked to my car. I was sore all over. I don't recall the drive home. I was going to drive to the home of a supervisor I knew I could trust. He would certainly help me. But Duncan's words were still ringing in my ears. "I'll see you're shot," he had said. This was no idle threat. The look on his face had said it all. His connections within the UVF were at the very highest level. No, I would make no complaints to anyone at this stage. I would wait to see what the morning would bring. If that young man's father did pursue his complaint, I would know Duncan was bluffing. If he did not, then that would mean that Duncan had alerted the UVF to Mr Cooper's intentions. It was worse than that. Mr Cooper had made his complaint to me only. He would now believe that I had tipped the UVF off. The irony of it all was not lost on me.

Duncan's words haunted me all night as I tossed and turned, trying to get to sleep in my flat in Abbotscoole House, Rathcoole.

"The men you stopped were on their way to guard the Cloughfern Arms," Duncan had said. "Decent men," he had said. I didn't have to speculate for too long as to where that information had come from. Nor did I have to wonder who had released the UVF commander Richard Moffet, or why. The fog was beginning to lift and I didn't like what I could see. These men identified more with the UVF than they did with me.

When it was time to go into work the next day, I was feeling downcast and very dejected. I was still very sore all over. Part of me wanted to go straight into the Chief Inspector's office to make a formal complaint, but I feared the reaction from Moffet and his UVF cohorts. Instinct somehow kept me from following what should have been normal procedure. As I got out of my car to go into the CID office, I saw Hurst watching my every move from a window. He stopped me in the corridor before I reached the office.

"You have to make a statement of evidence as soon as possible about those arrests last night so that it is available to the interviewers," he said.

Foolishly, I had half-expected an apology. But worse, he actually had the audacity to tell me that he wanted me to say that young Cooper could have had both guns, that Cooper could have passed them back inside when we stopped the van.

I nodded.

"Good lad," he said, as he walked off quickly towards the CID office.

Yes, he got his statement of evidence. But no, it did not implicate Cooper. I knew they couldn't change it. Duncan was in the CID office writing up his diary when I entered. I knew that there would be no reference of any assault upon me in it. My desk was just opposite his. I expected him to glare at me or to take me to the side and further threaten me. He did none of that. It was as if nothing had happened. He smiled at me. He acknowledged me with that quick nod of the head that was one of his traits.

I noted that he was wringing his hands anxiously. He looked down again and continued writing in his diary. He didn't look threatening. During the briefings, he would snatch the odd glance at me, and then look away quickly each time. I could see his hands shaking as he reached from time to time for his mug of steaming hot coffee.

Threatening? No. Pathetic? Yes. I almost felt sorry for him. Everybody loved this man: he was affable, funny and "one of the lads". In our small section, however, we knew better than to trust him as he was quite open about his unambiguously pro-Loyalist stance. But the authorities in the Division had a strong regard for him as a capable detective. They knew he had what were called "leanings", but they had not moved to deal with him thus far and probably never would. I confided in an older CID officer I knew I could trust. He was not surprised at what had happened. I told him that I intended to take the matter further.

"You're wasting your time," he warned me. "John Duncan is untouchable. All you'll do is get yourself transferred," he said.

"Transferred? They would transfer me? What for?" I asked.

"For stirring up a whole hornets' nest. They'll do a whitewash with Duncan and transfer him down the Division for a year or two, but they'll lose you forever. No-one supports a whistleblower, Johnston. Trust me," he said.

This was an old fellow with lots of CID experience, a man I trusted. He was a partner of mine. He patted me on the back as he moved to leave the general office.

"This Police Force is full of John Duncans, son," he said. "No-one is interested in ridding us of them. It's far easier to ignore them," he added.

I didn't agree with that at all. However, that ostrich syndrome was to pop up time and again throughout my service. No-one in authority seemed capable or willing to deal firmly and effectively with these people.

The day after I was brutally assaulted, I went to the guardroom to check the station C6. I wanted to see if Mr Cooper had followed up his complaint. He had not. His son would be charged along with the rest, and properly so. Any scheme to release the other suspected UVF men and charge him alone had been rumbled and was now dropped. On this occasion at least, the UVF would not dictate who did what inside our RUC Station. Ultimately, however, none of the six men was prosecuted for possession of the weapons: after a short hearing at Belfast City Commission, the judge pronounced that our evidence against them was insufficient.

A few days later, Duncan stopped me in a corridor in the Police station. I braced myself for another confrontation, but he offered me his hand. I didn't take it. It had happened so quickly the moment was lost. Somehow I knew that I had made another mistake.

For months afterwards I agonised about whether or not I should leave the Police Service. As a fully qualified electrician, I could return to "Civvy Street" and be better paid. But it wasn't about money: I knew that working as an electrician would not afford me the same measure of job satisfaction as being in the Police. Anyway, was that not exactly what people like Duncan wanted?

The vast majority of RUC officers were decent men. Many of them who heard my account of the beating found it too incredible even to contemplate. They would in fact have preferred not to hear it, never mind believe it.

Christmas 1974 came and went, and I finally resolved to remain in the RUC. At the same time, I swore that I would do all in my power to frustrate people like Duncan: I was determined to make a difference. So I decided to put the whole sordid affair down to experience. From then on, I just worked around people like Duncan and Hurst.

Late one evening in May 1975, I was on duty in the CID office. A number of my fellow officers were gathered, getting ready to go home. Some of these men had been drinking. A senior supervisor who was totally unaware of any friction between Duncan and me asked me to run Duncan home, as I was sober.

At that time, Duncan lived in North Belfast. Other Police officers helped him outside and into the passenger seat of the Police car. I got in to the driver's seat and drove off. As we were travelling along the Shore Road, Duncan spoke to me in a low, menacing tone:

"They think I'm drunk, you think I'm drunk, but I'll just show you how sober I am," he said.

He started to point out landmark after landmark as we drove past them: the Telstar Ballroom, the Golden Fry chip shop, the Mount Vernon Estate.

"You're finished, do you hear me, finished. I've given the UVF your new address in Monkstown. It's only a matter of time," he said and laughed. There was no mistaking the malevolence in his tone. He put his right hand up to his head in the shape of a gun. "Boom!" he said and laughed again.

He really appeared to think that this was funny. I did not speak, refusing to be drawn into conversation with him. I stopped the car outside his home. He hesitated before he stepped out onto the pavement, leaning over towards me in a menacing manner:

"You wouldn't listen to me, son. Well, maybe you'll listen to them

The author in 1973, one year after joining the RUC.

RUC Training Centre Enniskillen, Thursday, 27 April 1972. The new Constable Brown stands on the extreme left, fourth row back.

Sir Graham Shillington, Chief Constable of the RUC when Johnston Brown joined the Force. (*Empics*)

Victor Arbuckle, the first RUC man to die in the Troubles, killed by rioting Loyalists on the Shankill Road in October 1969. (*Alan Lewis/Photopress Belfast*)

Constable Frankie O'Reilly, the last RUC man to die in the Troubles. He died on 6 October 1988 from injuries received in a Loyalist blast bomb in Portadown. (*Alan Lewis/Photopress Belfast*)

The funeral of Constable Frankie O'Reilly. It was one of the ironies of the Troubles that the first and last policemen to die were both killed at the hands of Loyalists. (*Empics*)

Sir Kenneth Newman, one of the most influential RUC Chief Constables, leaves HQ for the last time in 1979. (*Pacemaker Press*)

Sir Jack Hermon, Chief Constable of the Force from 1980 to 1989. He was Sir Kenneth Newman's successor. (*Pacemaker Press*)

IN LOVING MEMORY OF
EDWARD WALKER
VOL. ULSTER DEFENCE ASSOCIATION
KILLED 12TH JUNE 1976
AGED 20 YEARS

QUIS SEPARABIT

The grave of Edward Walker.

The Pope's visit to Ireland in 1979 was a momentous event. Here he is shown in Phoenix Park in Dublin… (*Camera Press Ireland*)

…but the Pope did not cross the border during his time in Ireland, for fear of protest from extreme Protestants. This photograph shows the Pope being hanged in effigy in a Loyalist area of Belfast. (*Bettmann/Corbis*)

My colleague, Detective Constable Trevor McIlwrath.

Johnny Adair (centre) aged 18. (*Alan Lewis/Corbis*)

The Drumcree stand-off in 1988: Loyalist protestors confront RUC officers in riot gear. (*Empics*)

UVF boys. They're going to make an example of you," he said.

He pulled himself out of the Police car and walked unaided to his front door. He did not look back in my direction. I watched him fumble with his keys in the lock of the front door for a short time before he went inside. Certainly he had been drinking, but he was by no means in his usual legless state.

I sat there in the car outside his house, trying to take it all in. The malice, the sinister undertones, the hate-filled eyes. There was no doubt whatsoever that this man wished me harm. I got the distinct impression that whatever was about to happen, I wouldn't have long to wait. I had only moved into my new home in Twinburn in Monkstown the month before, in April 1975. Few people knew exactly where I lived. As far as I knew, no paramilitary group was aware of my new address.

About ten days or so after Duncan's threats in the car, I was out on the lawn in my front garden of 14 Twinburn Drive, Monkstown, a semi-detached dwelling. It was a beautiful sunny afternoon and I was making the most of the good weather to weed the flowerbeds. I was throwing the weeds into a black vinyl bin lid beside me.

Due to all of the friction with Duncan, I was in a constant state of high alert both at home and at work. It was mentally draining, but I couldn't afford to drop my guard. I had my personal protection weapon, the 9 mm Walther, hidden underneath the bin lid, out of sight but readily accessible to me.

Twinburn was a quiet estate. At times you could hear a pin drop. This was one of those times. The quietness of the estate was broken by the noisy arrival of a vehicle with a broken exhaust. I was alarmed when it stopped abruptly outside my next-door neighbours' house to my left. I heard a door opening and a gruff male voice shout: "His motor's there, make it quick."

I knew instinctively that this was a reference to me. My car was parked up the side of the house and my gate was closed. Fortunately, my glass front door was also closed. I knew I was in trouble. I reached below the bin lid and grabbed hold of my Walther pistol. I checked the little pin in front of the hammer. It was exposed, indicating that I had one bullet in the breech. All I had to do to fire the gun in double action was take the safety catch off. I did just that.

My grip on the handgun was firm, although my palms were sweating. I watched with trepidation as a youth aged between 18 and 20

years old approached my house. He was of slim build, not very tall, with very long, dark hair. His face was sombre, his expression intense. He was so engrossed in watching my front door that he didn't notice me in the garden only a few feet away, close enough to touch him. There was a three-foot high wall at the garden edge separating the garden from the footpath beyond. The footpath was on a higher level than the garden. I was looking up at this guy, studying his every move. He kept looking back at the car he had just left, as if for inspiration. I knew by his demeanour that he was going to become a threat to me.

Still oblivious to my presence, he walked past me and stopped at the front gate. I could see that he was very nervous. He had his right hand inside his large overcoat pocket and, judging by the shape of the bulge, was holding something there. He was trying with difficulty to open the wrought iron gate with his left hand. I was as nervous as he was. I didn't want to do anything quickly that would make him panic. There were lots of other people in the vicinity going about their business quietly. I was hoping to defuse this situation with the least possible threat to life. Especially mine.

Whoever this young man was, it was obvious that he was up to no good. I noted that the overcoat that he was wearing was two or three sizes too big for him, and of a fashion generally worn by much older men. He was still having great difficulty opening my gate. He was keeping his eyes fixed on my frosted-glass front door. I tried to compose myself, as I decided to challenge him.

"Can I help you?" I shouted.

He immediately looked in my direction and stopped trying to open the gate. He stared at me, totally taken aback. There was genuine surprise on his face. He looked back at his friend in the car.

"Is this 14 Twinburn Drive?" he asked.

The number 14 was clearly displayed on the wall, just next to the front door, in large metal numbers about a foot high and painted white. It is still there to this day. Now he was being ridiculous and he knew it. I glanced over at the numbers. He also looked at them.

"It's about the car for sale," he said.

I saw him staring at my right hand. Then fear left me as suddenly as it had set in. I was now ready to do whatever it was going to take to deal with this threat. This situation was not of my making. My right hand was still hidden below the bin lid, keeping the gun out of sight. I smiled at him in a bid to indicate that I had no idea that anything

was wrong. I could see the blind panic in his eyes. He knew I was calm and unrattled. He looked back yet again over his shoulder towards the car where his waiting friend pumped the car horn twice and revved the engine, creating a terrible noise.

Your move, mate, I thought.

I noted that he was sweating. He had moved slowly up from the gate until he was standing directly above me. He tried to remove his right hand from his coat pocket but it was stuck, so he pointed the pocket and its contents up in my direction. Something solid was pointing through the cloth.

I was afraid that he was about to shoot me. I removed my handgun from below the bin into full view. He couldn't take his eyes off it. He backed away a few steps at a time. He didn't speak. Then he panicked and ran to the car. I heard the car door slam. I was honestly glad to see him go. I had no wish to hurt him.

I knew that this guy had come to my home to murder me. I got to my feet. There was a loud sound from the exhaust as the car sped off up Twinburn Drive. It was a dark-coloured Hillman Avenger, but I could not see the registration number. I had no doubt that I had just been very lucky. I had never seen that lad before and I was never to see him again.

I went inside my house and called Belfast Regional Control (BRC) to report the incident to one of the Police officers responsible for "D" Division. The details of the car and its occupants were circulated to all stations. I had hoped the vehicle would be stopped, its occupants identified and my fears allayed. This was not to be. I did not see or hear of either the car or the occupants again.

I have no doubt whatsoever that they had come to my home at Duncan's behest. The proximity in time of their visit to the threat he had made to me was too much of a coincidence. With friends like Duncan, I didn't need enemies. I knew from then on in that I would have to be extremely careful regarding my personal safety. I had been lucky this time, but I would have to be lucky all of the time. Terrorists, those planning to attack me, only had to be lucky once.

Chapter 7
Every Copper's Nightmare

Friday, 11 June 1976 was a beautiful summer's day. I had started work at 8.30 am and had spent the morning and much of the afternoon in the collator's office filing paperwork with John, a Royal Military Policeman who was on secondment with us at the time. Since staff resources were so stretched in those days, it was the practice to send RMPs on short-term contracts to help us out, and we were always grateful for their assistance. John had a real interest in our work in CID and was always there to help us in any way he could. With his strong, lilting Welsh accent, sometimes I half-expected him to burst into song. His agreeable personality and warm sense of humour had endeared him to many of my RUC colleagues.

While John and I were working in the office, we would keep our respective firearms on the desk or put them into a drawer out of the way. I had recently noticed that John carried a Walther .32 semi-automatic pistol, which was considerably smaller and more compact than our more powerful Walther 9 mm pistols. I kept John going about carrying this "lady's gun". I also expressed my view that if we did encounter trouble, we would need a lot more firepower than that to get us out of it. The previous RMP placement to our CID office had carried a heavy-duty 9 mm Browning pistol. John laughed at the idea of trying to conceal such a bulky weapon while in plain clothes. We

amicably agreed to disagree on the matter, and neither of us said another word about it.

By the time we had finished for the day, we had done a great deal of paperwork. I was pleased with our efforts. The newly-appointed Chief Constable of the time, Sir Kenneth Newman, had instigated the setting up of these collators' offices, which were standard practice in all of the other Police Forces on the mainland. I had been charged with the task of setting one up in Newtownabbey. John and I had been working very hard on it.

We soon saw the obvious benefits that could be derived from such a resource. Intelligence on terrorists and criminals which had previously been held separately in our Criminal Records Office would now be readily available to all branches and departments in the Division. We also logged the photographs of all persons arrested in relation to crime and terrorism. It did not take long to build up a full and rounded picture of exactly who was who on the terrorist front.

Creating these records was a mammoth task, which could easily have taken up all of our working hours. On this particular day, we decided to go for a break at 5 pm and agreed to meet back at the barracks at 7 pm. As was our usual practice at the time, we were intending to spend the second half of our split shift patrolling the subdivision in our CID vehicle, until around midnight. We were keen to do our bit to put a stop to the senseless murders and attempted murders which were an all too frequent occurrence in the Newtownabbey area at that time.

Our thinking was to be seen regularly in the vicinity of the flashpoint areas such as, for example, the local Loyalist and Republican clubs, which we would frequently drive past. We knew that our very presence could well act as a deterrent to those involved in terrorist activities, making them think twice about even planning any such undertaking. We might even be able to spot any terrorists on the move and take appropriate action to deal with them. John and I had no fear of apprehending suspected terrorists in such circumstances. We would search them and make a note of their names and addresses, endeavouring to be as courteous and as tactful as was possible in such a situation. It was not ever going to make us friends.

John and I had a good track record for this kind of operation. It was less than a month earlier that we had arrested several UVF suspects in a garage at West Crescent in Rathcoole and had seized what was virtually an arsenal of firearms and explosives from them.

Some of our RUC colleagues did not agree with these CID patrols but that didn't particularly bother us and their criticism would fall on deaf ears. John had seen for himself, as I had, the advantages to be gained by our unexpected CID presence in the middle of some terrorist enterprise. All we wanted was to be able to achieve something in this way, while complementing the patrolling patterns of our uniformed colleagues and without compromising our own personal safety. I had no intention of press-ganging anyone to go out on these impromptu patrols who had no desire to be there.

It was in this context that John and I met again in the CID office at 7 pm. A new addition to our staff in CID, a detective constable, whom I will refer to here as Alan, happened to be there too. He promptly volunteered to join us on patrol. We were glad to have Alan as an extra man in the car: a CID volunteer for this kind of duty was not easy to come by in those days.

We walked out to the CID car, which was a standard "soft-skinned" (i.e. non-armoured) fleet saloon car. A green Ford Escort, with no markings to identify it as a Police car. It was, however, fitted with a radiotelephone and a Police siren. I got into the driver's seat, John got into the observer's seat and Alan got into the rear. I was wearing a light grey suit with a shirt and tie.

We had been on patrol for hours. The area was quiet. At around 10.30 pm we drove into Cloyne Crescent in the Monkstown Estate. We decided to take down the registration numbers of all the cars parked outside a UVF club there, with the intention of checking them out later. Two young UVF men who were on duty at the door of the club had apparently become agitated enough at our Police presence to run back inside. We were about to move off when a much older man ran out of the club. He waved at us to stop, then came across the street towards our Police car.

He told us that there had been an incident in the UVF club earlier. A fight had developed between some UVF men from Monkstown and some UDA men from Tiger's Bay, which ended with the UDA contingent being literally thrown out of the club. They were angry at this treatment, and the man who had approached us feared a reprisal. He was convinced that the UDA men had gone to get some of their friends to return for further fighting, or worse.

This man knew me by name, and was genuinely glad to see us on patrol. In those days, a counter-attack on the UVF club was more than a distinct possibility. We assured him that we would be about until well after midnight and we would be on the alert. He thanked us and went back inside the club.

We continued to patrol the Monkstown area for about an hour, vigilant for the sudden arrival of several cars filled with men which could be the precursor to an attack on the club. In the meantime, we also managed to recover a stolen Cortina car on the estate: this was one less car which could be used for terrorist purposes.

About an hour and a half after we had spoken to the UVF man, we left Monkstown and parked in the Diamond Rathcoole, a large shopping area in the estate. We were sitting in the car park with our lights off and our windows down, waiting for the untoward sounds of shooting or civil disturbance which were commonplace at that time. Several cars filled with locals had noticed our presence: some waved at us, while others just glared.

At a quarter to one in the morning, we decided that we would call it a day around 1 am. The expected attack on the UVF club had not developed; there had been no terrorist incidents in our subdivision all evening. We decided to sit out the rest of our duty where we were. If there were any calls, we would be in a position to respond immediately.

Five minutes later, at ten to one on the morning of 12 June 1976, we heard a call on the radiotelephone from Belfast Regional Control (BRC) at Castlereagh that was broadcast to all stations. An 1100 car, registration number AOI 6396, had just been stolen on the Shore Road. The owner had left it parked outside his bakery only long enough to allow him to go inside to light the ovens, as was his nightly routine. When he returned, his car had been stolen: it had last been seen heading away from the city along the Shore Road.

The stolen car was heading in our direction. So I drove out of the Diamond Rathcoole and then to the Shore Road, where I parked the Police car outside a Chinese restaurant. I positioned our vehicle so that it was hidden amongst other cars, while still affording us an unrestricted view of any cars coming from the Belfast direction.

We had not long to wait. I saw the unmistakable silhouette and lights of an 1100 car approach us from Belfast. I started the Police car, so as to be ready in case it was the stolen car. The car under observation was racing up the Shore Road towards us. I checked the registration number as it sped past our vantage point.

"That's it," I said excitedly to my two colleagues.

Turning on the headlights of the Police car, I set off in pursuit of the stolen car. There were four young men in it. I swung out onto the Shore Road only yards behind it and I switched on the two-tone siren that designated us as Police. I repeatedly flashed the headlights in a bid to get the driver to pull over and stop. The two men in the rear seat kept looking back in our direction.

Suddenly, after only a short chase, the stolen car stopped outside the old Merville Inn, opposite the Merville Estate. I had been communicating with BRC by radiotelephone since our first sighting of the stolen car and throughout the chase. This contact with BRC serves two purposes. The first is to keep the Control Room appraised so that they can deploy assistance if necessary. The second is to enable them to alert any patrols in the district of our non-uniformed presence and thus to avoid any chance of a "blue on blue" situation. I was later to be very thankful for the highly sophisticated communications system which would record every call on tape. Luckily for me, as it transpired, it was able to record more than just voices.

When the driver of the stolen car pulled over, I positioned our CID vehicle alongside it in the middle of the Shore Road. I got out of the car and ran to the driver's door of the 1100. I was armed but I did not draw my pistol. The driver wound his window down. I produced my warrant card from my top pocket and showed it to him. He nodded in acknowledgement.

"You are in a stolen car. Switch off the engine and apply your handbrake," I ordered.

I saw him fiddle with the ignition and put on the handbrake.

"What is your name?" I asked him.

"Ingram," he replied.

Everything was going well at this stage. My two colleagues were standing behind the stolen car to cover me. These men could well be armed. I realised this and I was as cautious as I could be.

I had left the siren on in the Police car in my haste to deal with this situation. The awkward position of our Police car and the noise of the siren were causing confusion to other motorists. They were slowing down and stopping. This could place them in danger. I asked a colleague to switch off the siren and move the CID car. He never got the chance.

I had decided to speak to the occupants of the stolen car from the kerbside at the front-seat passenger's window. As I walked from the driver's side around the front of the stolen vehicle, I was startled by the sudden high revving sound of the car engine. I realised that the driver, Ingram, had no intention of staying to be questioned or arrested: he was trying to drive off.

At the same time, but too late, I noticed that the rear of the stolen car was moving up and down. The driver was riding on the hand-brake! Before I could get out of the way, the stolen car leapt forward and knocked me down. There was nothing I could do to avoid it. It had happened in an instant.

The sound of me at sixteen and a half stone hitting that thin tin bonnet, coupled with my yells of blind panic, caused my colleagues to fear that I had been seriously injured. I wasn't. I had received only minor bruising in my fall to the ground from the bonnet of the stolen car.

I heard my colleagues shout at the driver to stop. Then there was the unmistakable sound of gunfire: there was an exchange of shots, it seemed, between the Police and the occupants of the stolen car. I rolled over and over, trying to find cover. There was none. I was at the mercy of these young gunmen.

As I lay on the ground, I heard two distinctly different types of gunfire. There was the familiar "crack, crack, crack, crack" of the RUC Walther pistol and the more thunderous report of a weapon of much heavier calibre which must have come from the terrorists. My heart was pounding. I was lying face down on the ground, looking up at my two CID colleagues still firing at the stolen car as it sped away from the scene.

My colleagues helped me to my feet. I limped over to the Police car. They looked at me in disbelief. They could not believe that I was not more seriously injured. I got into the driver's seat only seconds after the stolen car had fled the scene. Our Police siren was still blaring, adding to the confusion.

We had no time for discussion about exactly what had happened. My colleagues immediately joined me and we set off in pursuit of the stolen 1100 car. We had to catch these boys. I had a sneaking suspicion that they had been heading for the UVF club in Monkstown before we stopped them. I was amazed that no-one had been injured in that exchange of gunfire. Certainly no Police officer had been injured except me. We had reason to be grateful. Encounters of that nature with terrorists had often resulted in the loss of RUC life.

I was convinced that, as the stolen car sped off, the occupants of the vehicle had opened fire on the Police and my CID colleagues had returned fire. My gun was still in my holster. I had not fired a shot. The stolen car now racing along in front of us broke through a uniformed RUC checkpoint at the junction of Rathcoole Drive and the Shore Road.

With sirens blaring, we passed the checkpoint a split second later. We were so close that we could clearly see the men inside the stolen car panic.

All through this second part of the chase, the shattered glass from the rear window of the stolen car was falling out in pieces both large and small, and smashing into hundreds of pieces as they hit the roadway. This was happening in such a way as to give me the impression that the glass was being thrown out of the fleeing stolen car. I was half-expecting a gun or guns to fall onto the roadway too. I was also expecting to come under fire at any moment. Terrorists being chased in this manner are prone to kill anyone to make good their escape.

The stolen car swung erratically left from the Shore Road and onto the Doagh Road. We were aware that a number of Police vehicles were on their way to intercept it. It was no surprise to me when I saw the stolen car brake suddenly and pull in to the left. Police Land Rovers were in front and alongside it. As we pulled up behind it, we ran forward to assist other uniformed officers in dealing with the gunmen.

I fully expected to find a weapon or weapons in the stolen car. The terrorists inside had had no chance to throw any weapons from it. The uniformed Police were dealing with three of the youths from the stolen car and had them spread-eagled face down on the roadway.

"I've been hit! I've been hit!" one of the men on the ground shouted.

I could see the fourth youth lying down in the rear seat of the stolen car. I thought he was making a vain attempt to hide, which seemed rather foolish because of the posse of Police surrounding the stolen car. I asked him to get out of the car. He did not reply. He did not move. I reached into the back seat and attempted to pull him out. He was moaning deeply. I realised that he must have been injured in the exchange of gunfire.

It was obvious from the position in which I found him that he had attempted to crouch down as low as he could when the firing started. He was exactly where he had been when he had been hit. I was not sure if he was bluffing or not. His moans sounded genuine but I was still afraid that he was armed. I shook him roughly. He did not move. I pulled him as hard as I could, but no matter what I did I could not shift him. A uniformed officer behind me shone his torch inside. The youth was obviously now unconscious.

I helped a uniformed colleague to pull the young man out from the back seat. Other officers shone their flashlights into the rear of the car so that we could see what we were doing. I could now see his arms hanging loosely at his side. He was not armed. There were no obvious gunshot injuries to his body.

It was then I realised that it was his head that was stuck tight to the rear seat. Not realising why, I leaned further in and pulled the youth's head by his hair towards the front of the car. I felt his head come away slowly from the seat. It seemed that something was holding him back. I can vividly recall how in that moment the youth's head suddenly came loose.

I could see in the torchlight that two metal wire springs from the back seat, both in the shapes of a "V", had obviously been struck by bullets and had been forced forward. They had entered the young man's head, leaving him stuck tightly to the rear seat. Parts of his brains were now dangling from those wires. His blood was dripping onto the back seat.

It is this image more than any other that haunts me from that particular incident. I know that for as long as I live, I will have flashbacks to that scene. There is no training in the world that can prepare anyone to cope with something like that.

I had seen many such scenes. I had witnessed at first hand the carnage of explosions, dismembered bodies, suicides of all descriptions, but these had been perpetrated by criminals and terrorists, or they had been self-inflicted. Every one was a tragedy, yes, very much so, but this time was different. This time we were responsible. The Police, our patrol, had caused this. I had not fired a shot; nonetheless I was overwhelmed with guilt.

Even as the very welcome blue flashing lights and the siren of the ambulance approached, I knew that this young man would die. I just knew it. I felt sick.

No matter what this man had been involved in, he did not deserve to die like that. Our saving grace from a legal point of view was the fact that these young men had stolen the car and had attempted to murder members of an RUC patrol. In the eyes of the law, our actions were justified. At least the other three had survived. It could have been worse, much worse. I wondered what sort of a ballistics history the recovered weapons would have.

I was still in a trance, with all of these thoughts going through my mind, when I heard a Police officer speaking to me. His voice was weak, as if he was speaking from a distance. I strained to hear what he was saying. There was so much happening around me, I was only half-listening.

"No guns, Jonty," he said.

"What's that?" I asked.

I had only half-heard him. I was hoping that I had heard him wrongly.

"They weren't armed, Jonty, they couldn't have opened up on your patrol," he said.

Not armed? That couldn't be true! I had heard the two different reports. The men *had* fired on my patrol. I went over to my two CID colleagues. I asked them what was happening. Didn't the youths in the stolen car open fire on them? They both shook their heads in the negative.

Then why were there those two distinctly different types of gunfire? I had heard my CID colleague fire four shots at the car. But I had also heard the distinctive report of a much heavier gun. Who had fired that gun? At that point, John pulled his coat back to reveal a large Browning .9 mm pistol in his side holster. After my recent jibes, it seemed he had exchanged his "lady's" .32 calibre pistol for this heavier calibre weapon. Now it all made sense.

"I thought you were dead," John said awkwardly.

This was a tragedy. A string of events that could well cost a young man his life. It was also a very graphic illustration of how things could go so horribly wrong. I was filled with a sense of dread. I had totally misread the situation in all the confusion. These youths were from Tiger's Bay, indeed, but they had nothing to do with the contingent of UDA men who had caused trouble in the UVF club in Monkstown.

I wondered if the car had been properly searched. I decided to search it for myself. Grabbing a torch from a uniformed Police officer, I proceeded to do so. After a short time, I realised it was true: there were no weapons to be found. My sense of guilt deepened. I watched as the youth was placed into the ambulance. The white sheet was not placed over his head.

He's alive! I thought.

I ran over to the ambulance attendants.

"Will he be okay?" I asked.

"Not good, doesn't look good, son," the ambulance man said as he jumped into the passenger seat of the ambulance.

I watched with trepidation as the ambulance sped off, blue lights flashing but its siren silent.

I stood back and surveyed the grim scene. The bullet-ridden stolen car. The ambulance disappearing down the Doagh Road in eerie silence. The three surviving youths now under arrest and being placed into different Police vehicles. The realisation of what we had done hit me like a hammer. Joy riders! They were just young joy riders! My former confidence in our actions evaporated. This was something entirely different. I glanced over at my two other crew members standing not yards away from me. The three of us could only guess the ramifications of all this.

The protection of life: those words from the principles of Police work. The protection of life: I went over it again in my head. But it was too late for regrets. Too late for anything like that. We were already being summoned to return to base. I was filled with dread. The adrenalin in my body was ebbing and I was beginning to feel the pain from my injuries. We made our way back to the barracks. This was not a time for recriminations. There would be plenty of time for that.

At the barracks, we had time to take stock of our situation. Time to reflect upon the gravity of what had happened.

A young man could have lost his life because my colleagues had believed that I had been very seriously injured. There were words of support from some of our colleagues. Inevitably, there were also those officers who revelled in the fact that we had made such a terrible mistake, that we had left ourselves open for criticism, or worse.

The duty inspector arrived from York Road to commence initial investigations. He asked us to hand over our guns. I refused to furnish him with mine.

"I did not fire a shot," I said.

He didn't appear to believe me. He insisted that I must do as he said. I had no fear of any future enquiry, but I did, however, know better than to go home to Twinburn in Monkstown with no means of protecting myself. The local UVF knew that I was one of the three CID officers in the patrol that was responsible for the encounter with the young men.

They had already threatened to kill me on a number of occasions for arresting their volunteers and seizing their weapons. In fact, as I have already recounted in this narrative, two of their volunteers had arrived at my home on one occasion the previous year in very sinister circumstances. I had been lucky to escape with my life on that occasion. I feared that this latest incident would serve only to add fuel to the fire. If I was to lose my personal protection pistol, I should be given a replacement at once, I insisted.

The duty inspector, a polite Englishman, was keen to accommodate me. In fairness, he tried without success to obtain a replacement for me from our own armoury. We were all assembled in the station sergeant's office which was linked to the guardroom by a half-door affair that opens to allow the passage of post and telex messages from the guardroom.

Suddenly, without warning, the hatch opened and a constable, who was one of our most vociferous critics behind our backs, addressed us quite flippantly:

"He's dead," he said, and then he immediately closed the hatch.

I will never forget the way in which that constable rolled his eyes as he delivered that body blow, as if to say "you're for it now!"

I couldn't believe it. I had to sit down. I know how sick I felt; I couldn't even begin to imagine how the other two lads felt. The look on their faces said it all, as the enormity of what had happened began to dawn on them. The name of the deceased was Edward Walker. He was just twenty years old, a single man from 11 Hogarth Street in the Tiger's Bay area of the city. The other three youths were also from "the Bay".

We were joined by the Divisional Commander, a Chief Super-intendent. A Christian man and a strict disciplinarian, he brought immediate order to the mayhem that had proceeded. He had been the Commandant in the RUC Training Depot during my time there some four years before. He enquired as to what exactly had happened. Interested only in the facts, he made no judgements or criticisms.

Turning to the duty inspector he said, "Issue this officer with a Sterling submachine-gun and adequate ammunition."

He enquired about my injuries and told me to take care at home in case of reprisals from paramilitaries. He informed me that a senior CID officer from a neighbouring Division or from Headquarters would be appointed in the morning to fully investigate the incident from a criminal responsibility perspective. A prosecu-tions file would be prepared and submitted to the Director of Public Prosecutions. Once the Chief Superintendent saw that I had been given the Sterling submachine, he wished us goodnight and left the barracks. I was grateful for his intervention.

It was not until around 6 am in the morning of 12 June 1976 that I was able to leave the barracks for home. I had been on duty for eleven hours. I looked down at the Sterling submachine-gun and the two magazines filled with bullets on the passenger seat of my car. I was hoping that I wouldn't need to use these. I didn't sleep well that night, but lay wondering what the next day would bring.

I knew that people in the background, those who had had just about enough of my style of policing, would not miss this chance to have me transferred. There would be little if anything I would be able to do about it.

I was back at my desk at 1 pm that day, ready to be interviewed by senior Police from a neighbouring Division. Most of the day was spent explaining exactly what had happened to countless numbers of senior Police officers, Scenes of Crime Officers (SOCOs), CID and uniformed officers. The majority of them were supportive; however, the critics of such CID patrols were having a field day. They came back at me with all sorts of jibes.

"That's you finished, Jonty, you're out of here," one of them said with more than a hint of glee.

"You'll be lucky to stay in the CID," said another.

It was perhaps strange, but that last threat didn't really worry me. I had loved uniform beat and patrol duties and I regarded the uniformed branch as the cream of any Police force. Somehow I had always felt like a fish out of water in the CID. They after all had approached me to join them, rather than it being the other way around.

Since joining the CID, I had been bombarded by my CID colleagues to stop patrolling in plain clothes. Despite the successes I had achieved by this means. It was illegal, they argued. You are compromising our CID cars, they claimed. An off-duty member of the Security Forces will shoot you, they warned. They'll expect us all to do it, they argued. I believe it was the last they feared most.

I would come back with valid arguments to the contrary. The facts spoke for themselves. I had had many successes in the detection of criminals and terrorists whilst on patrol. They didn't like that, preferring to dwell on all of the negative aspects of such patrols. I had to concede that there were dangers, but then anyone could always find excuses not to do something. In the absence of any positive alternative, CID patrols were a helpful supplement to policing.

I reminded them of the old "Q" cars—traffic cars manned by uniformed Police wearing coats to cover their uniforms. If it was good enough for the Traffic Branch, it was good enough for the CID. Also, I ever only patrolled with volunteers, men who wanted to participate. My greatest and most valid argument I always kept for the last: I had never yet caught a criminal or terrorist while sitting at a desk, but had caught many red-handed whilst patrolling our subdivision. Common sense and experience applied, there was, I argued, a place for plainclothes patrols to supplement the work of our uniformed patrols. Finally, I would refer to neighbouring Divisions where CID patrols were accepted practice.

Realistically, however, I knew there were practical difficulties associated with what I was advocating: the possibility for example of a "blue on blue" situation arising, where two plainclothes patrols with no means of identifying one another as Police could encounter each other at an incident and engage in a shootout. This had happened more often than one cared to imagine, but in the final analysis, it did not deter us.

We continued the CID patrols. I believed that my CID colleagues in West Belfast were doing the same thing, although I was later to discover at first hand that this was not the case.

In any event, no senior officer had ever asked me to stop patrolling in this fashion. They could see the obvious benefits. They just chose not to detail us to patrol in plainclothes.

Now here we were in a "worst case scenario". This was every copper's nightmare. All three of us would have given anything to turn the clock back. However, there was nothing that we could do except wait and wonder what the outcome would be.

That afternoon, a Detective Chief Superintendent and a Detective Inspector interviewed me. The Detective Inspector did most of the aggressive questioning. He was a small-framed, wiry individual with an air of authority.

After caution, he recorded a full and detailed statement from me. The atmosphere and the setting were very formal. He left me in no doubt that every aspect of what we had done and had tried to do would be the subject of very searching scrutiny. He emphasised that the death of this young man, Edward Walker, was a very grave matter and that he intended to leave no stone unturned.

It was put to me directly that all three of the youths who had been arrested in the stolen car had alleged that I had stopped alongside them without warning. They had further alleged that I had not identified myself as a Police officer when I approached their car, and there had not been any Police siren sounding as I had claimed. I replied that we had applied the siren at once upon commencing the pursuit. I pointed out that whilst it could be argued that a motorist with a car radio on at a high volume might not hear the siren initially, over a prolonged pursuit, he could not avoid doing so. In any case, our siren was still going once the two vehicles were stationary. I also pointed out that the driver's window of the stolen car was wound down when I was speaking to the driver, and so it was inconceivable that they did not hear the Police siren.

It was as I was recounting the sequence of events to the investigating officers that I recalled my voice transmissions during our pursuit.

"That's it," I exclaimed, "Of course!"

We had independent technical evidence that we were telling the truth. All voice messages were recorded on audiotape at Belfast Regional Control (BRC) in Castlereagh: the siren blaring in the background as I spoke to the controller would be on tape. These tapes were kept for a long time before re-use, precisely because they might be required for evidence. The officer reached for the telephone to call BRC.

This man was a professional detective. He researched the whole affair meticulously. He was as good as his word: he left no stone unturned. He submitted his report on the incident to the Director of Public Prosecutions. In fact, and much to my advantage, this man and I were to meet again at a later date. Without realising it at the time, I had made a lasting impression upon him.

The Director of Public Prosecutions marked the papers "No Prosecution". There were to be no further legal consequences for John, Alan or myself. When I received the news, I was actually on a Junior Initial CID course at Hendon, London. I was still on the course between October and December 1976 when the inquest was heard and so, in my absence, someone read my evidence to the coroner and the jury. I would have much preferred to have been there in person. The inquest confirmed incidentally that the deceased was a member of the UDA's 2nd Battalion based in Tiger's Bay.

By August 1976, wheels were moving within wheels. The Special Branch was not about to miss this opportunity to get rid of me. They insisted that a new UDA death threat on me was very real, and that they wanted me out of the Belfast region—for my own safety, of course. I was in favour of moving house to lessen the danger to my personal security, and had bought a new property in Victoria Park, Newtownards, Co. Down. But I did not want a transfer from Newtownabbey RUC Station: I had invested too much time and effort in establishing myself there to turn my back on it now. I had also met Rebecca by this time: she was later to become my wife. There was the added consideration that I still had so much more to achieve in the Newtownabbey area. The real problem was that I was inadvertently stepping on Special Branch toes. Now I was in a situation where they could have me transferred on the pretext that it was for my own benefit. I was at their mercy: I had handed myself to them on a plate.

In my bid to stay where I was, I canvassed the support of my senior CID officer. Detective Chief Inspector Sam Stewart was aware of my success in crime investigation and he fully supported my application to remain in Newtownabbey CID. In fact, he did everything in his power to keep me there. He knew that it would be a battle, but neither of us had any idea of the lengths to which the Special Branch would go to ensure that they got their way.

Sam argued that I was being punished for something I was not guilty of—that, after all, forensic scientists had established beyond a doubt that I had not fired any shots. In fact, I had been knocked down and was therefore as much a victim of circumstances as the men in the car.

About a week before the proposed transfer date, however, I was called into Sam's office. He was red with anger, and recognising the expression on his face, I waited for a roasting. In fact, it never came. His fury was directed at the Special Branch, not me. He said that he had attended a meeting of senior Police at Divisional Headquarters in North Queen Street at which, amongst other things, there had been a heated discussion about my pending transfer from the division. During the debate, Special Branch officers had made non-specific but scurrilous allegations about me to senior Police officers in a bid to swing the argument in their favour. Sam was incensed. He had asked them to put up or shut up. They refused, however, to detail exactly what the allegations were or their source.

Sam told me that he had seen the Special Branch use this ploy before to move men who were causing them problems. He had also heard that in this case, the Special Branch were insisting that I was to remain in Newtownards for at least four years. He had stormed out of the meeting. There had been nothing more that he could do. He stood up and shook my hand.

"You have made some powerful enemies in your short time here, Johnston," he said, shaking his head.

We had not always seen eye-to-eye, but I knew this man was straight and if he said there was nothing that could be done, then I believed him. I was furious, forced to acknowledge yet again the extent of the power of the Special Branch. But I was not known for lying down for any man, and I wasn't about to do so here. At the time, I did not have the sense to fear the Special Branch.

My transfer went ahead as scheduled. I had already moved house to Victoria Park, in Newtownards, Co. Down. I did not want to be stationed in the town that I was policing ever again. My new Detective Inspector, formerly of Holywood CID, was a man I knew well. He was aware of my family background well. He supported my application for a transfer to Bangor CID.

———

The awful events of that terrible night of 12 June 1976 were well behind me. Or so I thought. The truth was that no matter what the facts were, no matter what I said about not having fired any shots at the stolen car, the UDA were still convinced that I was responsible. After all, I was the only member of that patrol to be transferred out of Newtownabbey. They saw the "dirty transfer" as clear evidence that it was me who was responsible for young Edward Walker's death. It mattered not what RUC officialdom alleged: the UDA were convinced that "Jonty" Brown had murdered their young volunteer. They have never forgiven me for this, not even to this day. And yet nothing could be further from the truth. It is a source of personal pride to me to be able to say that I did not discharge my firearm and that I was not responsible for the death of that young man. *The truth of the matter is that in my 30 years' service in the RUC, I was never directly responsible for the death of any person.*

Even today, years into my retirement, when I hear that a Police officer has opened fire and killed a suspect, I am thrust back to that traumatic scene on the Doagh Road in June 1976. Despite the passing of almost 30 years, I can still vividly recall every second of the chase, the standstill and the discovery of the body in the rear of that stolen car. Those dramatic images are accompanied by the unforgettable smell of the hot engine of the Police car and the sound of glass from the broken windows of the stolen vehicle on the road. I still have recurring nightmares in relation to the tragic death of that young man.

I know that I will take those images with me to my grave. The whole regrettable incident was aggravated by the fact that no firearms were recovered from the stolen car. The young men in the car were unarmed. Events such as this are the stuff of every copper's worst nightmare.

My heart goes out to the Police personnel involved in such confrontations. Generally speaking, no Police Officer sets out to deliberately kill or to maim anyone, unless he believes that his life or the life of one of his colleagues is threatened. I know exactly how they feel as the intensive investigation that properly follows in the wake of such an event leaves them feeling like criminals.

Chapter 8
The West Belfast Years

My transfer from the CID in Bangor to Andersonstown CID in West Belfast on 1 January 1978 was a welcome development. The Special Branch instruction that I would remain in "G" Division for at least four years had been overruled. By the day of my transfer I had served only one year and four months in Bangor. I had volunteered for service in West Belfast in October 1977. A senior CID colleague who was in overall charge of the CID in the RUC's "B" Division and had assured me of his support had kept his word, and it had taken only two months for him to organise the transfer.

Bangor had been a very busy CID office, and I had very much enjoyed my time there. The team was a wonderful bunch of people and there had been harmony and genuine comradeship. At my leaving function at a hotel in Donaghadee, a number of the lads told me that they thought "my head was cut": that I was mad to volunteer to go to West Belfast. We could not have known it at the time, but CID authorities at Headquarters had just taken the decision to double CID manpower in West Belfast. Many of those fellow officers who wished me farewell and said that they would be praying for my safety and well-being were to find themselves being drafted out to West Belfast only a few months later.

The RUC's "B" Division policed the whole of West Belfast at that time. The Divisional Headquarters were located in Springfield Road RUC Station near to the junction of the Falls Road. Set in the notoriously

Republican areas of West Belfast, the other RUC stations in the Division included Andersonstown, Hastings Street, New Barnsley, and later Woodbourne and Grosvenor Road. It was difficult for us to patrol the area, as the entire Division was in the grip of PIRA terrorists. Heavily-armed RUC patrols, whether on foot or in armoured vehicles, were necessarily accompanied by Army vehicles to provide cover from terrorist attack while they went about the everyday duties that would be expected of any Police service.

It was well known of course that the RUC did not enjoy the same level of support from the people of West Belfast as they did in the Loyalist areas. It is only with the support of the public at large that any Police Service can be successful. The lack of support for the Police by a large majority of the public in West Belfast, whether because of intimidation by the paramilitaries or some political or religious standpoint, impacted very negatively on the ability of the RUC to fulfil our everyday obligations. Yet in spite of this, we were determined to do our best. There were still an awful lot of decent people living in those areas who wanted us there. People who quietly and at times anonymously would move to help us get to grips with those responsible for terrorist atrocities, despite the fact that to be seen to be helping the Police in any way could be punishable with death at the hands of the paramilitaries. There are many examples of the brutal murder of decent Catholics by the same PIRA killing machine that purported to be there to protect them. In one particular case, a pensioner who came forward to assist us in a murder enquiry in Lenadoon was brutally murdered by the Provisionals. The very real fear of retribution that incidents such as this engendered meant that only exceptionally brave individuals would volunteer any kind of information or input which would help us with our enquiries. Without such people, however, I know for a fact that the difficulties that we experienced out on the ground while investigating crime would have been far greater.

I reported for duty at the Andersonstown CID Office in Springfield Parade on 2 January 1978. The RUC had leased an old industrial complex opposite the Protestant Highfield Estate on the corner of the West Circular Road and adjacent to the Springfield Road. We affectionately called these buildings "The Oaks". Behind the high walls was a massive, dismal-looking complex of large Portakabins®, which housed the CID officers responsible for criminal investigations in Andersonstown, Springfield Road, Hastings Street and the two small report centres at Roden Street and New Barnsley. Morale was high and the comradeship experienced in West Belfast was second to none. The constant threat to us all of a sudden and violent death at the hands of Republican terrorists doubtless created a strong bond between us. There was little, if any, backbiting or in-fighting. The uniformed branch was almost over-protective of us when we were called to investigate serious terrorist incidents in the area. Even the Special Branch did not fight with us at Andersonstown. They were kept far too busy with their own primary function: protecting the State from what was very quickly becoming the most dangerous terrorist threat in the history of Northern Ireland.

In those days of the late 1970s and early 1980s, the Provisional IRA had become a very proficient killing machine. Their ability to inflict heavy casualties upon the Security Forces and their absolute disregard for human life was truly awful to witness. We were following too many coffins of brave RUC men who had been cut down by cowardly PIRA attackers. It was not just the burgeoning membership of the PIRA that was the problem: it was the technology which they were constantly developing and refining which would enable them to place and detonate explosives to deadly effect in the most innocent of places. They put bombs in and behind walls, in "wheelie" bins or in the downpipes of buildings. Litterbins and various other containers would explode as the Security Forces passed by. Or PIRA snipers would simply randomly "pick off" any soldiers or RUC officers who might stray into their "frame".

We received on-the-job training and advice on how to get from one RUC station to another without becoming the next victim, the next statistic on a board at Headquarters or the next Police death to be reported on the fifth or sixth page of the local newspapers. The sad fact was that at that time the murder of RUC men no longer seemed to merit a front-page headline: the public were simply sick of hearing about what seemed to be a never-ending litany of death and destruction.

Some of the advice given to me during the first months of my service in Andersonstown would later be instrumental in saving my life. I was trained *never* to stop at a red light whilst moving around the Division if it was safe to go through it without causing an accident. One of our detective chief inspectors had been shot in the head and body when he stopped at a red traffic light on the Springfield Road, not 100 yards from the gates of the barracks. In another case, a young soldier was shot dead in his car on the Monagh Road not far from his military base because he had stopped at a pedestrian crossing to allow people across. The "pedestrians" he had stopped for were in fact part of a trap. The Provisional IRA had realised that the Mini car he had been travelling in was in fact an army undercover car. He had taken the same route many times before. Routine could be fatal: that had become patently obvious.

I was told *never* to indicate my intention to turn left or right into a barracks. An IRA sniper holed up at the window of a house taken over by the Provisionals would welcome those extra few seconds to get a "bead" on you. Rather, you should approach the barracks slowly in a line of normal traffic and then swerve suddenly in through the gates. This reduced the sniper's chances of getting a clean shot, as well as ensuring that anyone sympathetic to the PIRA did not get a chance to note your registration number. I remember clearly one older detective sergeant, a man in his late forties, telling me sternly,

"This is not Newtownabbey, nor is it Bangor, son. Here you have at most between five and eight minutes at the door of any house you may call at on an enquiry. You have that much time to conduct the enquiry and get the hell out of those areas, because five to eight minutes is all the time it takes for the Provos to get a hold of a 'surface' weapon and a volunteer who will be only too keen to kill you *before* you conduct your enquiry and leave."

He continued, "If you are ever unfortunate enough to fall into the hands of a group of armed Provos, do not try to talk your way out of it. They are not interested: history tells us that they will try to kidnap and interrogate you *before* they kill you. Use your service revolver to extricate yourself from such a situation. As you fire, count the shots. Fire only five. You will not have the chance to reload. Save the last bullet for yourself. Put the gun to your temple and pull the damn trigger! It will all be over in an instant. Believe me, son, that is a much quicker way to die than any those boys will give you. As far as they are concerned, you are Special Branch. You are in plain clothes. They hate the Special Branch, son. You are their sworn enemy," he said.

"But I'm not in Special Branch," I said.

"That's irrelevant, son. As far as they are concerned, you are," he said.

I soaked all of this in. I was about to lift a black manual of the RUC Code down from a shelf to study a finance query when the older man's hand reached out to stop me.

"You won't find any of the stuff I've told you in the Code, son. It is a jungle out there. There are no rules. Get it wrong, stray into an IRA trap or checkpoint and you are finished. Do you understand me? Dead. Over. History," he said.

I had been listening assiduously and was beginning to wonder just what I had let myself in for.

"How long have you been here?" I asked.

"Too long," he answered.

"Why don't you ask out?" I enquired.

"I have, son. I've applied three times on paper for transfer to somewhere nearer home but they can't get people to serve here. It's a blocking station, somewhere you're only sent when you've done something wrong. What did you do to deserve being sent to this god-forsaken hole?" he asked.

"I volunteered. I wanted a challenge," I replied truthfully.

He looked up at me with a quizzical expression on his face: "Really?" he asked.

"Honestly," I replied. "I didn't like the type of crime I was investigating in Bangor."

The old fella shook his head in astonishment.

"Well, there were no Provos in Bangor, son, now, were there? You'll have to be careful here," he said.

I brought it to his attention that there were in fact "Provos" in Bangor, and that they had conspired to murder two RUC men who lived there. The terrorists had targeted the pair as they attended a local chapel: they were planning to murder both of them at their place of worship! I explained how we had moved against that Bangor PIRA unit. Two of them had recently gone to prison for substantial jail terms and the trial of a third was pending.

"Well, this place is a hive of Provo activity. We recently lost two of our detectives. Both were shot dead by the Provisional IRA before they even realised there was a problem," he added.

During the next few months, I learned a great deal about self-preservation. I also learned that there were new unwritten rules about the policing of these "hard Green" areas. For instance, CID officers were only allowed to recruit and run ordinary criminals as informants. If anyone wandered in to our Police stations to volunteer information about terrorists or terrorist incidents, we were obliged to immediately contact the Special Branch and arrange for them to interview such individuals. The handling of Republican terrorist informants in West Belfast was deemed by our CID authorities to be a function better left to the Special Branch. I had no intention of arguing with the logic of that rule. During my time in West Belfast, which spanned almost nine years, I never on any occasion "locked horns" or found myself at odds with the Special Branch.

We worked entirely separately from the Branch. The general public and the terrorists knew us by name. We did *not* enjoy the Special Branch cloak of anonymity that has so protected them over the years. Like so many other CID officers stationed in West Belfast, I found myself allocated to a Divisional pool of CID men whose duty it was to interview terrorist suspects in the Police Office in Castlereagh RUC Station. This was the holding centre for all terrorists arrested in the Belfast region and further afield. All persons arrested under emergency legislation were brought to Castlereagh for interview. If a prisoner did confess to their crimes, and hundreds chose to do exactly that, we had to attend the Crown Court at Crumlin Road, Belfast to give evidence in open court against them. There was to be no hiding place for us, no way to prevent ourselves from being targeted by those PIRA members who remained at large.

Yet it was not all gloom and doom in "B" Division. I met some very, very decent people in those sprawling housing estates in West Belfast. The main Andersonstown Estate was, I found, very reminiscent of Rathcoole in Newtownabbey. The layout of the two estates was very similar; their houses were of exactly the same design, and had obviously been built at around the same time. But that was where the similarities ended. This was a very dangerous area for all RUC patrols and that included CID patrols. There were people who were national-ists but who had absolutely no time for the Provos. Some even hated the Republican paramilitaries with a passion. Many a time I broke that golden eight-minute rule and remained at a house in the heart of Andersonstown or Ballymurphy at great personal risk to myself, simply to be able to enjoy the hospitality of people who could not afford to be seen to be openly supportive of the RUC. I am glad today that I took the time to do so.

Pope John Paul II had visited Ireland in 1979 and I had listened with interest to what he preached about the evil of violence. "Murder is murder is murder," he said. There was no mistaking the genuine admonishment in his tone. There was also no room for argument or discussion on what he had said: his condemnation of murder was unequivocal. He told the gathered masses and anyone else around the world who might be listening that there could be no other word for the taking of a human life. Terms such as "assassinate", "execute", "kill" and "slay" were intended to detract from the inhumanity of the brutal act of murder. They should not be allowed to do so. No other word was appropriate.

I welcomed this development. I knew from interviews with PIRA "soldiers" that the ordinary Provo volunteer had always assumed that what he was doing in the name of Irish freedom was morally legitimate. Many of the terrorists that we interviewed believed wholeheartedly that they had at least the tacit approval, if not the full support, of the Catholic Church. Yet now Pope John Paul II himself had made it abundantly clear that the taking of a human life could never be justified, that no political cause could *ever* be advanced by the ruthless murder of a fellow human being. Even with only six years' service, I had stepped over enough dead bodies to last me a lifetime—the actual corpses of people whom the majority of the population know of only as statistics.

Following discussions with Catholic friends on the occasion of the Holy Father's visit, I decided to buy an LP of Pope John Paul's address which had been released at that time. I took it home and played it over and over again until I knew most of the lines by heart. Sometimes I would quote some of these lines during interviews with terrorists, and always to great effect. Many of the Republicans who personally confessed their involvement in murder to me were moved to do so by those words of Pope John Paul II. They went to prison at peace with themselves. Hardened paramilitaries would listen intently as I argued that neither their Pope nor their Maker would ever forgive them for such abominable and disgusting murders. Yet for me, this was no cynical exercise in psychological manipulation: I firmly believed in the truth of what I was saying. I fully understood that before any man can kill another, he has to dehumanise his intended victim. The PIRA found it easy to dehumanise the Army or the RUC. Further, the tactics of their leaders—the hostility, the Republican rhetoric and the threats of brutal disciplinary action against their own men—ensured that only the very bravest of men would question the order to kill.

Problems would, however, arise later when the volunteers, those who had committed murders, would find themselves revisited by the horrific images in their dreams or even in broad daylight in the form of "flashbacks". They had not expected this, but it is a fact of life. Guilt is a terrible thing and man is not born evil. Men from the para-militaries could kill—they did kill. But at home in later years, in the quietness of the night, they are revisited relentlessly by images of the dead. By the enormity of their crimes. I know this to be the case, because I recorded long and detailed statements from many IRA volunteers who broke down in tears during interview and confessed to their involvement in such crimes.

Any detective or former detective who reads this narrative will understand exactly what I mean. The first thing a murderer feels once he has confessed his crime is *relief*. He feels better. The atmosphere in the interview room is suddenly transformed by the sense of euphoria which emanates from the prisoner just after he or she has confessed. Yes, they have to go to jail, but they have realised that prison is in fact the very least of their problems. To somehow atone for the atrocity they have committed is far more important.

On occasion, I have found myself unexpectedly face-to-face with men who have confessed such crimes to me in the past and who have served out their sentences through many years of incarceration. None of these men have ever shown me any animosity. All of them, without exception, expressed only thanks. All of them spoke of the sense of being absolved of their guilt. They were no longer visited by night-mares or flashbacks to the same extent as they had been prior to their "confession". In a way, these men were the lucky ones. I know many men too, now in their forties and fifties, who cannot sleep at night. Every time they close their eyes, they are haunted by the same horrible images. As a former detective, I have no sympathy for them. I can only advise them to go and speak to the Police. If they could only hear the testimonies of those who have done so, and the release from guilt and return to some sense of normality they speak of, I believe that they would come forward without hesitating. The reality is too that the fear of long prison sentences is no longer valid. Executive political decisions have removed the possibility of terrorists facing the full rigour of the law, as the most recent example of the Ken Barrett case clearly illustrates.

On Monday, 12 May 1980, I was transferred from Andersonstown CID to Woodbourne RUC Station. The Woodbourne site had once been a local hotel, now long gone. In its place was a small RUC Portakabin®

manned by several RUC men as a "reporting post". There was also a large military contingent present. Plans were afoot at RUC Headquarters to turn this site into a major new Police station. But that would take years. In the meantime, we would have to make do with the usual Portakabin®-on-top-of-Portakabin®-scenario.

The site flooded in the winter and we had to call upon the services of a soldier in a flat punt to get us from our CID quarters to the enquiry office through a stream of rain water about two feet deep in places. Despite the fact that several female officers were stationed there, they had no toilet facilities. Someone in planning had simply forgotten. Women had to travel by armoured car to nearby Dunmurry RUC Station to use the facilities there.

Still, Woodbourne was a happy place. Nothing unites men more than the fact that we were all facing the same extreme adversity. Being a new station at the frontline of West Belfast, it was always going to be a challenging posting, to say the very least. Nevertheless, I have many fond memories of my service in Woodbourne RUC Station and of the characters that I met there. During the next four years I would experience sad times too, times when we had to lift and bury our dead colleagues. My experiences in that close-knit, volatile environment were many and varied and I could not do them justice by condensing them into this present book.

I cannot overstate the enormity of the pressure we faced as we went about our task of trying to afford a Police service in the most difficult of circumstances. I knew that we were not alone in our endeavours. Many other frontline RUC stations faced difficulties of the same nature. It was here in West Belfast that I would be initiated into the tiresome routine of trying to evade death each and every day. Every move we made out of our secure barracks had to be weighed up. A balance had to be struck between affording the locals a policing service and protecting ourselves from the constant threat of attack.

Our vehicles were heavily-armoured and two military vehicles always accompanied us to the scenes of crimes. In the CID, we enjoyed the facility of "ghost fleet" vehicles—non-armoured foreign saloon cars that could not be readily identified as Police vehicles. We used these for routine enquiries outside the Division or whilst on patrol during the hours of darkness. We only kept the "ghost fleet" vehicles for a short period of time before swapping them with other Divisions in order to confuse those Republicans targeting us for murder. Our

CID standard fleet vehicles were armoured and these were used during the daylight hours whilst moving around the Division from station to station. Our station came repeatedly under attack from high velocity gunfire and PIRA-improvised mortar bombs.

Policing West Belfast was to be a whole different ball game from anything I had previously experienced. My old colleague Joe had not exaggerated when he had said that the danger from Republicans would be ever-present. I would experience times when I was lucky to escape from the Provos with my life.

During those years of my service, I would find myself living for months in England with a PIRA member who had been fortunate enough to escape a Provo death squad just minutes before they intended to murder him. I would see the absolute brutality of PIRA-driven violence at first-hand. On another occasion, I witnessed one young RUC uniformed officer being sent needlessly to his death by a supervisor who expressed an unbelievable and profound indifference to his plight. These years were indeed a roller-coaster of a journey into what was known at that time as the "Wild West".

But the journey would eventually take its toll upon me psycho-logically and emotionally, and so insidiously that I had no awareness of just how much I had been affected until years later, when I left the Division to police in more normal environments. Yet despite all of this, I still look back at my time in "the West" with pride, tinged with more than a little sadness for those other brave Police officers who did not make it through.

Chapter 9

The Case of the Provo Turned UVF Man

It was in 1985 while serving at Greencastle that I first encountered Trevor McIlwrath, at that time a detective constable in the CID there. My initial impressions of Trevor were not perhaps the most favourable, because of his scruffy dress and at times droll sense of humour, but all of this belied the fact that he was a gifted detective. Once we started working together, it quickly became obvious that our respective skills and temperaments complemented each other perfectly, and that we would form a formidable duo. Our subsequent partnership as detectives was to last for twelve years, from 1985 to 1997, with a gap of only seven months in 1988, when at the behest of the Special Branch I was posted to Carrickfergus. The intention had been to keep me there, out of the mêlée, so to speak, for at least four years. Luckily, Detective Superintendent Alan Simpson from North Queen Street had intervened only seven months into my posting at Carrickfergus, inviting Trevor and I to join a newly formed Divisional Murder Squad based at Antrim Road RUC station.

As a partnership specialising in the area of Loyalist terrorism, Trevor and I achieved hitherto unparalleled successes. For the three years we were stationed at Greencastle, we had had a 67 per cent clear-up rate, which represented something like three times the national average. We arrested more prisoners and cleared more crimes on a monthly basis than any of the other stations in the Division, despite the fact that they had twice the manpower at their disposal. Inevitably our successes created jealousy, especially in the ranks of the Special Branch, and the friction that ensued was ultimately to destroy us as a partnership. My time with Trevor was cut short in 1997 when he was forced to leave the job on medical grounds. The truth was that in addition to the inevitable stresses and strains which our job involved, the cumulative effect of years of conflict with Special Branch had taken a terrible toll on Trevor. After his departure, a succession of other officers was selected by supervisors to work alongside me as his replacement. With one notable exception, these men fell one by one by the wayside, through no fault of their own, either because they failed to "gel" properly with informants or because they did not have the stomach for the continual friction with the Special Branch. The exception was Detective Constable John Allen, the only officer able to go any distance: he was my partner during the final two years of my service.

I first met "Tommy" (not his real name) in 1985 while I was conducting enquiries into the brutal murder of Stephen Megrath, a member of the UDR. Megrath had been shot dead by the Provisional IRA in the kitchen of his home in the Loyalist Tiger's Bay area of North Belfast. He had just arrived home and was followed into the kitchen by his murderer and shot from behind. Tommy was a friend of the young man's family, and the cowardly murder had sickened him.

At that time, Tommy, a Catholic, lived in a nearby nationalist area. He was extremely knowledgeable about local PIRA members. He appeared to co-operate with us, agreeing to do all in his power to help us bring those responsible for the murder of the UDR man to justice. I say "appeared to" because initially he was cautious. He would speak in riddles, saying an awful lot but telling us very little.

Tommy remained in touch with us for years. He soon got over his initial fear of working with the RUC and quickly learned the value of straight-talking. He would be in touch frequently and showed himself willing to assist us in identifying persons or places on both sides of the religious divide.

By his own admission, he was a former PIRA Fianna (Junior IRA) member. Fortunately for him, his father had got wind of his association with the Republican movement and sent him off to England out of the grip of his Provo masters. On his return to Northern Ireland, he did not renew his association with the Provos. Due to his family ties in nationalist areas and his friendships with Protestants living in Loyalist areas, Tommy was able to move freely among both communities. He had lost all the respect that he once had for the Republican movement, and when he first came forward to help us, he was actually under a death threat from the PIRA for reasons he did not want to reveal. His warm and affable personality, along with his heavy build and his ability to handle himself against any man, made him a formidable figure. On a one-to-one basis, no Provo would dare to tackle him. But then cowardly Republicans would never make an approach to him on a one-to-one basis: he knew that if they did come after him, there would be at least three or four of them and they would most certainly be armed. Tommy feared no man, but he always tempered his movements around the city with caution.

Only a fool would pour scorn on the information Tommy was able to offer: we certainly could not afford to. Lives depended upon our ability to obtain information from people just like him. Within a short time, he settled down and began to trust us completely. Mutual trust was vital in our dealings with these people. Tommy was always very willing to take on tasks from us. He would report back quickly to us and always with more detail than we had asked him to obtain.

In 1991, Tommy began to develop a close friendship with a local senior UVF man, "X", from the notorious Loyalist Mount Vernon Estate. At that time "X" was a well-known UVF activist. It is a measure of Tommy's personality and ability to relate to others that he was able to get so close to "X". What he did not know, however, was that he was not the only one close to "X". Trevor had in fact recruited "X" some years before and we had been running him very successfully as a CID informant.

Now that "X" was in the UVF and actively involved in terrorist crimes, he had been passed over to the Special Branch, in accordance with the Walker Report. Trevor had remained with "X" as a joint CID handler. I was removed from "X" in October 1991 when the Special Branch became involved. I was already very busy anyway with other sources, including the UDA commander Ken Barrett, nonetheless I kept my finger on the pulse as regards the "X" handling scenario. Trevor would keep me fully briefed.

Other CID sources in "X"'s UVF group were reporting that he was becoming vicious and uncontrollable, and that everyone in his local community feared him. This was a sad development, because initially he had co-operated fully with us and had always moved to save life and to frustrate UVF operations. I was aware that the Special Branch was doing little or nothing to limit their source "X"'s nefarious activities. Trevor and I had long since resolved to put him "on the floor" by way of arrest at the earliest possible moment. No informant had a licence to commit crime, particularly such serious crimes. Our only obstacle in taking "X" out of the picture was the absolute *carte blanche* he had been afforded by the Special Branch. We would have to think of a way to get around that.

Certain unscrupulous officers within the Special Branch made it clear that they did not share our enthusiasm to bring "X" to book. As far as they were concerned he could do whatever he liked. As long as they did not report his criminal activities into their intelligence system, they were sure of the unqualified support of their authorities. In fact, it was not what their agents actually did that would result in the withdrawal of that support. It was only what was logged against the agent on his file that would ultimately result in the Special Branch "red-lining" (striking off) an agent. This system was open to abuse, and I saw it being abused often. There are none so blind as those who will not see.

Some Special Branch supervisors encouraged their subordinates to turn a blind eye to the criminal activity of an agent, loathe as they were for him or her to be removed from their pool of intelligence resources. If none of an agent's more dubious activities were kept on record, he could be kept on by his handler without breaching the law and RUC regulations. And so, in the unlikely event of some outside agency arriving to investigate wrongdoing within the Constabulary, everyone involved would be legally covered. Unfortunately, however, this was a double-edged sword, giving those terrorists who did enjoy the status of a Special Branch agent the impression that they had what was effectively a licence to commit crimes, even murder. They could repeatedly admit their involvement in such crimes to their Special Branch handlers, absolutely safe in the knowledge that there would be no legal consequences and that they would be protected from the CID.

In the case of "X", the Special Branch handlers took the view that he was far too valuable to them at that time to consider removing him from the picture. We disagreed with this, our argument being that we had other informants in the same UVF grouping, and that as such, "X" would not have been as great a loss as the Special Branch would have us believe.

We watched with interest and some fascination as the strange relationship between Tommy and "X" blossomed. "X" came to trust Tommy implicitly and Tommy reported back to us. However, we had other sources so well-placed in that particular area that we did not benefit from much of what Tommy told us. There was no distance for us, however, in telling Tommy this. One never knew when he would be able to afford us intelligence that some other source would or could not deliver. In an environment such as North Belfast, lives depended upon our ability to gather such information.

Tommy moved to a new home just outside Belfast. Both he and "X" had common-law wives. They also had other girlfriends: they played hard. As long as Tommy was in "X"'s company, he was made welcome in all the UVF haunts in the Province. He even frequented the UVF Headquarters on the Shankill Road in Belfast. It is known locally as the Historical Club. Very few Roman Catholics would ever dare to venture in there. But the truth was that Tommy was walking on egg shells. I knew from experience that it would only be a matter of time before his new-found UVF friends would turn on him, and we often warned him of this possibility time and again.

In 1995, Tommy contacted us to tell us that he had been asked to supply a car for the UVF: it was their intention to use it in the murder of a young Catholic who habitually walked his Protestant girlfriend home to a Loyalist area just off the Antrim Road. The UVF murder team had been targeting this youth for some time. Unfortunately, however, Tommy did not know the identity of the intended victim. Nor was he in a position to ask the UVF any questions about their murderous operation. He had merely been asked by "Y", a senior UVF man, to supply the car for use by the murder gang.

We had an urgent meeting with Tommy in a car park in North Belfast. "X" was out of the country on a foreign holiday. He told us that "Y", the UVF gunman, who was well-known to us, was keen to carry out the murder personally in order to elevate himself in the eyes of his Shankill Road bosses before "X" came back home from holiday. Tommy did not like "Y". There was no particular reason—he was just unable to warm to him. What Tommy did not, could not, know was that "Y" was also a Special Branch agent. Worse still, his handler was none other than Alec (not his real name), a particularly unpleasant Special Branch officer.

Tommy's task was basically to obtain a roadworthy car and supply it in good working order to the UVF murder team. They would collect it from outside his house whenever it was ready. Tommy volunteered to make the vehicle available to us so that we could do with it whatever was required to monitor its movements and arrest these UVF men intent on murder. From experience, I knew that this would be a straightforward matter. We had done it often before, ably assisted by genuinely decent Special Branch officers.

The theory was simple. The operational capability of the Special Branch to deal with these situations was indisputable, as experience had proven. It wasn't their capability that was the problem, however: it was the fact that Trevor and I were asking them to move against one of their own agents. My previous experience with Alec had made me wary. I did not trust him, and so did not want him to become aware that Tommy was setting up one of his agents.

I decided to involve a decent Special Branch officer, a man I could trust from the Tennent Street Special Branch office. The only way that I could ensure that he would become involved in this life-or-death scenario was to allege that someone other than "Y"—some UVF man from the Shankill, perhaps—had asked Tommy to supply the murder car. This would keep Alec out of the equation. I submitted a CID 50 (intelligence input document) to that effect.

I had serious doubts as to whether the Special Branch would set in motion an operation to arrest "Y". I had come up against this before. They would take some overt action to abort the UVF operation, thus obviating the necessity to arrest anyone. The only problem with this form of response was that at a future time the UVF murder team might very well move against the same intended victim again, but at a time when our sources were not in a position to report on their intentions.

There was no time for delay. A life was at stake. I did not want Alec interfering with this one. I reported the intelligence to my authorities and through them to Special Branch, in accordance with our regulations.

Within a very short time the Special Branch officer from the Tennent Street office contacted me. I enjoyed a good rapport with this officer at that time. I knew that he at least would not deliberately do Tommy any harm. I set up a meeting between Tommy and the Special Branch. I assured Tommy that although the matter was now out of my hands, he could trust the Special Branch officer in question implicitly.

Tommy later informed me that he had met them and had handed the vehicle in question over to them. I was kept abreast of developments. The vehicle was kitted out with a tracker at a location in East Belfast.

Following the return of the car, a very concerned Tommy contacted me. Tommy had no problems with the Special Branch man he had met, referring to him as a "decent fella". He was, however, perplexed as to why the Branch man should tell him to be very, very careful. According to Tommy, the Branch man himself was shaking and the whole experience had greatly unsettled him. He asked me how many people knew of the bug in the car. I assured him that very few people were aware of what was happening.

Tommy employed several of "X"'s UVF men on a casual but daily basis. It was a rare day when there were none at his home, even when their commander was away on holiday. We asked Tommy to keep us appraised of the situation. Days passed without us hearing anything from him. This concerned me greatly, but I knew better than to try to ring him at home. I did not want to draw undue attention to him at such a crucial time. Nor would it have been prudent for me to ask the Special Branch what was happening.

The next I heard from Tommy was at 2 am a few days later. I received a telephone call from a woman detective constable from the Tennent Street CID office. She told me that I had to ring Tommy at home. This man had my home telephone number. Why would he ring in to Tennent Street to contact me? Something was obviously very wrong. I feared the worst.

I contacted Tommy a few minutes later from my home telephone. He told me that the UVF had never come near him to collect the car. It was still there. He told me that all of "X"'s UVF men had stopped calling at his home, and that "X" himself had now returned from holiday abroad, but had not come to see him. This was very odd because before he had left on holiday, "X" had embraced him and had told him that he would see him as soon as he got home. So why had he not been in touch? The only logical explanation was that the UVF somehow knew about the bug in the car. He told me that only a week before, a UVF commander had sworn him into the UVF in a flat in the Loyalist Rathcoole Estate.

I tried to pacify him. They could not know! How could they? But why then were none of the usual UVF men visiting his home? I could not reassure him. Tommy was, generally speaking, not easily rattled.

He just knew that his waters had been muddied and he feared an attack from his UVF cohorts at any time. The source was clearly panicking.

"How could the UVF know?" he asked me again.

I had no idea. The Special Branch was in charge of what was happening, so it wasn't in their interests to have the operation compromised. I spent at least an hour or two on the telephone with Tommy that night. I advised him to go back into UVF company: he should attempt to brazen it out. I suggested that he turn up unexpectedly at UVF haunts and stay for just a short time to test the temperature. He was afraid—terrified, in fact—but he agreed to do this. As it happened, he was due to attend a UVF meeting at a top commander's home in Shore Crescent within the next day or so.

I came off the telephone, perplexed. The life of a young Catholic man was at stake. Why had the UVF decided not to use the vehicle? Now that "X", the military OC, was back from holiday, why was he not contacting his old pal, our source Tommy?

I knew that at the end of the day our duty was to save life, but what of our "duty of care" to our source? If he was right, then his life was indeed in very grave danger. I slept very little for the rest of that night. There were a lot of options open to me to help our source. For instance, unknown to Tommy, we had other sources in his unit far better placed than him to report on UVF activity. We could call on them to find out if Tommy was under suspicion.

The next day I discussed the telephone call with very senior Police officers. They were not convinced, taking the view that it was more likely to be something that Tommy had said or done that had resulted in the UVF abort. I had to concede that without anything to suggest the contrary, this could well be the case. It was back to the drawing board.

We had not long to wait. A second call from Tommy prompted an immediate source meet. He had information in relation to an overnight arson attack on the Roughfort Inn, a bar on the outskirts of Glengormley and a well-known UVF haunt in those days. I was aware that a Headquarters unit from the CID's Serious Crime Squad had an on-going operation in the bar, which they were confident would result in the arrests of some very sinister UVF men involved in attempting to extort funds from the owner. Men that included the two Special Branch agents, "X" and "Y". Expensive RUC covert cameras had been installed to detect the offenders.

I had already spoken with the detective sergeant from the RUC Headquarters C12 Anti-racketeering team. The fire had been malicious and he wondered if the UVF were onto his attempted sting. I could smell a rat. I had good reason to suspect that certain Special Branch officers had betrayed the CID operation.

As Tommy was a member of the UVF team under observation by C12, I believed that he might be able to assist the detective sergeant in charge. I set up a meeting between them at my home in Ballyrobert. Both Loyalist and Republican terrorists knew where I lived. They had been targeting me there for years. My house was a virtual fortress.

I arranged to meet Tommy an hour before the meeting with C12. This would give me all the time I needed to discuss the suspected compromise of the Headquarters' sting operation. Tommy arrived first. He was ashen-faced. As a former PIRA member and now a fully sworn-in member of the UVF, he was clearly not a man to scare easily. So I knew by his demeanour that he was aware of the fact that he was now on a UVF death list, and why.

Once inside my house, Trevor and I attempted to calm Tommy down. I asked him to start at the beginning. Had he gone to Shore Crescent to the UVF meeting? He nodded. He said that most of the UVF men had left by the time he arrived, so he only had to face the stragglers who had stayed on to talk with the supreme South East Antrim UVF commander. When he had walked into the house, some of his former cronies had made as if to pinch their noses with their fingers, one of them saying, "F***, do you smell that?" They then continued to laugh and joke about the supposed bad smell. They asked Tommy pointedly, "Are your mates Jonty and Trevor out there, Tommy?"

He saw them going outside to check for any sign of a Police presence. Tommy said that he had tried to convince the UVF men that he had no idea what they were talking about, but that the atmosphere was so bad that he had to leave quickly amidst a barrage of profanities from his former friends.

This was bad. Our worst fears were confirmed. But how had the UVF got onto our source? What he said next made me extremely angry. He told us that the other local UVF commander, "Y", had called at his house alone. He was angry and he ordered Tommy to get into his car. Tommy was afraid not to comply. He got into "Y"'s car and was driven to the Roughfort Inn. When they got there a short time later, "Y" pointed to the burnt-out area of the bar. He barked at Tommy:

"Look at it!"

The damage was considerable.

"What do you see?" asked "Y". "What you see is what we do to peo-ple who f*** us about, Tommy," he continued.

He told Tommy that the UVF had become aware that the bar owner had been attempting to set them up for arrest. That the UVF had been tipped off about the concealed cameras. So they had burnt the bar a "wee bit", to teach the owner a lesson.

"What has this to do with me?" Tommy asked.

"It's simple, Tommy. We know all about the bug in the car too. We don't want the f*****g car. We know you are working for Jonty Brown and Trevor McIlwrath. You have been f*****g us about, Tommy. This is what happens to people who f**k us about. Do you want a fire at your house with a wee baby there? Do you?" "Y" asked forcefully.

Tommy said that his first gut reaction would have been to reach over and pull the head off "Y". God knows, he was capable of it, but he strove hard not to betray any reaction other than to deny all association with Trevor and myself. He told "Y" that it was probably just Brown and McIlwrath "putting the mix in". (We had briefed our contacts always to suggest when challenged that it was us who were trying to cause dissent in their ranks.) "Y" quickly retorted that the UVF didn't get the infor-mation from Brown and McIlwrath. He drove Tommy home and told him as he dropped him off that the UVF would be in touch.

As I listened to Tommy, I became incensed. It was obvious that someone had tipped off the UVF about the CID operation in the bar and the device in the intended murder car. But who could benefit from such a course of action? Why would anyone in the RUC put the life of our source in danger? We were fully co-operating with our friends in the Special Branch in relation to this murder car at least. So why would they alert the UVF? How? Despite the friction between myself and some of their more unscrupulous officers, even I did not think that they would deliberately jeopardise one of their own operations. I still had a lot to learn.

I certainly had my suspicions. The fact that our old Special Branch friend Alec was involved was more than a coincidence. Alec was now a prime suspect, but it wasn't enough. My authorities would be loath to tackle the Special Branch on these grounds alone. I had been down this road many times before. This UVF man, "Y", was not just saying that Tommy was an RUC informant—he even knew that Tommy was reporting to Trevor and I. Someone inside the Force who was aware that the murder car had been bugged was talking out of school. I intended to find out exactly who was it was.

Tommy met the detective sergeant from the Anti-Racketeering team as intended. We discussed the bar fire only, and were able to conclude that someone must have tipped off the UVF that covert cameras were in place to catch the UVF men who were attempting the "extortion". I did not tell the detective sergeant what we knew about the compromise of the bugging of the car. I needed to discuss my fears about that with senior Police and receive clearance first. There was now no doubt that our friend Tommy's life was in grave danger, and that someone within the RUC had deliberately placed him in this situation without any regard for his personal safety. Someone who was acting contrary to every principle of policing.

Trevor and I returned to Castlereagh Barracks and discussed our fears with one of our senior supervisors. We trusted this man implicitly, but I also knew that he was a staunch supporter of the Special Branch. He agreed that the whole episode was highly suspicious, but he did not share our view that we had enough to "pull" Special Branch. As much as I didn't want to, I had to agree with him. What if I was wrong? What if there was some other harmless explanation? Why would the Special Branch undermine its own operation? It didn't make sense. And yet without any evidence, we were flogging a dead horse.

Trevor and I agonised over what on earth to do next. We were weighing up all the options open to us when we realised that there was a very simple answer to our problem. We both knew a person who would have all the answers. "X"! But by this time, I had been taken off "X" as a handler and even Trevor, still his joint handler with the Special Branch, was forbidden to meet him without one of their officers being present.

We had been effectively forced to hand "X" over to Special Branch officers. Yet it is a fact that while the CID was solely responsible for handling this individual, he had at all times acted in a manner appropriate to his status as an informant: "X" knew the rules. Trevor and I had reminded him of them often enough. He was fully aware at that time that he did not have a licence to commit any crime. We could honestly say that in all the time that we had handled him, he had never taken a life. Further, it is a matter of record that he worked to save lives. It was a source of pride to us that none of our CID sources ever took a life while we handled them.

By the time Special Branch had finished with "X", he was taking life after life after life. When we brought his murderous activities to the attention of our CID authorities, they assured us that they had often made the Special Branch aware of them. Yet "X"'s handlers repeatedly told us to back off when we moved to deal with him, accusing us of "embarrassing their valuable source". Tough. I had more in mind for him than embarrassment.

It would have been easier to put "X" in jail than it was to put Johnny Adair away. Yet no-one was interested. We were not allowed to meet or speak to him. In any case, he feared me: he knew it was my intention to jail him. His Special Branch handlers had warned him often enough. He did, however, know and trust Trevor, his joint handler.

We knew "X" could answer a lot of our questions. He might even be in a position to save Tommy from certain death. That is, *if* he agreed to meet us at all. We also had to ensure that he met us without first informing his Special Branch handlers. Especially our old friend Alec, who would move to stop any such meeting.

I sought and quickly received authorisation from the CID at a very senior level to meet "X" with Trevor McIlwrath. Part of me was hoping that I was wrong, that there would be some unexpected twist that would show our suspicions of Alec to be unfounded.

We had had many such previous difficulties with Alec. We knew what he was capable of. But surely even he wouldn't jeopardise a Special Branch operation and scuttle the detective sergeant's extortion enquiry? It really didn't make any sense at all.

We picked "X" up and drove out into the countryside near Templepatrick. He asked Trevor at once, referring to me, "What is *he* doing here?" My presence made him feel uncomfortable, but then for years I had played the official guy, the "bogeyman" with him. He knew of my reputation for putting people like him in jail. He respected me for it but he was never going to warm to me in the way he did to Trevor. None of them did. Such was the nature of the roles Trevor and I adopted. We played it hot and cold, using the well-tried and tested good cop/bad cop, friend/foe scenario to perfection. In a very short time, "X" had settled down as Trevor reassured him.

I allowed them to exchange pleasantries. It was important that they did so. Then I went straight for the jugular: why had Tommy been ostracised? What did the UVF know about the car Tommy had made available for their pending murder attempt? "X" had all the answers. He said that an uncle of "Y's" was an RUC Reserve man at Whiteabbey RUC Station or was very friendly with an RUCR man there. Anyway, apparently this Reserve Policeman had overheard a Special Branch group at the table beside him discussing the fact that a tout called Tommy had allowed them to put a bug in a car which was to be used in a murder by the UVF.

"X" said it was very lucky for "Y" that the conversation had been overheard, because "Y" had volunteered to be the actual gunman and thus one of those UVF men who would have been getting into that car. I was really angry. I told "X" that members of the Special Branch do not discuss their informants or their operations openly in a Police canteen. He said he hoped not, but that "Y" had gone with that story to the Shankill UVF and they had given it sufficient credence to abort the operation and ostracise Tommy. We now knew exactly what had happened.

"X" told us that Alec and his other Special Branch handlers had warned him not to go near the Roughfort Inn as the CID had video cameras hidden there to catch UVF men blackmailing the owner. He said it was more than likely that Alec had also warned "Y" because Alec had told him that "Y" was working for Special Branch too. He told us that Alec was clearly anxious to elevate "Y" to a rank above his own as an informant. According to "X", the UVF suspected "Y" to be a tout but they couldn't be sure. He also had no doubt that it was Alec who warned "Y" about the bug in the car. He said he didn't know many senior UVF men who believed that Reserve man story.

As I sat in that Police car, I became more and more outraged. I asked about Tommy. "X" told me that Tommy was doing a good job on the denials but, since he was a "Fenian" (Catholic), it was likely that the UVF would err on the side of caution and kill him. Not just because of the bug, but because they couldn't risk him running to the Police and going Queen's Evidence on a lot of other UVF men.

"X" talked about the likelihood of Tommy being shot dead as casually as if he were an annoying fly which was going to be swatted. His indifference to his best friend's plight further angered me. This was not a game: Tommy's life was in danger. We now had a clear duty to do all in our power to change this course of events if at all possible.

We spent hours with "X". He had always suspected that Tommy

passed information to Trevor and I and here we were confirming it by our questions. He couldn't care less. Like Tommy, he needed the insurance of a bolthole, somewhere to run and someone to turn to if the UVF ever turned on him. As they inevitably would. We appealed to him to use his authority to put doubts in the minds of senior UVF that Tommy might not be a tout after all. He agreed that it was feasible that he could turn the situation around if he took a mind to.

"What if I can't, Jonty? What if Tommy gets whacked [murdered]?" he asked nonchalantly. He had touched a nerve, and I lost it. I told him that if anything happened to Tommy, then I would set in motion enough "mix" to see that he met the same fate. I had no intention of doing any such thing, but he wasn't to know that. He had been with the Special Branch now for so long that he knew exactly how treacherous elements of the Police were capable of being when it suited them. His perception of me was as someone like this. My threat had the desired effect. He glared at me. The tension between us was almost tangible. I brought the meeting to an abrupt end, telling him that his Special Branch friend Alec would know nothing of our meeting unless he spoke of it.

We had not logged our meeting with "X" with our Regional Intelligence Unit (RIU) as we were expected to. Nor had we cleared it with the Special Branch, as was required of us by regulations. We did, however, have authority to meet him from a senior CID level. "X" understood the position clearly. He promised us that he would do all in his power to try to cast as much doubt as possible upon the current UVF suspicions that Tommy was a tout.

As we were about to part company, "X" made a reasonable request. He wanted us to set up a meeting between himself and senior CID officers. He was getting very wary of the Special Branch, and especially of Alec. I could see the merit in such a meeting. If you didn't hear this catalogue of betrayal at first-hand, you could be forgiven for not believing it. I knew some very decent Special Branch officers who would not believe it. "X" was also keen to ensure that I didn't "put in the mix" about him with the UVF, as I had threatened I might. I knew that any help that we would get from "X" would be as much about his own self-preservation as about protecting Tommy's life. This was a dirty war and some Special Branch officers were obviously not averse to putting lives in danger—as long as it wasn't their own lives. These people would not hesitate to take any course of action that would benefit their own agenda. For some of them, the legality or indeed the morality of what they were doing was never an issue, it seemed. It was the stuff of fiction, like operating in a world of mirrors. I was fully aware that my RUC status would not shield me from this type of Special Branch ruthlessness. One could so easily find oneself at the wrong end of a Special Branch dirty trick, and I had been there often myself.

Trevor and I drove "X" back to his car and dropped him off. I could see that "X" was none too pleased, but I couldn't have cared less. As far as I was concerned, he was no longer a suitable person to be a source. Those involved in murder had no place in that regard. There was no place for a murderer other than in jail: I had always made that clear. "X" was a walking nightmare. An absolute liability. Why could the Special Branch not see that? Or was it the case that they knew exactly what he was but they chose to ignore it, as long as they could still use him to do whatever was necessary inside the UVF to promote their own twisted agenda. If people were murdered in the interim by him or on his direction, did this not matter to them?

This was to be the last time I ever met or spoke to "X". By this stage, he was the epitome of everything that could go wrong with source-handling. He had been used and abused by the RUC Special Branch. The tally of the brutal murders he was responsible for was mounting unchecked. Yet it would have been so easy to stop it: even we as CID officers had enough sources close to "X" to enable us to take him down. But he was what we called in the Police a "protected species". For some reason, someone in a position of authority in the Special Branch had decided that we should not be helped to bring him to book for the atrocities he had committed.

Trevor and I headed back to Castlereagh barracks. Now everything made sense. The deliberate compromise of the murder-car bug had been necessary to protect the Special Branch agent "Y". The deliberate compromise of the C12 Anti-Racketeering operation had been necessary to protect both "X" and "Y" and any other agents that might have fallen into that CID trap. Where would it all stop? Who did these people think they were? Did the Special Branch hierarchy support the likes of Alec in this blatantly unlawful obstruction of CID operations? Did they see our crime fighting efforts as ultimately expendable, unimportant? Was human life, Tommy's life, so worthless? How many of our operations had they scuppered without our knowledge? Who in the Special Branch decided on the propriety of it all?

These questions and many others were spinning around in my head. Surely now our senior CID officers would support us? Yet I had good reason to question their resolve: I had never been fully supported in any of my clashes with the Special Branch.

It seemed an age before we got back to Castlereagh. I made these new revelations of Special Branch betrayal known to one of our senior supervisors. I was sure that he would be as incensed as I was. He did indeed become angry, but was loath to approach the Special Branch, even at his level. He took the view that there was a "strong suspicion" of untoward activity by Special Branch, but still he insisted that nothing against them was proven. I had and still have a great respect for this officer, but what more evidence could we gain, I wondered? I had convicted criminals of serious crime on far less.

I firmly believed that our new findings would ruffle a few feathers and make these people think twice about doing something similar again. Damn the evidence, I thought. This was not a court of law. Surely we should take what we had up to RUC Headquarters? The lives of our source Tommy and the young unidentified Catholic were being played about with as if they didn't matter. What about our "duty of care" to both of these people? Had the Special Branch been able to identify and warn the young Catholic lad who was to be the target of the UVF murder operation? Or would he die in a hail of bullets weeks or months hence, at a time when we were not ahead of the UVF?

I told the senior CID officer that if anything happened to Tommy, if he died, I would immediately go to the Press. He laughed, and told me that he believed that I was far too professional to do that. In any event, he didn't think that the *Belfast Telegraph* would be interested. I told him that I would go to the *Times* newspaper. He just dismissed me. As I grabbed the handle of his door, he said, "Johnston, I will not fight with these people."

That was something I had not expected. This senior Police officer was as afraid of Special Branch as the rest of them. Ironically, the fear was mutual. I knew that for years Special Branch officers were frightened of working closely with him because they believed that he was too straight.

So there was to be no support, no assistance for us in dealing with these people. Nothing would be done or said by any CID officer that would embarrass the Special Branch. Nor would any senior CID supervisor meet "X" as he had requested. "X" had made his bed: now he could lie in it. They really did not want to know. All we could do now was to help Tommy to weather the storm. We told him that the UVF were not sure enough of his betrayal to kill him. We asked him to keep contacting his UVF associates and insist on an enquiry. I knew very well that no-one wants to start an enquiry in an organisation like the UVF, where every fifth or sixth person is a Police or MI5 informant. Within a few weeks, Tommy had convinced enough people to allow him to pop up here or there without too much danger, but it took months before he felt reassured that his denials were accepted.

Later Tommy complained to us about a UVF man called "Z" from the Mount Vernon unit. He was extremely worried about this particular man's behaviour, describing how "Z" would appear at well attended UVF meetings and drop accusations that he (Tommy) was a tout or that he had been seen talking to Trevor or Jonty. These outbursts were always put across as a joke with a jag. Each time that Tommy was sure that suspicion about him was a thing of the past, "Z" would stir it up again. In addition, Tommy related, "Z" would tell everybody he met— whether it was the Shankill or the Portadown UVF—where I lived. He said "Z" was pushing and pushing to have me "done" (murdered), and would keep mentioning my address and asking why the UVF had not taken any kind of action against me. I was intrigued. What Tommy did not know, could not know, and what I found extremely interesting was the fact that "Z" was also a Special Branch informant. His handler? Yes, of course! It was none other than our Special Branch common denominator, our "old friend" Alec.

Was Alec now deliberately using "Z" to stir the UVF up against me? Did he really make no distinction between me as an RUC officer and the terrorists that he pursued?

In this dirty war of his, was I really so expendable? I knew for a fact that the Special Branch was not averse to using their agents to target other terrorists. This was an acknowledged policy of theirs, whether official or not: to "use a rat to kill a rat." Had this idiot Alec decided of his own accord to use the same dirty trick against me? Would he have the UVF move against me just to get his own back for my constant attempts to take down the murdering reprobates he used as agents? And if this was indeed the case, was he acting alone or did he enjoy the support of some like-minded senior Special Branch officers? I had seen so many of their dirty tricks by that stage that nothing would have surprised me.

I appreciated Tommy's information, and asked him to keep an eye on the situation for me. I did not tell him that "Z" was a Special Branch agent. Tommy was paranoid enough. He agreed to keep me appraised of the situation.

Any rivalry that I encountered with the Special Branch was of their own making. I had no wish to fight with them. I wanted to assist them, not work against them. On one particularly auspicious occasion, I received information from a well-placed source that two Special Branch officers were to be ambushed by a group of Ulster Freedom Fighters (UFF) men at a source meeting in East Belfast, the source in question having tipped off his UFF masters that he had been asked to meet the Branch. This timely information allowed the Special Branch to mount a counter-ambush to protect their two vulnerable officers. It is a matter of record that their Headquarters Mobile Support Units (HMSUs) stopped several cars in East Belfast and very quickly had a large number of UFF men on the floor.

Loyalty like that was lost on our "friend" Alec. Special Branch men like him did not see it as a two-way street. If the boot had been on the other foot, he would most certainly have allowed the terrorists a free hand to deal with Trevor and I as they pleased. Alec was loyal only to himself. He was loyal to his Special Branch authorities only when it suited him.

Our entire Constabulary and its investigative ability was fettered by regulations properly put in place to protect all informants. These ensured that the Special Branch had total control of who was arrested and when they were arrested, as well as what searches were conducted and when they were conducted.

Clearance by uniformed Police or by CID officers to arrest suspected terrorists or criminals, or to search premises (including wasteground), had to be granted by the Special Branch. Such clearance could be refused or deliberately delayed by the Special Branch out of hand and certainly without question. There had been good and very valid reasons for giving the Special Branch such power in the first instance, but often proper clearance was refused for all of the wrong reasons. In order, for example, to enable the Special Branch to get their sources offside before they could be tackled by wholly legitimate CID operations which were being conducted, after all, in the best interests of the public. This aspect of the Special Branch's powers was open to abuse and sadly officers like Alec frequently abused it.

Alec was so blinded by his hatred for me that he cared nothing for the fact that I was also a husband and a father. His professional jealousy of me, which is something I never understood, put me totally at odds with him and individuals like him in the Special Branch. It also placed me at his mercy. He was handling some very vicious terrorists who would not hesitate to kill me if he was to point them in my direction. My reputation was such that it would not have taken much to prompt an attack by such terrorists. Alec knew this and he would often threaten to turn his terrorist sources on me: death threats, in effect. My own CID officers had done the same thing in 1975. I was lucky to have survived on that occasion. I was to find out later that there really were no depths to which Alec would not stoop to get me out of the picture.

Alec's UVF agent "Z"'s constant drone about Tommy being an informant began, however, to fall on deaf ears. Soon the only person listening to him was our friend Tommy himself, who knew from his days in PIRA that even a sneaking suspicion that you are a tout was often reason enough for you to be murdered. For this just reason, Tommy was in the grip of constant anxiety.

I remember how Tommy contacted me, about five or six months after he was accepted back into the UVF fold. He asked me not to contact him again until further notice. This development did not surprise me: often a source would get spooked and ask for space in this fashion. When I asked him how long he needed, he begged me never to contact him by telephone or call at his house again. He certainly could not contemplate a face-to-face meeting with us for a very long time, he said. "X" had warned Tommy that the UVF were watching him and even an innocent encounter with me or Trevor could cost him his life. I reminded him that he was a volunteer just like all the rest of our contacts. That it had, after all, always been him who had contacted us. I gave him my word that the next time we spoke, he would be the one to initiate the contact. I advised him moreover to take care, because there was no-one in the environment in which he moved in whom he should trust. It was to be a long time before he rang in to us again, but when he did, he was once again in fear of his life from his UVF cohorts . . .

———

It was Wednesday, 2 April 1997 when we received an urgent telephone call from Tommy. He said that he was in danger of being shot dead by the UVF and he wanted to "come in". At his request, Trevor and I went immediately to his home. He was extremely agitated, speaking about a proposed UVF bomb attack on a Sinn Féin office in Monaghan, in the Republic of Ireland. He explained to us that at the last moment, the UVF had told him that the car they were intending to use in that bombing was needed for some other job. They had subsequently instructed him to hire a car in his own name or to use his own car to plant the bomb. Paranoid or not, Tommy believed that too many UVF men knew of the plot for the information not to have reached the ears of the CID or the Special Branch. Too many junior UVF men had been congratulating him weeks before the bomb was to be planted. He pulled his best friend "X" and asked him what was happening, but "X" assured him that the information was being kept very tight. Tommy complained to "X" that other UVF volunteers who had no need to know about the operation were obviously already aware of it, that so many people knew about the proposed bombing that it was more than likely that the Police were aware of it too. He reminded "X" about the small uniformed Garda road stop that they had encountered on one of their dummy runs. "Pure coincidence," retorted "X". Tommy said he detected a coldness in "X"'s attitude, and that he had noticed in recent weeks that "X" had been distant with him. He feared that the UVF were trying to set him up. He then told us of his visits with "X" to the Rex Bar on the Shankill Road, where they had been given a large quantity of Powergell, a very recent explosives addition to the UVF armoury at that time. Eddie Sayers, a top Shankill UVF man, had chatted and laughed with them as they loaded the explosives into their white van. The explosive on its own was harmless and inert, but the UVF had now acquired a number of detonators. Tommy knew that the UVF were working harder than ever at developing their explosives capability, even during the Ceasefire.

We listened to Tommy for the best part of 30 to 45 minutes. He became even more agitated as he recalled how the previous night at around 2 am he had seen four or five UVF men, some of whom he recognised, at the rear of his home. The fact that they didn't ring him or call at his back door was ominous. He got the distinct impression that they were trying to draw him outside, so that they could "whack" him.

The UVF had turned on him when he took cold feet about hiring the car to go on the Monaghan bombing mission. He had suspected that they had been setting him up to be shot by the RUC or captured by the Gardaí in the Republic of Ireland. He outlined the difficulty of his position in a nutshell: "Can you imagine what it would be like for me, a Fenian in Portlaoise jail, on remand for a UVF bomb bid on a Sinn Féin office in Monaghan?"

I told Tommy that it was his own fault for joining the UVF. No-one had asked him to join. Did he not realise that the only way the UVF could benefit from his membership of their group now was to have him caught like that? They could then use his case as propaganda. Here was their Catholic UVF man, caught red-handed bombing a Sinn Féin office in the Republic of Ireland during a paramilitary ceasefire. Surely he could see how much more valuable he would be to the UVF as part of such a scenario? Apart from anything else, they would be able to use his story and his involvement in the organisation as powerful evidence that they were a non-sectarian outfit and that their cause was a just one, since even members of the Catholic community had joined their ranks!

Tommy agreed and said he wanted to "come in". He said we owed him. I did not agree. As a source, he had been of limited value, although he perhaps did not realise this fully himself. For the fact was, that in spite of his close association with certain UVF members, his religion meant that he would always have only limited access to their inner sanctum. I was concerned for his family. I warned him that if the UVF became aware of his flight into Police safety, his family would be their next port of call. Tommy disagreed, explaining that he no longer lived with his common-law wife and children, but had a new girlfriend now, and it was more likely that the UVF would go for her instead, because "X" knew how much he cared for her and that this would hurt him more.

We remained with Tommy long enough to obtain all the information we would need to brief senior Police. It was they who would make the decision as to whether Tommy would be accepted "into the fold". Due to the last débâcle of the bug in the car Tommy had not been in regular contact with us except for a few telephone briefs: hardly the sort of contact that would sway senior Police deciding whether to allocate tens of thousands of pounds to reward and resettle him!

We outlined to Tommy exactly where he stood. He didn't like it, but he had little choice but to accept it. I explained that in order to help us convince our authorities that he was worth their trouble, we needed more from him at this stage—more in terms of weapons or explosives or information which would get a result for us. It was as simple as that. He would have to work well with us over the next few days if we were to be able to help him at all. He didn't like this. He believed, and I mean truly believed, that his previous assistance had been invaluable to us. I pointed out that one factor heavily in his favour was that "X" had made him a trusted quartermaster for some of their best "gear", including a large quantity of Powergell and a brand new vz58 assault rifle. These two items would be valuable prizes if Tommy could produce them.

I knew too that our saving grace would be the RUC's "duty of care" to their informants: this was a card which I hoped we could play successfully to swing a decision in Tommy's favour even if he failed to produce a weapon. As it transpired, our job of convincing those responsible for making such decisions was to be even more of an uphill struggle than I had first expected. In fact, had it not been for the "duty of care" safety net, I doubt very much if we could have convinced the authorities to move as quickly as they did.

I took the opportunity to warn Tommy that our old Special Branch friend Alec was very much on the scene and working to his own agenda. Without a doubt, Alec would move heaven and earth to ensure maximum damage control as regards the loss of UVF weapons or explosives. I alerted Tommy to the fact that Alec might go as far as alerting UVF men to any intended betrayal. Tommy had met Alec on occasions and said he knew only too well how ruthless he could be. We tried to allay his fears by assuring him that we would do all in our power to keep this development from the knowledge of Special Branch. He would, however, have to stay on the outside for a couple more days and lie low. Tommy reluctantly agreed to do so. I asked him to use the time to get his hands on weapons and explosives and isolate them from the UVF. At this, he smiled: "Jonty, I wasn't born yesterday. I have already done that. The weapon and the explosives are safe from UVF interference. They are now in a hide that was previously used by Republicans. 'X' and the UVF will only be able to recover their gear while I am alive. They don't have a clue where I have it," he concluded.

I told him to keep it like that. It was time for us to go, however. As we were leaving, Tommy asked for cash. I reached for a £20 note, but before I could get to my pocket Trevor handed him a bundle of notes, confirming that there was almost £400 there. Tommy was surprised, but he was not half as surprised as I was.

When we got into our car, I asked Trevor why he had given Tommy so much money.

"I'll get it back," he replied.

I asked him why he had been carrying so much cash around with him.

"Oh, it's my mortgage money," he said.

Trevor had just given Tommy his own money, cash he needed to pay his mortgage! It was an odd thing to do. As far as cash rewards for informants went, official guidelines were in place relating to the sums of money available for our sources from government coffers: there was in fact a carefully conceived sliding scale of strictly results-based payment terms for source-handling! On occasion, however, and at our own discretion, we detectives would pay out tens or twenties from our own pockets, sometimes (though rarely) up to £100 each. But never hundreds of pounds we could ill-afford. What Trevor had done was to be the first warning sign that he was not well, but I missed it at the time. The truth is that after twelve very intense years of our partnership on the job, he had been suffering for some time from the accumulated effects of the many stresses we faced, and he was already far down the road to a shattering nervous breakdown. Unfortunately, I was not aware of this at the time. However, in relation to the immediate situation, I did reflect that it was more important now than ever to ensure that we got funds for Tommy—so that at the very least Trevor would get his money back.

On our arrival at Castlereagh RUC Station, we briefed a senior supervisor. In order to strengthen my argument that we should wait before alerting the Special Branch to what was afoot, I played for time by warning the senior officer that our friend Tommy was unpredictable and could be unreliable at times and that we would have to see if he delivered on his promises; that, in any case, we would need time to isolate the weapons and explosives that he said he could recover for us from his UVF cohorts. Then, cutting to the chase, I reminded my supervisor of instances of previous Special Branch betrayal. I warned him that I knew from experience that certain Special Branch officers would move to abort our operations without any regard to the danger in which they placed us, our families or indeed our sources. I did not relish yet another foray "into the Dark".

Fortunately, this particular officer was a man of the world. He had been around as many corners as we had and said that he knew what the Special Branch were capable of. He also knew something about the friction which existed between Special Branch and Trevor and I. He asked to meet Tommy the following Saturday morning when there would be little or no Special Branch about, saying that he expected that by that time Tommy would have isolated whatever weapons or explosives he could. The Mount Vernon UVF unit were known to be well-equipped. They were also notorious for their penchant to indulge in violence even all these months into a ceasefire.

In a situation like this, I was particularly concerned about one of our senior detectives. He was to all intents and purposes spineless, never able or willing to make a decision for himself and easily flustered when challenged by his subordinates. He baulked at the idea of taking direct responsibility for anything, and surrounded himself with sycophants who would constantly praise him and do his bidding without question. I was not one of his "people," and had little respect for him either as a leader or as a Police officer.

Our fear was that this man would run straight to the Special Branch and tell them about our proposed operation on the UVF in Mount Vernon. It was not that he had any love for the UVF—it was not that at all. He knew, however, that at least half of their numbers were Special Branch informants, which meant that he would be certain to ingratiate himself with the Special Branch if he were to alert them to our intentions. Integrity came a very poor second to this man's struggle to be one rung higher up the promotion ladder.

Luckily our senior supervisor was aware of the difficulties which dealing with this individual would pose. It is telling that even though the man was in fact his own superior in rank, he agreed that it would be best to work around him and go directly to the officer in charge of the CID in the Belfast area. Now this was a man who was not afraid to make decisions, who had a sense of when he could or could not hold things back from our colleagues in the Special Branch and was prepared to act on it. We got ourselves the 48 hours we needed to safeguard "Operation Mechanic", which would consist of a series of extensive, carefully co-ordinated raids on the weapons hides of the Mount Vernon UVF, as specifically and precisely identified in advance from the intelligence Tommy had provided. Regarding the weapons he had in his personal possession, Tommy was as good as his word, handing over the Powergell explosives and the vz58 rifle as promised. Our senior supervisor examined them at our offices in Castlereagh RUC Station and instructed us to move them to a safe place. There was no discussion as to where that safe place would be.

I knew that the searches were scheduled for the morning after next. I placed the bag of Powergell explosives and the vz58 rifle into the boot of one of our Police cars. It was a staff car belonging to a senior CID officer, which he had left at our disposal as he rarely used it himself. The Assistant Chief Constable (ACC) Belfast's staff officer was the only other person who would drive it, but that was only ever very rarely. I knew that there were only two sets of car keys for this vehicle and made sure I obtained both sets to ensure that the car couldn't leave the complex.

The explosives and the rifle were in a very safe place: in a locked Police car in Castlereagh RUC Station. If Tommy did take cold feet, he would have a hell of a job getting his "gear" back from there. We could go home and take it easy. Get a good night's sleep. For the first time in a few days I felt better. Now that the safe-keeping of the munitions was well catered for, I felt I could relax somewhat. Tomorrow senior CID officers would brief the Special Branch in relation to "Operation Mechanic". I could just imagine their rage and panic. We were about to reap the whirlwind. I had been down this road many, many times before.

I was not to be disappointed. The next morning, I was summoned to the Detective Chief Superintendent's office. Our senior supervisor was there also. The Chief Superintendent did not waste any time: according to the Special Branch, our source Tommy was not able to produce the Powergell or the vz58 rifle because he had no access to them. Our senior supervisor, who was standing behind the boss, shook his head, to indicate that we should say nothing. It seemed that the Special Branch had intimated that they could electronically monitor any movement of either of the munitions. They had said that it would be ill-advised of our source to get involved in any such venture. I listened intently. What could I say? It would have been almost laughable, if it had not been so serious.

We were informed that some of the searches would go ahead, but that the Special Branch had put a bar on the more important ones. For instance, a virtual arsenal in the Shore Road area would not be touched. The Special Branch had conceded that a lot of UVF "big gear" was there, but they did not have to give any reasons for their decision of non-clearance. A number of other arms dumps in hides identified in various parts of North and West Belfast would not be raided either, for reasons best known to the Special Branch. And so the UVF would hold on to all of these weapons. I found this intensely frustrating.

The rest of what the boss was saying was going over my head. I was looking over his shoulder: I couldn't believe my eyes! The ACC Belfast and his staff officer were getting into our boss's staff car and were obviously about to leave the Castlereagh complex. But how could they? I had both sets of car keys in my pocket. My heart sank. The staff car was an unmarked Vauxhall Astra, a prime target for car thieves. We knew this and would never leave it unattended in a public place. Would they? Worse, what if one of them decided to put something into the boot or they got a puncture and had to fetch the spare tyre? I panicked as they disappeared out of the complex. I was oblivious to what was being said around me. All I could think about was that I had find out where on earth that pair had gone.

I was suddenly jolted out of my mesmerised state by the boss's voice, addressing me with a tone of formal authority which he would not normally use: "Do you understand, Johnston?" he said.

"Yes, Sir," I replied.

The truth was, I didn't hear about half of what he had said to me. My stomach was churning over, and I had a sudden irresistible need to visit the toilet. I excused myself politely at the first possible opportunity and left the boss's office. Trevor followed quickly in my wake, and was confused when I ran past our offices and on down to the guardroom in the main complex.

"Did you get a load of that?" asked Trevor as he rushed to follow me. "Putting the searches off like that for another day and refusing clearance on the biggest arms dumps!"

I stopped dead in my tracks. "Who said that?" I enquired. "The boss did," said Trevor, "The Special Branch have put a block on Operation Mechanic for 24 hours."

Damn it, I had missed that. I had been so caught up in the departure of the Police car that I hadn't heard it. I realised immediately what the Special Branch were at. They were obviously having difficulty in getting in contact with some of their informants, and the "force within a force" had now set its machinery in motion to warn UVF terrorists and murderers that we were coming after them.

With their veto on the raids of some of the most important dumps, they had already succeeded in ensuring that the terrorists would hold on to the majority of their weapons. Now they had bought themselves the time needed to allow their sources to move themselves and their weapons around so that they would not get caught up in our raids. Who knew or cared what their arguments for doing so were? I was not in the least surprised.

How on earth were we supposed to impact upon this vicious UVF unit with our hands tied behind our back? If I had been given a free rein and a few detectives, I could have put the entire UVF unit out of business. This pussy-footing approach to the problem was merely ensuring that the UVF perpetuated their violence. All in the name of source protection? I'm afraid I didn't buy into that one.

"Where are we going?" asked Trevor.

"To the guardroom," I replied, "They've just driven off with the staff car, and the explosives and the rifle are still in the damn boot."

"Who has just driven off?" asked Trevor.

"The ACC and his staff officer," I added.

I saw his face fall. "What?" he asked in total disbelief. "But we have all the keys of that car," he said.

I ran on into the guardroom. "Morning, Skipper," the guard greeted me with a cheery smile. I lifted the phone in the guardroom and rang the ACC's office. In the most authoritative voice I could muster, I asked to speak to "Bill". I knew of course that he wasn't there.

"He's out at the moment, Sir," came the polite reply. "He's gone out for a short time with his staff officer, Sir. He'll be back soon. I will get him to ring you if you'll just give your number to me, Sir." His secretary was a great girl and I hated to deceive her. She had assumed that anyone calling the ACC "Bill" must be of a higher rank.

I didn't have to ask where they were—I could hazard a very good guess. It was highly likely that they were making a quick trip to Sainsburys to buy some of their favourite scones for their usual coffee break! If I was right, they'd be back in no time. I was still very concerned. The fact that they were out of uniform could mean that they had a longer excursion in mind.

Trevor and I remained at the window of the guardroom in Castlereagh, watching the traffic coming into the Police station and waiting for the arrival of the staff car. I was also monitoring the secure "E" Division radio net for transmissions from the staff car. This was the last thing we needed. "Who gave him the keys?" asked Trevor.

"No-one," I replied. I lifted both sets out off my crombie coat pockets to show that I still had them.

"Shit!" Trevor and I both said the word at the same time, and I remember laughing nervously. We stayed there for about twenty minutes until the car drove back into the barracks. I could see both the ACC and his staff officer laughing as they entered the complex. We knew then that there was no way that they had opened the boot. I rushed to the ACC's entrance and challenged the staff officer. Where did he get the keys?

"Keys?" he asked, grinning from ear to ear.

He had got another set of car keys cut the day before.

"Why?" I asked him.

"You told me weeks ago to get a set cut, Jonty," he replied.

I explained that we needed the car. He nodded. He said he wouldn't need it for the rest of the day. That 20-minute wait in the guardroom had been interminable. It was the longest 20 minutes that I had ever spent. All sorts of imaginary scenarios had flooded through my head. I could imagine the headlines: "Crime Squad Unit puts life of ACC in danger", or "Crime Squad Unit loses Police vehicle and weapons and explosives". It didn't even bear thinking about. I sat down in my office and thanked God that it had worked out all right. It was also a lesson: perhaps the boot of a Police car inside one of the highest security Police establishments in the Province was not after all the safest place to store semi-recovered munitions.

It was back to porridge. I knew that the Special Branch would be coming back on us hard. The whisperings would start. The allegations of CID impropriety, of "taking shortcuts", were all to come. For now at least, we had the support of our own authorities. Would they waver in the face of Special Branch "bully boy" tactics? We had yet to see. For the present, the safety of Tommy and his girlfriend was our top priority. Following liaison with the Headquarters' "minders", or Witness Protection Unit, Tommy was installed in a small hotel in County Down. He remained there for several days, being taken to Castlereagh each day for a full debriefing by CID.

The Special Branch was housed on the second and third floor of the complex at Castlereagh. They would occasionally have cause to walk past our offices on the ground floor. We noticed a marked increase in the flow of Special Branch North (i.e. North Belfast) officers past our offices. There was more than a hint of hostility in the air. It didn't bother me: I wasn't expecting anything else. However, it certainly did bother my colleague Trevor.

"What did they expect us to do?" he kept repeating. "Leave Tommy out there to be killed?" Trevor was wasting his time with these speculations. There was no point getting upset about the attitude of Special Branch.

"But what if they *can* track those explosives and the vz58 assault rifle?" he asked.

I told him not to worry. I knew that strictly speaking, from a legal point of view, statutory defences were built into the legislation which allowed us to be lawfully in possession of those munitions we had recovered from terrorists. That was our position exactly. Our methods might not suit the Special Branch, but they were born out of the necessity for us to frustrate them in allowing their UVF agents to hold onto such munitions. In any event, our own senior authorities knew exactly what we were doing. We had not moved left or right, up or down without the authority of at least a Detective Chief Inspector. If he had chosen not to allow the Special Branch or anyone else into his confidence, then that was his prerogative. It also incidentally said a lot about his confidence in their ability to handle matters of this nature without first informing their agents on the ground. The fact that we agreed with his decision was neither here nor there.

I spent one or two days attempting to convince Tommy that he should go Queen's Evidence. This term refers to the scenario in which a criminal who has already been convicted and received a sentence decides of his own volition to give evidence against his criminal associates, relating to any or all crimes they have been involved in. I put the argument to Tommy that it would be in his interests to admit to all of the crimes he committed with the UVF, as he would then be sentenced with the full support of the Police. He could then come back as a prosecution witness against some of the more hardened UVF terrorists. I had some very nasty ones in mind, men who were under normal circumstances very hard to bring down, including "X" and "Y".

Tommy asked me what sort of sentence he could expect. We explained that this was dependent upon what sort of crimes he had committed. Robberies can carry up to ten years, UVF membership five to ten years, and so on. He said he would think about it, that he would need guarantees. We told him we couldn't give him any guarantees. He was later to abandon any suggestion of going Queen's Evidence: he just wanted a lump sum of money and the chance to get out of the UVF and Northern Ireland. Resettlement somewhere in England and a new start, away from terrorists and terrorism. Later, on reflection, I realised anyway that we could not use Tommy as a converted terrorist or Queen's Evidence. The whole idea was flawed. For a start, he had a long criminal history, albeit for relatively minor offences. Also, he had been in too deep with the UVF. He would tell a lie to hang himself if it meant ingratiating himself even just a little with people he needed to use, and that included the RUC.

As the hours passed, I could feel the sense of urgency going out of the entire proceedings. The euphoria that had surrounded the initial briefings for Operation Mechanic had evaporated. I was summoned to the offices of senior Police, where I was asked pointedly if I had actually seen the rifle and the explosives. I said I had. When asked if the source was still familiar with the location of the munitions, I lied and replied that he was. A senior Police officer then ordered me to move the munitions as soon as possible.

"Just in case Tommy changes his mind, eh! We don't want to end up with any more egg on our faces, now. So get to it and remember, the Special Branch is probably monitoring all that we do. They are still insisting that they have total control over the munitions and that they can locate and recover them," he said.

Good luck to them, I thought. But I knew to keep such thoughts to myself. Three of us set out to move the munitions as instructed. In fact, they were still in the boot of our squad car. Even Tommy couldn't move them from there and if the Special Branch could track them, it would confound them. The evening before the searches were to commence, we set out to put the munitions "down".

We left East Belfast and went along the M3 and onto the M2, stopping eventually at a roadside marker on the hard shoulder. Trevor and I removed the munitions from the boot of the Police car and climbed over the barrier and entered the waste ground not a mile or two from the Mount Vernon Estate. As we walked from the light of the motorway hard shoulder into the darkness of the waste ground, I turned to Detective Constable Trevor Neill who was standing near the car and asked him to stay where he was and keep watch. I had only walked a few paces behind Detective Constable McIlwrath into the darkness when I heard a call from behind, a shaking, timid voice.

"Who am I looking out for, Skipper?" Detective Constable Neill asked. "You said to keep dick, you know?"

"The Police," I replied.

"But we are the Police," he said. I pointed to a large CCTV camera to my right situated on the Mount Vernon flyover.

"It moves, so if it points this way, we can assume that an operative can zoom in and monitor our activities," I said, "Traffic Branch is only a stone's throw away. Now do you really want to explain what we are doing to the Traffic Branch?"

Detective Constable Neill shook his head, and seemed to be placated. I turned and headed back into the darkness. He called me back again. I knew by his face that he was less than happy with the whole situation and properly so.

"Does the Chief know about all this?" he enquired.

I smiled. I knew that no attempt at reassurance was going to convince him. I also realised that things had happened so fast that he had not had the benefit of my audience with senior Police, nor had I had any time to properly brief him in relation to our instructions. I took my RUC mobile telephone from my pocket and scrolled for the home telephone number of our Detective Chief Inspector. I handed it to the constable and invited him to ring the Chief Inspector. At this, he seemed much happier, and declined to ring the number.

We put the munitions down and withdrew. We knew that they would be safe until 6 am the next morning. We had put them in two separate places, so that recovery of one would not necessarily have meant recovery of the other. Fearful of such tracking devices anyway, Tommy had long since moved the explosives to a different bag. He had assured me that he had stripped and checked every inch of the vz58 assault rifle. We would be returning tomorrow to recover those items with the Ammunitions Technical Officer (ATO) and other Police.

If this did not suit the Special Branch, that was too bad. I could not understand their stance. They were supposed to be a part of our team, so to speak. As much of an ally to us in our investigations as the Scenes of Crime officers, Photography, Fingerprint Branch or Forensics. There was no hint of professional jealousy from any of those other agencies. As far as I was concerned, personalities or office politics should never come into the equation when we were dealing with terrorists.

"Operation Mechanic" went down the next morning, with the searches being conducted as planned. The explosives were located and removed by the ATO, who was able to confirm that this was the biggest find of Powergell to date in the Province at the time. The vz58 assault rifle was also located and recovered. We breathed a sigh of relief. Now all we had to do was await the results of the other searches.

I returned to Castlereagh to monitor progress, only to have my boss launch an attack upon me for some alleged failing in relation to Tommy's girlfriend. Without waiting to hear my answer, which should have been more than satisfactory, he stormed out of the building. I had a lot of time for this man. This was not like him. He was in fact more hated by the Special Branch than I was. On this occasion, however, it seemed that the Special Branch poison was already in. They were injecting it where it would cause the most harm. It is human nature to want an easy life. No-one wanted to be caught in the crossfire as the Special Branch moved to deal with us and anyone who would dare to support us.

And so once again the Special Branch had decided to "pee on my fire", as they so aptly put it. I watched as each of the house searches came in negative. The operation was failing to have the impact on the UVF that we had intended. One after another, CID officers returned their search folders marked negative, negative, negative. Trevor and I became the butt of jokes and ridicule from other inept CID officers who loved to see us fail. The whole operation was starting to look like the use of a sledgehammer to crack a nut. The Special Branch had indeed done their damage control very well. With the agreed instructions of nothing found, no arrests, we had only one arrest. Thank God we had made Tommy isolate the two big items: without them, the operation would have been an unqualified disaster.

Towards the late afternoon on the day of the searches, a very senior CID officer arrived at our offices. Visits by men of his rank were occasional and usually meant trouble of some sort. He was wearing grey trousers and a well-cut blue blazer: this man was always dressed immaculately. He motioned me into the Detective Chief Inspector's office. The Detective Chief Inspector was elsewhere. We were alone. He told me to close the door.

"What would you say, Johnston, if I were to tell you that the Special Branch have suggested to the Chief Constable that he consider handing the explosives and the rifle back to 'X' in the UVF?" he began.

"That he is very badly advised, Sir," I replied.

"Nonetheless, the Special Branch fear that the loss of munitions of this nature might unseat 'X'. He could lose his life," the officer added.

Tough, I thought.

So what on earth were we supposed to do? Compassion was something I preferred to keep for victims. The protection of serial killers never did sit easy with me. "X" had made his bed—let him lie in it! Isn't that exactly what had been said in relation to Tommy only a few days previously? So what had changed?

I had too much respect for this officer to argue with him. I couldn't imagine what sort of arguments the Special Branch must have put up that would make them think that someone as astute as Sir Ronnie Flanagan would contemplate such an illogical decision. I listened to the senior officer as he went on to inform me that when the dust settled there would be very little to show for our effort.

As CID officers we had moved against the UVF in good faith and in the public interest. Many of the officers involved in "Operation Mechanic" had never encountered Special Branch obstruction before. They couldn't believe it. We had been robbed of a valuable opportunity to seriously impact on a notorious UVF unit, whose leader "X" was now known to have been responsible for the brutal, senseless killings of Protestant after Protestant in his own community. We had been given a chance to send a signal to that terrified community that the RUC would not tolerate such activity. Why were we to be obstructed? In the absence of any valid argument, I reserved the right to take men like "X" down.

Now bear in mind that this same vicious UVF unit was continuing their murderous activities well on into the Ceasefire. We were also aware that the same unit was targeting the Republic of Ireland for bombings! What on earth was the reason for not taking them out? What operational imperative could possibly be more important than the removal of such a bunch of thugs from a community which had suffered so terribly at their hands? What was this alleged bigger picture? I really would like to have known.

No matter. The decisions were made and no-one dared to question them. Such was the absolute power of the Special Branch. They had taken this self-confessed killer, a man hated and feared by his own community, had dressed him up in some intelligence "glad rags" and had convinced our most senior Police that he was something holy, something good, something vital to their future operational strategy. Was he? Even if he was, did this really warrant maintaining his credibility? They had argued vehemently that it did. The force within a force had moved to protect him and God knows how many of his co-conspirators.

My intolerance of any conduct of a criminal nature by informants outside the guidelines of the Home Office was well known by this time, and for years now the Special Branch had no longer even bothered trying to convince me that they were right. I didn't give a damn about the calibre of an informant or the quality of his intelligence: if he wouldn't toe the line, he should be imprisoned or "red-lined". We would get him in the long grass.

On more than one occasion, I warned Special Branch officers that to suggest crimes to terrorists or criminals and then to orchestrate who was to be involved in them was a crime in itself. Such conduct would be frowned upon by the courts and was totally against the Home Office guidelines. The Special Branch officers would claim ignorance of this concept and then ask me, "How do you ever catch anybody?" One very clever Special Branch supervisor, who would quote the guidelines verbatim as if to demonstrate his intimate knowledge of procedure, would go on to qualify this by declaring that these guidelines did not apply to the Special Branch. Listening to him used to give me the shivers. I was glad to be in the CID, and was proud of our staunch adherence to the rules and to fair play.

I remember one young detective I worked with in Andersonstown asking me why I had such a reputation for fighting with the Special Branch. "They must be a bunch of bastards," he concluded.

"On the contrary," I replied, "Like us in the CID, they have been a bastion of strength in the face of anarchy. There is a pressing operational need for their services. Unfortunately, there are individuals within that department who abuse their powers. Such is life. We have some such people in CID as well."

The difference, I told him, between our two departments was very simple. We as investigators were concerned only with the facts and the collection of evidence. We had many tools in our armoury to enable us to do this. The Special Branch, on the other hand, was concerned only with the gathering of intelligence, to be analysed and acted upon in due course. They say information is power and they are right. It is what one does with such power which is so important.

I told that young detective that the majority of Special Branch personnel were decent men who would be shocked at the conduct of the some of their colleagues. That in my experience, however, and at the risk of sounding melodramatic, there was an almost tangible sense of evil and corruption about some of the men I had encountered in the Special Branch thus far. I told him that these cloak-and-dagger Special Branch men did not care who they offended or hurt. They were not interested if their target was a friend or a foe. They would not hesitate to inject poison to eliminate anyone daring to challenge them.

I knew many, many decent, honest and highly courageous Special Branch officers, men I would have liked to have had beside me in any situation. Unfortunately, the converse was the case too, and some of the worst specimens of humanity I had ever encountered in my life were Special Branch men. It would be a great mistake however, I reiterated, to tar them all with the same brush.

That conversation took place in 1984, just before I left Andersonstown for York Road on transfer. Today that young man is a senior officer in the Special Branch. He is a tremendous fellow.

"Operation Mechanic" was over. Interviews of the one prisoner who had been taken were ongoing. Now that the dust was settling, I prepared myself mentally for the criticisms, the allegations and the accusations that would be levelled at me. I was all too familiar with the routine by this stage. They would set out to blame me for the "breakdown in communications", or my malicious endeavours to identify and prosecute, or "burn", their informants. They never really changed their tack. It was like a record that was stuck.

I had to agree that to officers who knew no better, some of the Special Branch arguments were valid. Why did McIlwrath and I have such a free hand? Were we not out of control? Could they really afford to allow us to continue as we were, in the face of Special Branch warnings that we were unprofessional? What if something did go wrong? This was exactly the response that Special Branch were aiming for. They would imply that although we did get some good information, our methods were crude and unprofessional: we should be split up and put back to ordinary CID work. The handling of informants of this calibre was a function best left to the professionals, the Special Branch themselves. They argued that there was no place for a two-man amateur CID team like Trevor and myself.

The truth was that we *were* out of control. We were beyond the control of the Special Branch and they didn't like it. I was one of the most successful CID officers in the Belfast region: the results spoke for themselves. Yet here I was again, standing before senior Police officers having to justify our actions.

Trevor was in an awful state. He saw that our endeavours, initially praised and celebrated, were being held up to ridicule. Worse still, we were now at the mercy of the Special Branch and whatever allegations they cared to throw at us. Trevor was downing tablet after tablet—the painkillers he was rapidly becoming dependent on. The inevitable stress and anxiety caused by all the friction and backbiting was taking its toll on him. His health was deteriorating badly: that much was clear. Deeply concerned on his account, I brought this to the attention of my supervisors. Far from moving to help Trevor, they accused me of disloyalty. Was I trying to get Trevor in trouble? He would be transferred out, placed in some desk job: is that what I wanted? The truth was that I was sick of it all myself, of fighting with the Special Branch with little or no support from my authorities in the CID. I had already asked to be transferred out of the Crime Squad twice and was at that time waiting for a suitable post at Headquarters. What did these people want? Blood?

We were brought before the Detective Chief Superintendent. We could see he was not pleased. I couldn't have cared less. I waited for the barrage of Special Branch criticisms and allegations. It never came, however: this man was far too professional to pass on to me any of the issues raised by the Special Branch. He had obviously accepted the criticism on our behalf. There was no doubt that whatever had been said had had the desired effect upon him. It was a turning point in our relationship. Only months earlier, he had referred to Trevor and myself as "the jewel in his crown". It was he who had opposed my transfer out of the Crime Squad to Headquarters. Now here he was seated before us, obviously battered. He had absolutely no wish to hear any of our cries of "foul" by Special Branch.

He ordered us to put Tommy outside of the gates of Castlereagh and give him just £30. "But . . .," I started.

He stopped me. There was to be no arguing. Tommy was due a reward and resettlement, that he conceded. But for tonight, we were to hand him £30 and tell him he was on his own for the time being. Trevor tried to inject humour into the proceedings, but it was no use. As I got up from my chair to leave the room, the boss told me yet again, "Not a penny more than £30, Johnston, and tell him that *I* said that!"

I nodded but I knew in my heart there was no way I could do that. I hired Tommy a car from a local garage that same evening. I took him home and fed him and bid him good luck for the next few days until "the minders" on his resettlement operation could get started. I was saddened as I watched him drive off on his own. He had his faults. He was no angel. In fact, he was now a UVF man. But I felt that we were not dealing with him in a professional, responsible manner and that we had let him down. He had been caught up in a tangle of office politics.

There was a pre-resettlement post-mortem in relation to Tommy's case. We looked at what munitions we had recovered. We examined what intelligence had been gleaned to date. It was considerable. His future potential in the Province was nil. We appealed to our authorities for as large a reward as possible to boost his chances of being resettled successfully in Great Britain. I was surprised at the final amount agreed: it was only £10,000, a pittance for someone who now had to turn his back on everyone and everything he held dear in the Province. It had been his choice, of course, but £10,000 was by no means a true reflection of the assistance he had given us. Many of what should have been the most productive arms finds had been blocked by the Special Branch for reasons of their own.

I can recall how someone in authority, listening to my appeals for more cash, asked me pointedly what assistance Tommy had offered us. I referred to the explosives and the vz58 assault rifle.

"The recovery of those items has caused more problems than they were worth," he retorted. "Oh!" I interjected, "tell me about that. Should we have left them in the hands of the most vicious UVF unit in the Belfast region?"

He did not reply for a short time.

"All we really got was a few bullets," he said finally.

"So what about the large arsenal of weapons on the Shore Road that Special Branch conceded was there, or the house in West Belfast with the three handguns and God knows whatever else the Special Branch has blocked without our knowledge? Is our source to get no credit for what we should have seized?" I asked.

There was silence. The officer said £10,000 was agreed. It was all Tommy was getting. There were to be no arguments. No right of appeal. Everyone in authority simply wanted to put the whole episode behind them.

Tommy's resettlement was fraught with difficulty and friction. He was, naturally, extremely disappointed with how things had panned out for him. Trevor flew over to England with another officer to fully debrief him. They spent a few days there and Tommy later told me that he had benefited greatly from their presence. I remember receiving a telephone call from Trevor shortly after his flight from England touched down in Belfast. He was extremely agitated. He recounted how he had turned his RUC mobile telephone on as he approached the terminal building and took a call from "Y", the Special Branch source who had nearly cost Tommy his life. "Y" asked Trevor how "Tommy the tout" was doing in England, even naming the town he had been resettled in! He asked Trevor to give Tommy his regards and to ask him if it was worth it for £10,000.

The whole incident had rattled Trevor enormously. It was a graphic illustration, if we needed one, that our old friend Alec had once again told all to his source "Y" and God knows who else. Surely this was illegal, to say the least? Yet no-one would want to hear any allegations from us against Special Branch. Better to drop it for the time being. Note it, but then let it go.

Our next few encounters with our boss were strained. I believed he had fought our corner, but he had no doubt taken a pounding, and it was months before his attitude would improve. For me, it was over. I was consciously avoiding friction with Special Branch. Yet on the ground things were getting worse, with "X"'s UVF unit still very active. I couldn't ignore it, yet I knew that if I got pro-actively involved again in a bid against "X" it would thrust me back into conflict with the Special Branch. I didn't need that, but it couldn't be helped. It came with the job. So here I was again, bracing myself to go back "into the Dark". The first thing you would know of any untoward activity from Special Branch would be a warning from some very senior CID officer that they were "at it" again, injecting poison into the minds of our immediate supervisors. Then there would be the questions, "What are you working on?" or the instructions to "drop that enquiry into this guy or that guy". Our supervisors thought that they were approaching the matter tentatively or diplomatically, but it sent a clear signal to Trevor and I that we had touched a Special Branch nerve and in fact inadvertently alerted us as to who their informants were.

In any event, our friend Tommy was resettled eventually. At first he was suicidal, but then he settled down and got on with his life. Tommy lives today in self-exile in England and is doing well in business. I will always be grateful to him for his assistance to us in our fight against terrorism.

We were astounded to hear in later months that Tommy had re-established contact with "X": he even had him and some of his other former UVF cronies come over to England. We warned Tommy that this renewing of contact would end in grief, that "X" was evil. Tommy argued that we didn't really know "X", that he was a great guy, really. He reminded us that he had "stood" for "X"'s baby at the christening in the Republic of Ireland. Tommy would not listen to our warnings, and continued his relationship with "X" regardless.

Little did Tommy know that we had once been as close to "X" as he was now. It all seemed such a very long time ago. At that time, I would have agreed with Tommy. Then, "X" was not a killer, not a cold-blooded murderer. But now he was very different, a wholly evil man, very far removed from the amiable, helpful and respectful character Trevor and I had recruited and "run" for years. A man who obviously enjoyed inflicting pain on his own community and who ruled by fear alone. Tommy's warning that "X" was out of control was to prove extremely accurate. Even at that time, he was certainly not the model source that Special Branch were professing. I knew this; anyone with sources close to "X" knew this. He was still very much the focus of my attention. I reserved the right to take him down and to hell with Special Branch's objections.

Chapter 10
Agent Wesley

Trevor and I had been on our feet since 6.30 am on Tuesday, 1 October 1991. We had hoped to stand down and go home at around 11 pm. It was not to be. This was nothing new. It was hard to set a schedule for anything in those days, never mind plan a social life. Our detailed hours of duty were a mere guide. Our real itinerary would be set by the events of each day as they unfolded. Time off to spend with our families was a rare event.

At 10 pm that evening, a detective called Hugh who was in the CID office at Tennent Street contacted me. An anonymous male caller had telephoned and had asked to speak to me urgently. Trevor and I were on the way to Trevor's office at Greencastle RUC Station. I gave my colleague a direct-line telephone number, Belfast 700345. We gave that number to all of our informants. It was such an easy number to remember.

We were seated in Greencastle CID office at around 10.30 pm enjoying a welcome cup of tea when the telephone started to ring. Trevor nodded to me. I lifted the handset. I did not recognise the deep voice at the other end of the line. The male caller spoke in a gruff, almost guttural tone. As anonymous calls go, this was perhaps the most sinister such call that I had ever received.

The voice was chilling, to say the least. It sent shivers down my spine. He spoke slowly and with deliberation. By the time I realised that this man was offering me his services as an informant, I was already very sceptical as to his bona fides. His tone was aggressive and it carried a sense of urgency. I believed that Trevor and I were facing a possible "come-on" situation.

The account which follows of what happened that night and on dates subsequent to that night in relation to this man is taken from entries in my official notebooks and journals that were kept contemporaneously.

"Jonty, is that you?" the unknown caller asked.

"Yes," I replied. "Who is speaking?"

"Ken," he said.

This was like pulling teeth. I was about to ask him for his surname when he spoke again.

"Save a life, you said, Jonty. You told me to ring you if I could save a life. Well, I want to save a life. I need to talk to you," he said.

"Sorry, Ken, I didn't catch your surname," I said.

"I didn't give you it," he replied. "You know who it is," he added.

"Sorry, Ken, but I speak to lots of people. I can't place your voice," I said.

"Ken Barrett," he replied.

My interest picked up at once. This individual was well known to me. He was a self-confessed UDA man and was suspected of being the Officer Commanding the UDA's "B" Company UFF military team. This is one of the most vicious UFF units in the whole of the UDA. Prior to the evolvement of the mainstream UDA, this unit had been known as the Woodvale Defence Association (WDA). Barrett was also reputed to be a serial killer. I had interviewed him many times at Castlereagh Police Office in relation to serious terrorist crimes. On each of the occasions that we interviewed him, Trevor and I used the final interviews in Castlereagh with him to invite him to ring us if he ever had any information that could save a life. Any fool could take a life—the challenge for us was to turn terrorists into a medium to save life. I had honestly believed that our pleas to Barrett had fallen on deaf ears. Yet here he was, ringing and offering his assistance to us. But I detected something malevolent in his tone. There was definitely something sinister about his manner of approach.

"Jonty, I'm taking my life in my hands here ringing you. The only reason I trust you is that the UDA hates you, the UVF hates you. Look, I even know some peelers who hate you: you've got to be straight," he said.

"How can I help you, Ken?" I asked.

"Come up to my house in the Glencairn. I want to empty these bastards," he said.

He gave me his home telephone number. I didn't ask him for his address. He had assumed that I knew where he lived. I didn't have the heart to disappoint him. I told him that I would call up with him as soon as I could.

"Come up here on your own, Jonty," he said.

"No problem," I replied.

I had absolutely no intention of going to his home on my own. That was not an option. It was a shock to me that a terrorist of this man's ilk should come forward in the first place. I feared an ambush. Perhaps those "C" Company men who had spotted us in the Glencairn had gone complaining to their "B" Company counterparts. We could be drawn into a trap. I decided to do a number of routine checks before I responded to this man's request.

I rang a Headquarters extension and asked the constable on duty in the Criminal Intelligence Section (CIS) for some personal details on Ken Barrett. I could hear him tapping the details into his computer keyboard.

"128 Glencairn Way, Skipper," he replied.

"Do you have his home telephone number?" I asked.

He gave me the same telephone number that Barrett had given me.

"Who does Barrett live there with?" I asked.

"Just a minute," he said.

There was a period of silence.

"It's a Beverley Quirey, Skipper. She is listed as living there alone," he said.

I thanked him again and replaced the receiver. We had at least confirmed Barrett's address. But I still didn't like his tone. He had been very aggressive, short and demanding. And he was not as enthusiastic as someone who had just struck up enough courage to come forward with vital information for the Police would generally be. The urgency in his tone was different. He was somehow more cold and detached. Maybe some other terrorists were holding him in his home, forcing Barrett to draw us in. I intended to approach this individual very carefully. We were not going to leave ourselves open to attack. Trevor and I sat in Greencastle CID office and worked out a strategy that would allow us to get to this man safely to see if he was genuine. We decided to go into the Glencairn Estate in strength.

It was an unfortunate matter of fact that we could not call upon the support of our uniformed colleagues in Tennent Street RUC Station. History had shown us that there was a small hard core of individuals within our number who could not be trusted. Some would maliciously tip off the Loyalist paramilitaries as to the identity of anyone who was "touting" to the RUC. In situations like this, it was best to use RUC uniformed officers from outside the Division.

At 11.15 pm I lifted the handset and rang Belfast Regional Control (BRC). The White Mobile Support Unit (MSU—the "White" MSU was that attached to Tennent Street) was on duty and on patrol in our Division. White MSU call signs 1, 2 and 5 were placed at our disposal. These officers were based in Tennent Street RUC Station but they had absolutely no role in our day-to-day policing. I had every confidence in their impartiality. They agreed to meet us at the entrance to the Glencairn Estate at the junction of the Forthriver and Ballygomartin roads fifteen minutes hence. I now had sufficient manpower to deal with any threat that Barrett and his UFF cronies might pose. I lifted the handset again and rang Barrett at home. I asked him if he was alone. He said that he and his girlfriend Beverley were alone in the house. I asked him if he had any problems at the house.

"No," he said.

I explained that we had to go through certain procedures before I could visit him. He understood.

"Don't take all night, Jonty," he said.

At 11.30 pm, I pulled my car up alongside three grey, armoured RUC Landrovers parked at the bottom of the Forthriver Road. I had already briefed the White India (Inspector) that we were going into 128 Glencairn Way on an important CID enquiry. I made him aware of who lived there and of exactly the type of individual Barrett was. We agreed on a safety strategy. If Barrett was in there, Trevor and I would speak to him alone. The MSU officers would remain outside the house to ensure our safety.

I knocked the front door of 128 Glencairn Way. When Barrett opened the door, Trevor and I confronted him. Two burly, uniformed RUC officers armed with Hechlor Koch submachine-guns were standing at each side of his front door. Uniformed Police officers were crouching nearby for cover. Others were covering the back door of his home. Barrett was not impressed. He glared at us.

"We're off to a great start here, Jonty," he said. "How am I going to explain all this?"

I explained to him that there were rules and regulations that governed the way we met or had contact with people wishing to help us. He was not happy but he invited us inside into his small living room. Barrett was a dirty, scruffy individual and I was struck by how neat and tidy the room was. It was a credit to Beverley Quirey.

Out of courtesy I offered Barrett my hand. He abruptly refused to shake it. He said he wanted to make no friends, no handshakes. He stated that he was under no illusions as to what he was contemplating.

"I want to work for you for 6 to 9 months and then get out. I want to go to Canada and you can help me get there," he said.

God help Canada, I thought as I looked into Barrett's vacant stare.

"What about Beverley?" I asked.

"F**k her, I'm going alone. I'm out of here forever," he said.

At this juncture precisely, Beverley Quirey joined us in the living room. Barrett gave her a look that could have withered her.

"Stay you in the kitchen!" he said, dismissing her.

Beverley turned on her heels and walked back into the kitchen. Barrett asked us to speak quietly so that she would not hear us. He reminded us that he had been in the UDA for a long time. He was sick of the lot of them. He said that he was so well placed within the UFF that no operations were mounted anywhere in Belfast or further afield without his knowledge. He said that he was second-in-command to Jim Spence, the Brigadier of the 1 Battalion UDA/UFF. He offered to hand over UFF arms dumps in both North and West Belfast. He gave examples of the type of weapons he could deliver to us, including two SA80 rifles and two 9 mm Browning pistols stolen from the Malone Road UDR base. Barrett "forgot" to mention at that time that it was he and another UFF man who had stolen those weapons from the UDR base in the first place.

He was adamant that he knew of all UFF operations past and present. More importantly, he said, he would be made aware of any operations being planned in the future as high as Brigade level. He offered to expose RUC officers and UDR men who were actively meeting and passing on information to the UFF. I was impressed. If this was true, it was a welcome development. We needed that invaluable information to enable us to deal effectively with those responsible for such treachery.

"I've had it, Jonty. I've seen enough. I have seen them with big boxes of money from their drugs and their racketeering, sharing it out among them," he said. "There are no soldiers in it, Jonty. It's all a waste of time," he added.

Barrett noticed that my interest was mounting. He had been talking almost without caution and without interruption. He looked at me intently with that wild, wide-eyed stare of his. He continued but he was now obviously more wary than before.

"Talking hypothetically now, Jonty. I'm the military commander of the UFF in West Belfast. I'm willing to hand over all I know if the RUC will come up with a deal," he said.

Trevor and I just nodded at him. We had no wish to interrupt his flow. It wasn't every day that an evil man of his ilk comes over or offers to come over to the side of the law. We didn't want to say anything to make him have a change of heart. He said that the UFF knew of two RUC touts who had been identified in recent times. He said neither of these two had been shot dead as yet because the political climate was not right. He named William Stobie as one. He said that Stobie had been moved out of the military, so he could tell us nothing now. The other suspected RUC tout was from Rathcoole. He declined to name this man at first. He didn't have to. I knew exactly who he meant. A Special Branch colleague had made me aware that the man was well out of harm's way.

I decided that it was time to get down to the nitty-gritty.

"How much do you want, Ken?" I asked.

"I'd need a lot of cash up front," he replied. "I was thinking of a grand or so, Jonty. As a token of our deal, if you know what I mean."

I nearly laughed out loud. Trevor and I could easily scrape up £100 between us but he had no chance of getting anything like £1,000. I was going to have to put this man down gently. I explained to him that the CID only paid on results. There would be no money up front. No arrests or no finds meant no result and that meant no payout. We were not like the RUC Special Branch. We did not give informants monthly retainers. Our resources for this very necessary area of Police work were limited, to say the least.

"No Branch, Jonty. I want nothing to do with them scumbags," Barrett said. "Look, go and get the questions from your bosses. I'll answer any questions you ask me. Just try me out. If your Headquarters are not pleased with my answers then that's it, the deal's off."

I told him that we would do our best. I explained that we *had* to involve the Special Branch at an early stage in accordance with our regulations. Barrett lost it.

"No Branch, Jonty. No way. The back roads of Northern Ireland are littered with their mistakes," he said.

This was obviously a reference to the unfortunate individuals who had been murdered by both Republican and Loyalist paramilitaries who believed that they were informants. I repeated and explained the procedures that we must follow. Barrett was not impressed. Yet I had no choice. Barrett was in for a shock if he thought it was that simple to keep the Special Branch out of the equation. I wondered how on earth we would get around this one. It was Barrett who broke the silence.

"There is no way I'm selling myself out for buttons, Jonty. I'm not going to be risking my life for buttons. This has to be done at my pace," he urged. "I'm talking about saving lives here, Jonty, and then before I go, I'll give you the heap. All of their dumps."

It was useless to argue with Barrett. Our hands were tied. There was no way we could exclude the Special Branch from the Police handling of this man. I knew also that there was no way that they would let any informant, never mind a murderer like Barrett, dictate any terms.

I looked at the clock on the fireplace. It was 25 minutes past midnight. The lads outside must be freezing. I needed to bring this to a close as soon as I could without further angering Barrett. I knew that he had the potential to save life. I wanted to exploit this very welcome development. It was obvious to me that something had happened within Barrett's sick world of terrorism to make him take this leap in our direction. That could be explored later. It was not in the public interest to alienate him at this stage by questioning his motives.

"I want to be like Sandy Lynch, Jonty, without the court bit," Barrett continued. "If I go supergrass, I could put away half the Shankill."

Lynch, a well-publicised Special Branch PIRA agent, had been identified by the Provisional IRA as a Security Forces agent. When a PIRA internal security team arrested him and interrogated him in a house in Lenadoon, the Police moved in and rescued him before he could be murdered. Lynch had been very lucky. He later gave evidence in open court against some notable PIRA men, including the Sinn Féin Press Secretary Danny Morrison.

Barrett made it clear, however, that he would not be telling us anything that he had done personally for the UFF. He also made it very clear that that he was not interested in giving evidence against anyone or going supergrass on anyone in an open court.

Barrett spoke again about the alleged Special Branch informant from Rathcoole. He told us that the UFF knew that it was this informant who had handed over a few hundred home-made Ingram submachine-guns that had never fired a shot. He stated that the Branch informant was supposed to be living in the North Down area but the UFF couldn't pin him down. Barrett told us that if they did find him, he would be "away for his tea" (murdered). He stated that as far as he could see, the UFF knew far too much about Special Branch informants.

"Don't even tell them my real name, Jonty. I don't want them to know I work for you."

Now that last utterance intrigued me. I had previous experience of people who had said that and when they did, it usually meant that they were already working for the Special Branch or some other agency. They were only coming forward to the CID to try to get paid twice for the same information. I wondered if this was the case with Barrett. Was he already working for the Special Branch? Had he worked for the Special Branch in the past and possibly been dropped or "red-lined" by the Special Branch for some good and valid reason?

I decided to draw this initial meeting to a close. I had heard enough. We had a lot of enquiries to get on with before we could even contemplate using Barrett as an informant. There was also no doubt in my mind that if Barrett was genuine, he had great potential. But that was a consideration for another day. We could evaluate his worth at a later date.

In the meantime if Barrett thought he was going to stroke a couple of CID men for a thousand pounds and then give no information in return, he had another thing coming. On the other hand, if he was genuinely coming forward to help us save life then he should be financially encouraged to do so. Trevor and I could take what he had told us to senior Police officers in the morning. I got up from my seat to indicate that we had heard enough and we were ready to leave.

"Right, what about a meet in daylight, Ken?" I asked.

"No way, Jonty. It has to be in the dark. I'll tell you where. The lay-by at Nutts Corner where everybody learns to drive. Nine pm, next Thursday night," he replied.

It struck me that Barrett had done this before for someone. He knew the ropes. There was no sign of any of the usual questions or reservations people normally have when they first come forward.

Trevor and I walked to the front door. It would normally be expected to shake hands at that juncture. I was grateful that Barrett himself had ruled that out. This man was a despicable, low-life thug. He was the epitome of everything that was deplorable of his kind. We knew that he was going to be a very hard man to handle. Barrett had already made the mistake of believing that he could control the situation. He was wrong. I was about to introduce him to some real bullies. Special Branch officers who should be more than a match for him. I just had no idea how on earth I was going to swing it without alienating Barrett. As we walked away from the door, Barrett could not resist the last word.

"It is as simple as this, Jonty. I have the commodity. You want it. It's a seller's market at my level because I can ruin the UFF. No threats, Jonty. No blackmail. Just play it straight. I'll do the same. It's my life that's on the line here," he said.

It was 1 am on the Wednesday morning before Trevor and I reached Greencastle RUC station. By that time we had been nineteen hours on our feet. We had hardly spoken a word on our way from the Glencairn Estate. We were too tired. We could do all of our talking in the morning.

I had a fitful sleep that night.

I was under no illusions as to why Barrett had come forward to offer us his services. This was all about Ken Barrett and how he could get his grubby hands into the public purse. I understood that. But I also understood that we could exploit his weakness to enable us to gain vital information that could indeed save lives. The Special Branch would not be too pleased that he had chosen to contact the CID. That was their problem. In the public interest, we would have to work very closely together now to get the best from Barrett.

At 9.30 am on 2 October 1991, we attended the offices of senior Police in North Queen Street RUC Station, our Divisional Headquarters. We fully debriefed on the events of the night before. We were told that we would have to work closely with the Special Branch on this one. The Walker Report and its recommendations were quoted. There really was no choice. Barrett's information related solely to subversive matters. There would also be no chance of any cash up front for Barrett, never mind the £1,000 cash he was demanding.

Our senior CID staff would consult with the Special Branch. In the meantime we were asked to research the most serious crimes that had been linked by intelligence or ballistics to the UFF's "B" Company in the Woodvale, which Barrett commanded. We needed to be in a position to question him about who was responsible for the most serious crimes traceable to that UFF unit. This would test Barrett's alleged intention to help us.

Trevor and I knew that we were in for a rough ride from both Barrett and the Special Branch. We had just recently weathered a storm in relation to another CID source who would not entertain talking to the Special Branch. I knew that they would accuse me of trying to "keep them out" of the Barrett case in the same manner, as they had done in relation to our other source. They were wrong. I had many good examples of my CID sources being passed to the Special Branch without any problem. I always left it up to the individual source. Some were happy to go with the Special Branch within a short time, but others were not. Barrett was making it clear that he wanted absolutely nothing to do with them. He felt that this should have been his prerogative. He would soon learn that it was not a matter of choice for him.

Trevor and I left North Queen Street and drove to Antrim Road RUC Station. We called at the offices of our Divisional Research Unit (DRU). We drew up a list of the most serious crimes that had occurred in the previous three years that we could attribute to "B" Company. The list was awesome. Standing out from all the rest was the brutal murder of the criminal defence solicitor Pat Finucane. No murder is more important than any other murder, however one stood out mainly because of its brutality. A husband and a father had been gunned down in the kitchen of his home in the presence of his wife and children on Sunday, 12 February 1989.

The UFF gunman responsible had pumped round after round from a semi-automatic pistol directly into Pat Finucane's face. The ferocity of the hate-fuelled attack was unprecedented in Belfast. There had also been the additional exasperating issue of alleged RUC and Security Force collusion in that murder. I personally did not believe any of that. In any case I took the view that we had to get to the bottom of this particular murder. If our enquiries led us in the direction of some corrupt colleague, that would be investigated too. The Constabulary had moved against such people in the past. I had no reason to believe that it would be any different now. On a personal level, I had felt sick to the stomach when I had heard of the murder of Pat Finucane. I had met him in 1980, and in the years which followed had many encounters with him in a professional context, as he defended his various clients in court. I had always found him to be open, friendly and respectful.

The question of who was responsible for the murder of Pat Finucane was one that I intended to broach with Barrett at the earliest opportunity. But it was only one of many questions. He had intimated that he knew the identity of a number of RUC officers who were passing information to the UDA and through them to the UFF. This was a serious allegation to make. If Barrett did have information or evidence to identify those RUC men responsible, I intended to pursue it.

Trevor and I learned later that day at 2.05 pm that our first meeting with the Special Branch in relation to Barrett was to take place at their offices in Castlereagh at 10 am the next day (Thursday, 3 October 1991). We were not looking forward to it at all.

At 10.43 am that day Trevor and I made our way to a Special Branch office on the third floor of Castlereagh RUC Station. I knocked the office door before going in. I was going to give these boys absolutely no room for complaint. We were confronted by what I had come to call "the usual suspects". There was one notable exception: a Detective Inspector for whom I had a lot of respect. He was a squad mate of mine. We had joined the RUC together on "Bloody Sunday". He had also served alongside me in Newtownabbey RUC Station in uniform. He was a very decent man and I was grateful that he was present. He would certainly not move to do me any harm or misquote me. But he had little or no say in what would happen to Barrett. I had already had as much bother as I could stomach from the rest of those present.

We gave a full briefing in relation to what Barrett had said and what he had claimed his intentions were. These guys just looked at each other. I looked up from my notes to find them winking and nudging each other as if they were communicating in some silent language all of their own. I wanted this over as quickly as I could get it over with. I didn't like to spend too much time in the presence of these fools.

As I was briefing them, they went out of their way in a childish manner to let me know that no-one was interested. There were no questions. There were no remarks made to us about Barrett's insistence that the Special Branch be excluded. I thought this very strange. It wasn't. They had already decided how to deal with that problem long before I had arrived to brief them. In fact, it later became clear that our briefing was unnecessary. They had already had the benefit of a briefing by senior CID officers.

I had not stopped speaking for enough time to pause for a breath when a Special Branch detective who was present chirped up.

"Thanks for that, Jonty. Now this is how we will handle this," he said.

The officer had been in touch with the Tactical Co-ordination Group (TCG). He went over the level of security in manpower, firearms, and vehicles which would be deployed to cover this source meet. Personally speaking, I thought it was way over the top but I had to bow to their experience. They were allowing for any eventuality, including a "Judas" ambush of our car by Barrett or his cronies in the UFF.

I listened to the Detective Inspector going over the detail of the stringent security precautions. Then came the bottom line.

"Jonty, you and Sam will go together in a Special Branch car to pick Barrett up. Sam will use a concealed tape recorder to record the conversations that take place throughout the entire meet. Have you any problems with that?" he asked.

"None at all," I replied.

In fact, I did have a problem. I did not agree with his choice of Special Branch constable to go with me to pick Ken Barrett up. Sam (not his real name) and I went back a long way. We had never seen eye-to-eye on anything before. He represented everything that I despised in certain Special Branch officers. He was so full of his own self-importance and so engrossed in his futile attempts to "get one over" on Trevor and me that he could not see the wood for the trees. He saw the CID not as of any potential benefit to him, but as an adversary. But whether we liked it or not, Sam was to accompany me on this crucial first meeting with Ken Barrett. There was absolutely nothing that I could do or say to change it.

I had just one question for the Special Branch Detective Inspector before we concluded our meeting. I was anxious to see how he would cope with this little gem. I thought he had missed it during our briefing.

"Barrett has made it clear that he wants no involvement with the Special Branch. How do I explain the presence of Sam?" I asked.

"Simple," replied the Detective Inspector, without missing a beat. "Tell him that Sam is the link man to the cash in Headquarters. Sam is a CID officer from Headquarters as far as Barrett is concerned."

I nodded. This was good. It was inspired. Whoever had briefed these guys before me had covered everything. The Special Branch officers stood up and we all prepared to leave the briefing.

Trevor and I left the Special Branch Regional Headquarters and walked downstairs to the canteen. Sam had been unusually subdued. He had whispered to me that we (the CID) would not be allowed to handle this one. He had an odd smirk on his face. I had thought nothing of the remark at the time: it was typical of the sort of thing Sam would say. Trevor had not missed the quiet malevolence from Sam either. Nor had he missed the fact that we had not really been required at that briefing. We were simply needed to get the Special Branch into Barrett's favour. The minute we could be removed from the equation, the Special Branch would dispense with our services.

Sam would have to put on a very good act to convince Barrett, because Barrett knew most of the local CID men. His liberty depended on it. He might not have been highly intelligent but he was extremely streetwise.

Trevor and I had other business to conduct at Castlereagh RUC Station that evening. We arrived early at 6.30 pm and completed our enquiries. Sam arrived with his Special Branch car at 7.30 pm. I went over to join him. I got into the front passenger seat and Trevor got into the rear seat behind me. Sam looked at Trevor and then looked quizzically at me.

"We come as a team," I said.

The truth was I had no intention of spending an hour or two on my own with Sam on a one-to-one basis. I had enough to contend with. Trevor was infinitely more diplomatic with the Special Branch than I was. He would pour cool water over the hot coals of my fraught relationship with them. He would inject humour at times when he felt that it would lift the oppressive atmosphere. I did not want Sam making any false accusations about what I had done or said on this important source meet.

Sam explained where the tape recorder was and how he controlled when it was turned off or on. He assured us that there would be no electric whirring or clicks at the end of a tape. He said that there would be nothing to alert Barrett to the fact that his conversation with us was being tape-recorded.

We got to Nutts Corner at 8.30 pm, a good half an hour early for the meet. The area was swarming with Police. Civilians would not necessarily have noticed them but Trevor and I did. We knew that Barrett would identify them as Police immediately. This concerned me.

Sam drove up and down past the pick-up point a few times to ensure that his E4a undercover team and his uniformed Headquarters Mobile Support Unit (HMSU) were in place. We then drove off to let the surveillance teams monitor the area. E4a operatives positioned near Barrett's home in the Glencairn Estate reported to Sam that Barrett had left home in his car, alone, at 8.30 pm. He was on his way towards Nutts Corner to meet us. I was impressed. These guys were taking absolutely no chances.

At 8.50 pm Barrett drove into the agreed meeting place. Sam swung the Special Branch car around and we headed back to pick him up. I knew by the expression on Barrett's face as he grabbed the door handle of our Police car that he was none too pleased that Trevor and I were not alone. I assumed that his evident anger was due to the presence of our CID "link man". I was wrong. Nothing could have prepared me for the débâcle that came next.

Barrett opened the back door of our Police car and was seated beside Trevor in a flash. I got the distinct impression that he had done this before. At the same time I saw Sam reach in below his driver's seat to set the tape recorder. Sam drove off quickly towards the nearby roundabout at Nutts Corner. We took the exit onto the road toward Crumlin. Cars coming towards us and others parked at the side of the road flashed their lights at us. I leaned over to check the headlights warning lamp on the Police car. I honestly believed that Sam had his full headlights on. He didn't. The persons flashing the lights were not angry motorists.

Our friend Barrett was under no such illusion. He had twigged exactly what was happening. Sam swung the Police car into the first layby on the left. He pulled up beside a large black litter bin, switched off the ignition and turned off all of the car lights. Suddenly car headlights flashed once again from a car parked approximately 300 yards up the main road and to our right. I now knew exactly what was happening. Sam reached for his radiotelephone. Before I could stop him he pushed his transmit button. The bright red light that indicated that the Police radio was in transmitting mode seemed to almost light up the car interior.

"The bird is in the nest," Sam said. "The bird is in the nest."

"Roger," came the crackled reply.

Sam took his finger off the transmit button and the little red light went out. It was Ken Barrett who broke the seemingly interminable silence that followed.

"I told you no Branch, Jonty," he said.

I did not speak. I could not believe the stupidity of what had just occurred. It was almost as if Sam and his colleagues wanted Barrett to be aware that they were Special Branch. This show of strength and of obvious mistrust by the Police was not lost on Barrett. He had realised that it was not something that would have occurred on a normal CID meet.

"Who are these c***s, Jonty? I spotted at least four Police cars and there's another one up there flashing lights!" he said.

I was flabbergasted. I didn't know what to say. Barrett was no fool. What on earth could I say? Was all this rigmarole really necessary? I reached into the furthest recesses of my mind to come up with a plausible answer.

"Those people are here as much to protect you as they are to protect us," I lied.

"And who is he, Jonty?" Barrett asked, pointing to Sam.

"This is Sam, he is a CID officer from Headquarters. He is your linkman to the cash," I lied again.

The Special Branch were not making this easy for us. By this time my eyes were becoming accustomed to the darkness inside the car. I could see Barrett clearly. He was extremely agitated. I turned around in my seat to speak to him. There were some very important questions that I wanted to put to Barrett. I also wanted to look into his wild eyes while he was answering me. From time to time a car or a lorry would drive past, illuminating the layby and our Police car. It also shone on the other HMSU car that was parked up the road. Barrett leaned forward to see everything around him. He kept shaking his head to indicate his irritation.

"'The bird is in the nest', Jonty? Is that me?" asked Barrett. "How many people know I am here? Say there's three of them boys in each car. That's five cars and fifteen men, plus you three. That means at least eighteen people know I'm here and how many more?"

Barrett was infuriated. None of what had just happened had been done to help us to convince him that Sam was a CID man. In fact everything Barrett had seen had served only to show him that a "special" RUC unit had surrounded him. He knew that Sam and his colleagues were not CID officers. I needed help from Sam now. Only he could turn this situation around. I nudged him with my knee. He didn't turn around. I could not believe what happened next. Sam fired a series of intelligence questions at Barrett.

Barrett was even more incensed. These were not questions that a CID officer would normally ask and he knew it. Sam had obviously no intention of helping me convince him that he was not a Special Branch officer. If we wanted to convince Barrett that Sam was a CID colleague we would have to do it ourselves and quickly, if we were not to risk deliberately alienating Barrett. But why would Special Branch officers seek to deliberately upset this man? Why did they not want to exploit Barrett's potential? Things got gradually worse.

Barrett repeated Sam's questions almost verbatim. He had not missed a thing.

"He is a f*****g Branch man!" he exclaimed. "CID men don't talk like that," he added.

I had to agree with him. I could not believe what was happening. I could not for the life of me understand it. I decided that all I could do was to attempt to redeem the situation. I spoke quickly and with as much authority as I could muster. Barrett had to be made aware of exactly who was in control of this unnecessarily fraught situation.

"Now look, Ken. This security is for all of us and Sam's questions were set out for him at RUC Headquarters. You asked me for questions. Those are some of them and I have plenty more in the same vein once you have answered them," I said.

Barrett stared at us looking for signs of nervousness or that we were lying. He found none. He then settled down. But he was not happy and certainly not convinced that Sam was a CID officer. He started to answer the questions as quickly as they were put to him. His knowledge of the UDA/UFF, its operations and its personalities was profound to say the least. I remembered that the conversation was being tape-recorded. I did not want Barrett to realise this was happening. I turned the interior light on in the car to at least pretend to take a few notes. I started to write down some of Barrett's more important answers. Before I had written no more than two or three words, Sam turned the interior light off again. He winked at me and pointed to the tape recorder. Barrett could not see him do this. Sam thought that I had forgotten it was on. I hadn't. I just did not want Barrett to suspect that we were recording him.

I reached up and switched the car interior light on again. Before I could start to write anything Sam turned it off again. It was no use. Sam either did not understand my role play or he deliberately wanted Barrett to smell a rat. I guessed it was the latter. But why?

Our petty differences were needlessly spooking Barrett. Trevor was doing a wonderful job of distracting Barrett. We sat in that car for the best part of two hours questioning him. I cannot recall exactly at what juncture it happened, but he was in a fully unguarded co-operative flow when I decided to ask him who had murdered the solicitor Pat Finucane.

Barrett's composure left him. The look on his face was one of shock. Perhaps it was the brutal nature of the murder or perhaps it was because of the controversy surrounding it, but I realised that I had touched a nerve. I was keen to pursue this because at that time Republicans had alleged for over two years that members of the Security Forces were involved in the murder. If there was collusion at any level then it was likely that Barrett would know exactly who was involved. He had already intimated that he could pass details of RUC and UDR men who were passing information to the UFF.

Barrett answered my question almost immediately and certainly before he had regained his composure.

"Hypothetically, me," he said without hesitation.

Sam pushed his knee into mine as if to indicate that I should say no more. I did not know what his problem was and I couldn't have cared less. This was not an interview room in Castlereagh and Barrett was obviously in a mind to help us, even if it meant incriminating himself. I wanted nothing to interrupt this flow. Barrett stared at me without blinking in that wild-eyed manner of his. The atmosphere in that Special Branch car was electric. The headlights of vehicles passing on the main road lit up the interior of the car momentarily from time to time. The scene was reminiscent of the lighting in some horror movie. Barrett's pallid white skin was illuminated from time to time in those same headlights. He was certainly a disconcerting figure.

Thoughts raced through my mind of how I could advance his flow without alerting Barrett that we were too interested. I tried my best to keep my face expressionless. I did not want him to detect any sign of triumph or enthusiasm in my voice or my demeanour.

"Who was the second gunman?" I asked

His reply was immediate. "Hypothetically, Jim Millar."

My heart was thumping in my chest. I was glad that we were sitting in virtual darkness. But Sam was still digging his knee into mine. That last answer from Barrett was like a bolt out of the blue for me. I ignored Sam.

I was only too well aware that the Police had recovered the 9 mm Browning pistol used by Ken Barrett to pump those bullets into Pat Finucane's face less than five months after the murder. It had been seized on 4 July 1989 with another handgun in Jim Millar's (not his real name) home in a side street just off the main Shankill Road. It had been a fortuitous find. Millar was not at home at the time of the search. His brother David (not his real name) was found sleeping in another bed in the same bedroom. When the investigating Police officers questioned him, David admitted that the guns were his. He took full responsibility for them. He even went willingly off to jail for possessing them. We had had our doubts about his involvement. His brother Jim was a notable UFF suspect. Unfortunately there is little that one can do in such a situation. We later arrested and interviewed Jim Millar in relation to his suspected possession of the two handguns. Jim denied any knowledge of the murder gun or the other weapon. He was obviously happy enough to let his brother "do the time" for it.

Now here we were over a year later, and Ken Barrett was not only confessing to the murder of Pat Finucane. He was also confirming that Jim Millar had been the second gunman at the scene of the murder. My interest soared. I realised that this UFF suspected serial killer was more than likely telling us the truth. I decided to explore this new avenue of enquiry fully. I could find out later from the facts exactly how accurate his account was.

I explained to Barrett that I had not been at the scene of the murder of Pat Finucane on Sunday, 12 February 1989 and I was not familiar with exactly what had occurred. I asked him to go over the events of that fateful night. I expected him to falter. I half-expected him to be wary now that he could see that my interest was up. But to my surprise not only did Barrett continue to talk, he started to boast openly to us of his involvement in that brutal murder.

"There were three of us in that car, Jonty. Jim Millar and me were the two gunmen. The driver was a wee lad from Rathcoole," he said.

He went on to say that this murder was the first job the "wee lad" had been involved in with the UFF. He had not participated in anything prior to the murder of Pat Finucane.

"What is his name?" I asked.

Barrett hesitated. You could almost hear his brain whirring in the deadly silence of the Police car. I got the impression that his next answer was not going to be as honest as the previous answers. He was anxious and fidgeting.

"I don't know his name, Jonty, and that's the truth but I could pick him out from photographs," he replied.

I immediately realised that if that was the UFF man's first job then it would be unlikely that we would have any record of his involvement with the UDA/UFF, never mind a photograph of him. For some reason Barrett was being evasive and as an investigator of these matters for years, I knew exactly what that reason was. Not wishing to stem Barrett's flow, I dropped that question for the moment. We could go back to it again.

Barrett was now no longer in my sights as a potential informant. He was now a self-confessed murderer. Our rules governing the handling of informants meant that Barrett's confession ruled him out as far as ever becoming a Police informant or agent. It was one thing to suspect him of murder. It was a totally different matter to have evidence of his involvement in it. I fully intended to convict him of that brutal murder.

I knew that we would face counter-arguments from the Special Branch. We had heard them all before. We would deal with that if it arose. Yet even as we sat there in that Police car, I really expected that the Special Branch would assist us in this one. I knew of no reason why they would not do so. If Ken Barrett was the murderer of Pat Finucane, then we intended to vigorously pursue him for it. We would prosecute him and hold him up to the world as the UFF man *solely* responsible for the murder of Pat Finucane. Any allegations that he would wish to make about the involvement of members of the Security Forces could be equally vigorously pursued.

Perhaps it was because of the apparent lack of revulsion or negative response from the three of us in that car with him. Or perhaps it was due to the fact that Barrett believed that in coming forward to the Police in this manner it would somehow protect him from prosecution. But whatever the reason, Barrett obviously felt safe confessing his role in that gruesome murder to three RUC detectives. He spoke openly and extremely frankly to us. He went on to give us a chilling account of how the big outer door of the Finucane home had been open. He said he kicked the inner door so hard that the small and inadequate Yale lock had actually come off its mounting and had flown up the hall in front of him. He said that he ran straight up the hall and towards a glass door that led into the kitchen. He could see people gathered in the kitchen. He said that as he reached the glass door to the kitchen, Mrs Finucane tried to slam it shut.

Barrett sat there in that Special Branch car, his wild eyes blazing. He clasped his hands together and used one finger outstretched to simulate the shape of a gun.

"Bang, bang," he said.

He said that he had fired a number of shots in the hallway at Pat Finucane as he approached the kitchen and some even went through the glass in the kitchen door, striking Finucane as he made an attempt to close it. Barrett had seen him jump up from his seat at the kitchen table. He said bullets struck the solicitor, wounding him and causing him to fall onto his back on the kitchen floor just inside the door.

By now Barrett was reliving that traumatic event. He was obviously back there in that kitchen committing the murder all over again. But unlike the dozens of men who had solemnly confessed to their role in similar murders Barrett was not remorseful. There were no tears, no anguish as he recounted the horrific events. I was struck by his callous and inhuman disregard for life. Far from remorseful, he was in fact gloating, boasting of how he had murdered Pat Finucane. In Barrett's own sinister world, he was a hero. He went on:

"I stood right over him, Jonty, straddling him, and I fired shot after shot into his face."

Barrett looked at me with those scary, cruel eyes of his. He seemed to be seeking approval. I think he expected me to congratulate him. The fact was, he made me feel physically ill. But I knew better than to let him detect that. This guy was the stuff of nightmares. He was one of those uncommon psychopathic killers that we only encountered on the very rare occasion. Even as he paused, waiting for the praise that never came, he continued to hold his hands in the shape of a handgun.

His grip was so tight on that imaginary weapon that his knuckles were white. I studied his long, thin, white fingers. He looked down again into the floorwell of the car at his clasped hands.

"Bang, bang, bang, bang, bang," he said.

Each bang indicated another round going into the victim's head. Barrett looked up from his hands. His eyes were blank. They were staring straight ahead past me and out into the darkness of the countryside and beyond. This man was frightening. He was evil personified. An evil you could almost smell. I remember shuddering. It is an odd feeling you get, at times like that. It has been described well in the past as the feeling you would get if someone had just walked over your grave. Barrett broke the silence.

"You'd never tire of doing this, Jonty," he said. "Bang, bang, bang, bang."

Suddenly he stopped and looked up at me. His eyes were staring wildly as if he had just remembered something else from that bloody scene. He reached over to grab hold of my arm to make sure that he had my attention. He obviously did not want me to miss what was coming next.

"Them bullets were going into his f****n' head and coming straight back up at me. I heard them whizzing past my own head," he said.

I was intrigued. These were facts that only the murderer or someone who was at the scene could know. The statements of our Scenes of Crime Officers (soco) or our Forensic scientists would confirm if this monster was telling us the truth or not, but I needed more.

"Why was that?" I asked.

"The stone floor in the kitchen, Jonty. The bullets were going through his face and into the stone floor and whistling back up again past me. I nearly shot myself dead," he said, with a sudden expression of concern.

If Barrett was looking for sympathy, he was talking to the wrong cop. He paused again. He was sitting staring straight ahead, wide-eyed, reliving that horrific scene. All I could think was, how could anyone do such a thing to a fellow human being, let alone do it in front of screaming and terrified witnesses like Pat Finucane's wife and children?

"I'll tell you something else you won't know, then," Barrett said. "I killed that c**t so fast he was still holding his fork in his hand," he gloated in a sickening manner.

With facts like these we would be able to further incriminate or to eliminate Barrett from our murder enquiry. I had to bear in mind that it would not be the first time that someone for reasons best known to themselves had confessed their part in a murder to Police officers only for it to transpire later that they did not commit it. And yet there was something about the whole atmosphere, Barrett's entire confession, the nature and the flow of it and his frightening demeanour that struck me, that made me believe it was the truth. Such a frank confession to a most horrific crime had a distinct ring of truth about it. I was personally in no doubt that we were sitting in the presence of a psychopath. I was also totally convinced that this was not the only murder that Ken Barrett had committed.

Sam the Branch man had said nothing throughout Barrett's confession. He just kept nudging me with his knee from time to time. I wondered what that was all about. I intended to ask him later. I was just so glad that he had not said anything to interrupt Barrett. In fact, I was impressed. It had taken me everything I had inside me not to show my revulsion or ask a lot more questions as Barrett relayed that confession to us.

I was sitting there in the darkness of that car trying to think of a way that we could turn what we had just heard into evidence. How we could ensure that Barrett would be brought to justice for this crime.

As confessions go, it was one of the most open and frank confessions that I had ever heard. But unfortunately none of it was evidence against him. There is a vast difference between information and evidence. Our difficulty was due to a legal nicety. Barrett was not under caution. We were not in that car on an evidence-gathering exercise. We had gone there to meet Barrett on an *intelligence*-gathering exercise only. And that is the difference, subtle though it may be.

The problem we had now was that nothing that Barrett had said to us was admissible evidence against him. It could only be used to corroborate other evidence. It was not admissible against him in a court of law. I was half-hoping that he did not know that because, as a basis to launch a new avenue of enquiry, developments don't come much better than this. Until Barrett had enlightened us as to exactly who had committed the murder, Trevor and I had had absolutely no idea. We believed that we were shining the first light of discovery onto what had been a very elusive quarry. No other murder in the history of the Northern Ireland Troubles had been more frequently used to discredit us across the world than this one.

We had to move this enquiry up a level. That was going to be easy: all we had to do was to lure an unsuspecting Barrett into an evidence-gathering forum. We knew exactly how to do that. Trevor's glances and his nudges to my arm were a signal that he was at one with me on that. We let Barrett continue.

"She was f****n' screaming," he said.

It was a derogatory reference to Mrs Geraldine Finucane.

"I heard she was hit in the foot," he added.

Barrett said that after the murder, he ran out of the house and back to the hijacked taxi. He spoke of how he had jumped into the back seat and Jim Millar had jumped into the front seat beside the young driver. Barrett said that he told the driver to drive to the Glencairn Estate. He became annoyed and agitated as he recounted this. He grabbed my arm again.

"Aye, wait 'til you hear this, Jonty," he said as he held my arm. "The wee f****r froze as we got into the car."

Barrett grimaced. His hand was back in the shape of a gun again. He said he put the hot 9 mm pistol to the back of the young driver's neck and told him to drive, otherwise he would be shot too.

"Would you believe that, Jonty? He nearly got us all caught!"

Barrett stated that the young "fella" drove off up to the Glencairn, where they dumped the guns before they drove back down to the Woodvale Road. He said they dumped the car on the Woodvale Road facing the city and ran down the steps into the Woodvale Estate to get away. Barrett had finished his account. If all of that were captured on audiotape, it would assist us greatly in preparing to launch our newly revitalised criminal investigation.

I asked Barrett directly if he knew the nickname or the first name or if he could even give me a description of the young driver from Rathcoole. Barrett must have detected more that a hint of enthusiasm in my voice. I could see his guard go up. Realising that I was extremely interested in what he had said, he pointed his imaginary gun into my face. There was no mistaking the immediate change in his tone and his attitude. No mistaking the malevolence.

"I'm sound, take me to Castlereagh and I'm admitting f**k all. I know Jim Millar is sound. He will admit f**k all too. But that wee guy from Rathcoole will squeal the house down and you'll use him as Queen's Evidence against me. Nothing I've said in this car is evidence against me. But that wee lad could put me in jail for life."

I had been hoping against hope that Barrett had not realised that this was the case. I could dream on. This was going to be one slippery customer. I decided to lighten the atmosphere. I moved on to other topics. These were controversial too. Barrett also admitted that a senior UDR soldier had assisted the UFF to enter Malone UDR barracks to steal two Browning 9 mm high-powered handguns and two SA80 rifles. These were the standard Army-issue rifles allocated to all soldiers serving in the British Army and the UDR was a regiment of the British Army at that time.

Barrett boasted openly of his involvement in this crime. He agreed to help us recover all four of the stolen weapons. His difficulty was that very few people were aware of the "bed" (firearms hide) they were stored in. Recovery of them by the Security Forces would trigger a very unwelcome internal enquiry within the UFF. This was something that Barrett said he could well do without.

We spent about two hours in that Special Branch car quizzing Barrett. We then dropped him off back at his own car. I watched him stumble in the darkness as he made his way through the mud and puddles towards his car. My mind was racing as Sam drove the Special Branch car at speed back towards Belfast and to Castlereagh. Due to Barrett's confession we must now abandon all thoughts of recruiting him as an informant. He had admitted to murder. We now had a clear duty to put him in jail for life for that murder and our colleagues in the Special Branch had a duty to assist us.

They would. I just knew that they would. Yes, we had our differences on some minor source-handling matters. But this was black and white. This was sheer, unadulterated murder. We had a sworn duty to our community and a clear responsibility to the deceased and to his wife and family. I had never found the RUC wanting in any case like this before, so I did not expect any change of stance now.

I broke the silence less than a mile from the Nutts Corner roundabout.

"I'm going to knock that character for six. You may move over, Sam, we are going to put him in jail for life for the murder of Pat Finucane," I said.

Trevor spoke next, seconding my assertion that we would deal with Barrett.

"No, you won't," Sam said.

I couldn't believe what he had said.

"Yes, I am," I insisted.

"Move away from it," Sam said.

"What?" I asked.

"Move away from it," he repeated.

I brought it to his attention that we could clear the controversial murder of the solicitor Pat Finucane. It was in the best interests of our

Force and the solicitor's family that we did so. If we could prove that there was no involvement by any member of the RUC or other Security Forces in that murder, then it would augur well for the future standing and reputation of our entire Constabulary. Surely he could see that. What he said next astounded me.

"We (Special Branch) know he done it," he said.

"Pardon?" I replied.

Chapter 11
"We know he done it"

"We know he done it, Jonty. We know all about it," Sam was saying. I was dumbfounded. It was news to me that the RUC was aware of exactly who had murdered Pat Finucane. I had been questioning both UDA and UFF men for years about it.

I intended to exhaust this new avenue of enquiry. My own CID authorities would support me even if the Special Branch would attempt to work to some other perverse agenda. I decided not to argue with Sam any further.

En route to Castlereagh RUC Station, Sam spoke hurriedly and excitedly about some investigation into his conduct and the conduct of other Special Branch men in relation to their handling of a Special Branch agent called William Stobie. I did not know Stobie at that time. I wrongly assumed that the name was a pseudonym for Sam's agent. Barrett had mentioned the name Stobie on our first visit to his home. But what on earth had all of this to do with Barrett and the murder of Pat Finucane?

Here we were back "in the Dark". We had no idea what this Special Branch man was talking about. We were expected to just agree with the inexplicable view of the Special Branch officer without question. I had no intention of dismissing Barrett's important confession to satisfy some unknown Special Branch agenda.

I was now more than a little worried about the safety and integrity of that audiotape that was sitting in a tape recorder below Sam's seat.

I was tempted to reach over and seize it. Everything in my fibre told me to seize it and let the powers that be make the appropriate decisions about it.

I feared that Sam would destroy it or simply allege that the tape recorder did not work. I also had the distinct impression that he was never going to let me hear it, never mind give me a copy of it. I agreed that we should take the future direction of the case from our authorities. I put this to Sam.

"Yes, our Special Branch authorities," Sam asserted.

I wasn't going to argue. It would have been futile to do so. I was sure that my CID supervisors would come down firmly on our side. We stopped arguing. By the time Sam pulled that Special Branch car into Castlereagh twenty minutes later, the atmosphere in the Police car was electric. Trevor had been poking me in the shoulder from the rear of the car in an attempt to get me to stop pressing my point. As I left the Police car I decided to press it once more.

"Sam, I need a copy of that tape for my senior CID supervisors," I said.

He bent down and lifted the tape out of the recorder. He held it up to my face across the roof of the Police car in a teasing, childish manner. But this was no laughing matter.

"No way, Jonty," he said. "Tell your bosses to contact mine in the morning."

It was midnight as Trevor and I walked into Castlereagh Police Office to make our routine calls home. Rebecca confirmed that all was well. As I drove home my mind was racing once again. I tried to relax. I could let my CID authorities fight with the likes of Sam the Branch man. I was sick of their constant obstruction.

I was involved in law enforcement. The mollycoddling of killers did not rest easy with me. Even if they were Special Branch agents. I wondered what on earth it was that would make them want to protect Barrett from us. Whatever it was, they were certainly not about to share it with me. I would make damn sure that their reasons would at least be examined by my senior CID supervisors.

My notes show that despite an early start on Friday, 4 October 1991, it was not until 11.30 am that Trevor and I arrived at North Queen Street RUC Station to brief senior CID officers in relation to the events of the night before. We had been very busy on other urgent matters that had nothing to do with Barrett. We spent an hour briefing our supervisors as to Barrett's startling confession.

The Orange march from Drumcree church in 2003: a police barrier blocks them from a Roman Catholic part of Portadown. (*Reuters*)

A boy runs past graffiti on a wall on the Garvaghy Road in Drumcree. (*Reuters*)

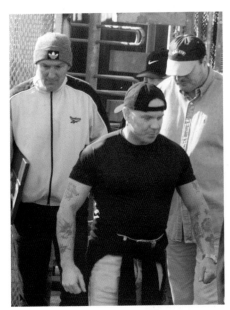

Johnny Adair being released from the Maze Prison under the terms of the Good Friday Agreement. (*Empics*)

Boundary Way, a street on the lower Shankill area of West Belfast where Johnny Adair lived. Police stand guard. (*Reuters*)

William Stobie, former UDA Quartermaster and Special Branch informer. He was shot dead on 12 December 2001. (*Getty Images*)

Pat Finucane, the outstanding solicitor whose murder was one of the great causes célèbres of the Troubles. (*Pacemaker Press*)

The scene outside Pat Finucane's house on the Antrim Road on the night he was murdered. (*Pacemaker Press*)

A Sinn Féin protest at Stormont on the occasion of the fifteenth anniversary of Pat Finucane's murder. (*Empics*)

Ken Barrett arriving at Belfast Crown Court to face the charge of murder of Pat Finucane. (*Alan Lewis/Photopress Belfast*)

Close-up of an RUC tunic, together with a personal issue .375 Magnum revolver belt and holster.

The aftermath of a bomb attack on the author's home, showing damage to the outside of the heavily armoured front door.

Johnston Brown and his family in 1999. From left, Lisa 24, Adam 15, Rebecca and Simon, 12.

With Rebecca. (*Alan Lewis/Photopress Belfast*)

We argued that we would have to move quickly if we were to set up a CID operation to take Barrett down. Time was of the essence. I did not want some unscrupulous Special Branch officer warning him of our intentions. That had happened in other cases before this. We would also have to move quickly before Barrett had any chance to change his mind. There was no room here for hesitation.

We pressed our case to our supervisors as strongly as we could. Barrett had spoken openly and in an unguarded manner in that Police car. It was likely that he would do so again. We should exploit this obvious weakness. We could place him into a controlled environment and go for evidence to convict him of the murder of Pat Finucane. I saw our supervisors glance at each other from time to time yet I noted an apparent lack of enthusiasm. There was a lack of interest in this chance of a lifetime to put a suspected serial killer in jail. I had not expected that. It became obvious to me very quickly that the Special Branch had capitalised on our short absence to get to these men first. I continued our briefing.

We knew that we were getting nowhere. The briefing ended with Trevor and I underlining the fact that we had a chance here to take a serial killer off the streets. This was our primary duty. How could the Special Branch argue against that? What on earth could be more important?

I was assured that the Special Branch had fully briefed my CID authorities. There was mutual agreement between the two distinctly separate disciplines that the entire matter be referred "upstairs" to RUC Headquarters for a decision. That was the end of the matter as far as my authorities in the CID were concerned. I could not argue with that. Our regulations were clear. Where there is a disagreement between the two disciplines i.e. CID and Special Branch, the Walker Report makes it clear that the matter should be referred to officers of ACC rank at RUC Headquarters for a final decision.

This was all very well in theory. But the fact was that delay of any kind in a case like this was the same thing as doing nothing. It was more than a little perverse for us to be even contemplating running a self-confessed murderer as an RUC agent. To run him as an agent now would substantially weaken any later attempt to prosecute him. I could see that. My senior supervisors must see that. It was my experience that the Special Branch were not that clever in relation to these matters.

We were told that we could not meet Barrett again until 10 October 1991, six days hence. Some people who did not want to move against Barrett had been up burning the midnight oil to out-manoeuvre us on this one. They had gained six more days to argue their case. That was six days more than I would have given them. But it was not up to me. In any case, I did not expect that we would ever meet Ken Barrett again as a potential informant. I had no doubt that my authorities in RUC Headquarters would examine all the facts and come down firmly on our side. Nothing else made sense. I decided to relax and let things take their natural course.

My CID authorities told me that Sam and one of his senior Special Branch supervisors were having difficulty transcribing some of the content of the audiotape. The Special Branch alleged that cars and heavy lorries thundering past the layby we had stopped in had drowned out the voice of Ken Barrett in some crucial parts of the recording. I feared that this was an attempt to say that the recording was of such a poor quality that it was useless. This fear was to prove unfounded.

The audiotape was safe for now and I was assured that it would be made available to us at a later date. The main thing was that Ken Barrett was far from out of the woods and I was glad to hear that. But until RUC Headquarters made a decision about the direction of the enquiry, we were to continue to meet Barrett to glean as much information from him as we could. We were to bleed him dry of every scrap of information about the UFF and its activities.

The Special Branch had allegedly given senior CID officers in Headquarters the other nine-tenths of the picture. That infamous phenomenon, "the bigger picture". I had heard that one many times before. My alarm bells never rang louder than when Branch men used that "catch-all" term, the "bigger picture".

My experience was that this "bigger picture" phenomenon was used like a shield to protect the Special Branch and their agents from what would for the rest of us be normal scrutiny of our activities or procedures. No-one was allowed to question the propriety of what the Special Branch were doing. Matters of concern about the Special Branch would be referred up to RUC Headquarters. It was there that their masters of spin would wrap up something apparently sinister in some Special Branch glad rags so that it would appear innocent to anyone without a discerning eye.

There was no system in place to oversee Special Branch activities as there was for the rest of the Force. They would try to hide their wrongdoings behind a cloak of secrecy. They would use their age-old arguments, such as "not impinging upon one of their ongoing operations" or "not embarrassing one of their valuable sources". These were just two of the excuses that no-one was allowed to argue with. When it came to challenging the Special Branch, Policemen who had stood up courageously against the likes of the Provisional IRA suddenly became gutless, spineless individuals. This never ceased to amaze me.

And yet Barrett came forward in 1991, six years after John Stalker had exposed the RUC Special Branch authorities to the world for what they were. No-one had listened. No-one had truly examined the enormity of his findings. No-one seemed to have any regard for the adverse effect that his serious allegations had on the rest of the Force. Everybody was expected to close ranks to protect the Special Branch.

As a CID supervisor operating in Belfast at the height of a terrorist campaign, I was incensed when I read in the national newspapers of how the Special Branch authorities had used their own HMSU operatives to kill Republican suspects in the most questionable of circumstances. How young uniformed Police officers who were sworn to protect life were put into the most unenviable situations where they felt that they had to take life. I read of how they had been ordered by their authorities to tell lies to their fellow CID investigators. I read with disgust how those same Special Branch authorities turned their backs on their junior men. How senior Special Branch officers had told John Stalker during interviews that the shoot-to-kill allegations and the circumstances surrounding them had been the result of a low-level conspiracy between the HMSU and E4a sergeants and constables. I was not surprised to hear of the treachery of certain senior Special Branch men. I had crossed some of them earlier in my career. But I was shocked when I saw the same treacherous men supported at a high level within the RUC at that time.

It was clear to anyone familiar with the facts that senior Special Branch officers had been the architects of all of those sinister and controversial incidents. They had then tried to wash their hands of any responsibility by pointing the finger of blame at the lower ranks. John Stalker saw right through it. He had some very senior Special Branch officers in his sights. There is no doubt that he would have ensured that they also faced prosecution for their alleged involvement in serious criminal activity. He would have done—had he not been abruptly removed from the enquiry before he could take any such action.

Allegations of minor disciplinary improprieties were made against Stalker to break his credibility and to ensure his timely removal from Northern Ireland. None of the allegations made against him were found to have any substance. I was not surprised. Stalker had dared to question the activities of the RUC Special Branch. That had been previously unheard of. There would be a price, and the RUC Special Branch wasted no time in exacting it.

Stalker appeared to be either very courageous or totally unaware of the ruthless nature of the agency that he had been sent to Northern Ireland to investigate. I believe it was the former. He set about his investigation in an open and honest manner. His findings shocked him. The deliberate obstruction by the Special Branch at RUC Headquarters shocked him. Nonetheless he tried his best to prove to the nation that the RUC Special Branch were out of control. His findings were clear. Certain Police officers within the Special Branch were operating outside the law to enforce the law.

Yet the RUC had learned nothing. Its inability to accept constructive criticism from any quarter was one of its major failings. History has now shown that the RUC would have been well advised to face up to the constructive criticisms made by John Stalker.

Back in that office in North Queen Street RUC Station, there was nothing more that Trevor and I could do to push for the prosecution of Ken Barrett. The decision not to move against Barrett for one of the most controversial murders in the history of the Troubles had been made. It was made in the first two and a half hours of our working day on Friday, 4 October 1991 and it had been made in our absence. Unfortunately there was nothing at all that I could do about it. I felt frustrated and powerless.

Later that same day, a senior supervisor told me that I was to go over to Castlereagh to help Sam the Special Branch man transcribe the audiotape. Once I got there, I opened the door of the small Special Branch office. Sam was seated on a chair in front of me with his back to me and the door. He was wearing a long-sleeved dark fine woollen pullover and a light coloured shirt. He had a pair of heavily padded black headphones on. He was writing frantically onto a number of blank pages on the desk in front of him. A block of new blue SB50s (intelligence input forms) was sitting on the desk to his left. He was totally unaware of my presence.

I stood there behind him and listened as the tape recorder clicked and whirred repeatedly as Sam stopped it, rewound it and started it again. He would listen to it for a few seconds before he repeated the same procedure. It was one I was familiar with. Tape transcription from audiotape to written statement of evidence was one of our core tasks in CID. It was a painstaking and thankless one. Ours had to be exact and precise in its interpretation. What Sam was doing was simply a note-taking job. This would never be examined later in any open court.

I put my hand on Sam's shoulder from behind. The constable jumped up from his seat. I had startled him. The headphone lead was very short and the headset was wrenched from his head. It swung from left to right at the side of his desk.

Sam was not happy. He did not like to see the CID on his floor. We were not part of his team. Therefore as far as he was concerned, we could not be trusted. He was not amused at the fact that I was going to hear the content of that tape. I had been present when the audio record was made. So why did it matter if I heard it all again? I decided to inject a bit of sick humour into the situation.

"My boss says that I have to bring him back a copy tape," I lied.

Sam's face was a picture.

"My instructions are that we are not to make any copies," he said, getting up and reaching for the door handle. I stopped him.

"I'm only joking, lighten up," I said.

Sam glared at me. The attempt at humour was lost on him. I saw the relief flood over his face. Now I was certain that whatever the reason was not to set up a CID operation to prosecute Barrett, Sam had to be at the centre of it. I would just have to go along with it all for now.

I was glad to see that audiotape. At least the Special Branch were not pretending that the tape recorder had malfunctioned and not recorded the meeting with Ken Barrett. They could so easily have done so. Perhaps that would have been far too simple. I got the distinct impression that Sam felt that they did not have to offer the CID any excuses or reason. The tape was the sole property of the Special Branch and as far as he was concerned that was the end of it.

According to my records, I spent the best part of two hours transcribing the audiotape with Sam. I was present as he wrote out his notes. I took a mental note of what he was submitting to his intelligence system. I asked him for a copy of the SB50s but he refused to give me anything. He was making it clear that the CID was going to be the poor relation in this exercise.

I listened to that tape recording over and over again. It was interspersed with sections of clear recordings of our meeting with Barrett. But other sections were hard to hear because of the loud background noises made by passing traffic, including one motorbike that seemed to take an age to reach our location and another age to pass it. That section of the audiotape was virtually indecipherable.

Sam stressed that he would never park in that particular layby again. The noise of the road traffic was horrendous. He said that he would choose somewhere much quieter the next time. But the important section on the audiotape where Barrett had confessed to the murder of Pat Finucane was clear enough to transcribe in full. In fact, Sam made out an SB50 that read something like this:

"Source (Ken Barrett) states that the following two men were the gunmen in the murder of Pat Finucane:

1. Ken Barrett

2. Jim Millar (not real name)."

The intelligence that Sam had entered into the Special Branch computer system made it clear that Barrett was the murderer of Pat Finucane. Normally this would be disseminated down to CID level. Then the fun would start. Barrett would have to be arrested and questioned for the murder. There was no getting around that. At least that was the theory. But we knew from experience that Barrett was not amenable to interviews in Castlereagh. We would have to be more resourceful than that if we were to take Ken Barrett down.

At least the Special Branch appeared to be playing it straight. Perhaps they had realised that Headquarters was likely to agree with the CID. We were due to meet Barrett again on 10 October 1991. That was only six days away. I didn't really expect that meeting to take place at all. I expected that our Headquarters staff would come firmly down on our side.

October 1991 was an extremely busy month for Trevor and I. We had dozens of informants to meet. We even had some that the Special Branch knew absolutely nothing about. They had betrayed one too many. It was an indictment on the Special Branch that we had to dupe some of its operatives but that was the case. We had to protect the people who came forward to help us. I was too busy that month to properly fight our corner with the Special Branch in relation to Barrett. They had pulled their ace card, the Walker Report, and we had to fall into line.

In the meantime Trevor and I visited the Divisional Research Unit (DRU) at Antrim Road RUC Station. We examined the records and the video and photographs on the murder of Pat Finucane. We were astounded at what we found.

Barrett's graphic description of the home of the deceased both inside and out fitted perfectly with the facts. His description of the position of the body of the deceased was also correct. Pat Finucane was still holding a fork in his hand in the photographs. There were two bullet holes in the glass door leading into the kitchen. There was a heavily tiled floor.

The horrific injuries inflicted were exactly as described by Barrett. We realised immediately that we had obtained a very important confession. The Special Branch had also conceded that they already knew that Barrett had "done it". All we had to do now was to move things up a level. Go after Ken Barrett. It was as simple as that. Trevor and I took a few important notes. The next time we saw Barrett, we intended to question him fully about the murder of the solicitor Pat Finucane.

Thursday, 10 October 1991 was upon us before we knew it. It did not seem a week since we had last met Barrett. We had heard nothing to indicate that there had been any change of heart by our authorities. Barrett was to be accepted into the fold as a Special Branch agent and that was it. There was no decision as yet from Headquarters to change that fact. It could take quite a while before someone upstairs made a decision as important as this one. Would they allow the Special Branch to lead them by the nose? I prayed that they would not.

The wheels at RUC Headquarters were known to grind very slowly. A thing as insignificant as the proper handling of one newly recruited and untested Loyalist source was obviously low down on their list of priorities. I had to settle down and accept that it could take weeks or even months before any such decision was made. I decided to use the time that I had available with Barrett to milk every little drop of information from him.

Nonetheless, I still harboured the notion that Special Branch had not fully debriefed our authorities at RUC Headquarters. Had they mentioned the existence of that audio recording? Had Headquarters even been made aware of the fact that Barrett had confessed so graphically, so dramatically to the murder of Pat Finucane?

On the other hand, even I had to accept that it might well be the case that the Special Branch or some other secretive unit at RUC Headquarters had the other nine-tenths of the picture. I would just have to bide my time. Was I being paranoid? Bitter experience had taught me that I was not being paranoid. It had also taught me that a certain degree of paranoia was healthy when dealing with these scheming gentlemen.

Trevor and I arrived at Tennent Street RUC Station at around 6.30 pm on 10 October 1991 to link up with Sam. This second meeting with Barrett at Nutts Corner was due to take place at 8 pm so we left Tennent Street in the Special Branch car at 7.30 pm. Sam was driving again. I was in the front passenger seat and Trevor was behind me in the rear.

Sam quickly brought it to our attention that his instructions from his own bosses were very clear. We (CID) were to take a back seat in this particular meeting. Sam was now in charge of Barrett. He produced a slip of paper from the inside of his jacket pocket. It appeared to be an A4 sized page folded in half. He stated that he had a list of questions from the RUC Special Branch at Headquarters for Barrett. He would question him. We were not to interrupt him until he was finished. This was an extremely unusual request indeed but we had no real problems with it. But then Sam dropped a further bombshell:

"You are not to mention the murder of Pat Finucane tonight. There are to be no references to the Finucane murder tonight, OK?" Sam said. "Anyway, we know he did it. We have known for a long time."

"So how long have you known that Barrett was responsible?" I asked.

"For years," Sam replied flippantly.

"Who in Headquarters is evaluating that confession of Barrett's?" I asked.

"I'm not sure," Sam replied.

I was fit to be tied. What was the point of the CID meeting Barrett with the Special Branch if we were not allowed to ask him questions about his confession to murder? We sat in silence while Sam sped towards Nutts Corner.

"Now you two must not mention the Finucane murder," Sam repeated.

He repeated that annoying phrase on the way to meet Barrett so many times that he sounded like a toddler who wanted a toy. It just got worse and worse. I turned around in my seat to speak to Trevor.

"Have you got that now, Trevor? We mustn't mention, *mustn't mention* the Finucane murder," I jibed.

The humour and the sarcasm were lost on Sam. He was too intense. He was looking straight ahead into the darkness as we drew closer to Nutts Corner. We pulled up at the spot where Barrett had parked the week before. I remember thinking this strange, after Sam's protestations that we would never park there again. Sam applied the handbrake as the Police car came to an abrupt stop. The sudden total silence was almost deafening. We sat there quietly waiting for Barrett to appear. This time any cover from Sam's uniformed support was out of sight and keeping a professional distance. I was glad of that at least.

In the event, Barrett did not arrive for that meet. It annoyed me at the time but I would later have good reason to be grateful for the fact that he did not appear. Our E4(a) and HMSU cover vehicles left the area, one by one informing Sam of their departure. They had obviously more to do with their time than to sit around waiting for Barrett. Sam kept looking at his watch. We sat in that Police car and waited until 8.50 pm before Sam finally agreed to drive off. He was obviously very agitated about something. For some unknown reason, Sam was inclined to wait longer for Barrett than was usual in the circumstances.

Some Special Branch officers worked in that world of shadows, of mirrors. A world where nothing was ever what it appeared to be. Special Branch officers like Sam worked "in the Dark". They had to. They certainly did not want the likes of me shining some legal spotlight onto their activities. But not all Special Branch officers were involved in murky areas like this. I knew of other officers who had opted to settle into administrative posts following the Stalker revelations.

That decent majority of Special Branch officers would have been as much at odds with some of their number as I was. You had to treat each Special Branch officer as you found him. The treacherous ones did not appear with a label. But it was foolish for anyone to have a blanket respect for the Special Branch. The same applied to the rest of the Force. Respect was to be hard-earned.

It worried me more than a little that Barrett had not appeared to meet us. I could see him getting cold feet. I could also see my quarry slipping away from me. Trevor had remained on duty with me for a while, so I decided to ring Barrett at home. I was surprised when he answered the phone. He insisted that he had appeared for the meet on time but he had not seen us. He alleged that he had waited for a time before going home. He agreed to meet us at 11 pm at the same spot.

The record shows that I contacted a senior CID officer by pager through BRC. He rang me back. I explained that Barrett had not appeared for our initial meet and he now wanted to meet us at 11 pm. I wanted authority to go without the Special Branch officer as he did not want us to ask any questions about the murder of Pat Finucane. The answer was an emphatic "no". We (CID) had agreed with Special Branch that there would be no CID meets with this particular source without the Special Branch being present. I was told to inform Sam of the new time. I complied with that instruction.

We contacted Sam and he agreed to be there. We linked up with him and got into the Special Branch car in the same seating arrangements as before. Sam was in total control of the tape recorder. He would record the conversation with Barrett. He again repeated his assertion that we must not mention the murder of Pat Finucane.

We picked Barrett up at 11.05 pm at Nutts Corner and Sam drove to the same layby as before. I remember thinking that this was odd because we had realised during the last tape transcript that the layby had been a poor choice of venue. The noise of passing vehicles would drown out our voices. Sam had said that he would never park there again. What was he thinking of? Little did I know it at that time, but the answer would only become clear years later. The Special Branch believed that they were being very clever.

When Barrett got into the Police car on this second occasion, he immediately spoke excitedly about two murders that had occurred earlier that night. Henry Fleming Ward, a 42-year-old man, had been shot dead by two hooded gunmen from the Irish Peoples Liberation Organisation (IPLO) in the Diamond Jubilee Bar on the Shankill Road. Barrett alleged that Ward was a member of the UDA welfare, i.e. not part of the military ring. He could not understand why anyone would shoot this man.

He spoke of how their UDA Brigadier, Jim, had told all of the UFF units to stand still. They would retaliate as soon as they knew which Republican group was responsible. Jim would pick a target from that group. Barrett went on:

"Then what does that wee b*****d Johnny Adair do? He sends his boys from 'C' Company to whack the first Fenian taxi driver that they could find!" he exclaimed.

Barrett was in an extremely agitated state. I was aware that he was referring to the murder of Hugh Magee, a 52-year-old Catholic taxi driver who had been shot dead in his taxi as he drove out of Rosapenna Street onto the Oldpark Road in Belfast, within hours of the murder of Ward. Loyalists had shot him dead obviously in direct retaliation for the IPLO murder of Henry Ward. We suspected that members of the Shankill UDA's "C" Company were responsible. Barrett was now confirming it. Adair was running rings around us on the Shankill Road. No other military commander in the UFF was as ruthless or as blatantly sectarian as Adair. I cast a glance over at Trevor. He rolled his eyes to indicate his despair.

We engaged Barrett in the usual introductory conversation. We allowed him to ramble on for a time with only a few questions before Sam jabbed me in the knee in his usual manner, which meant I should to be quiet. I told Barrett that Sam had some questions from RUC Headquarters. I was expecting some gems. I was annoyed when he went over almost exactly the same ground as we had done at the previous meet on 3 October 1991.

Sam kept referring to his notes on that sheet of paper as if it was a shopping list. We waited patiently until he was finished. Barrett commented upon the fact that we had gone over all of this before. He was referring to our previous meeting. I couldn't understand the reasons for it myself. During this second meet, Barrett admitted out of the blue that he had been the gunman involved in the attempted murder of an alleged drug dealer from North Belfast called Tommy McCreery outside the Heather Street Club in the Woodvale.

The fact that McCreery had not been shot dead was no thanks to Barrett. As far as Barrett was concerned, he had failed his UFF masters. Now he was sitting in a Police car confessing to yet another horrific crime. How much more would my authorities need before they decided to move against this killer?

The record shows that we remained there with Barrett until 12.45 am on the morning of Friday, 11 October 1991. That was one hour and forty-two minutes, all told. It was towards the end of the meet that I asked Barrett a question that had been annoying me for years. I deliberately broke the rule that we were not to mention the Finucane murder. I could not resist this one question.

"Was Johnny Adair involved in the murder of Pat Finucane?" I asked.

I felt Sam's knee jamming against mine with a little more aggression than usual. I had half-expected that. His tape recorder would not pick up that little gesture. It was done simply to remind me not to question Barrett about the Finucane murder. I was not expecting Barrett's reaction to be so forceful. He came forward in his seat. He leaned over towards me and grabbed me by the arm as he always did when he wanted your undivided attention.

"No way, Jonty. Adair is a chocolate soldier. He is an armchair general. He has never shot anybody in his life," he said. "He hasn't got the balls for it. Everybody in the military knows that," he added.

"Really?" I asked.

Barrett deflated again like a balloon. There was no mistaking the animosity, the enmity he felt for Adair. That interested me. Trevor and I were studying Adair with a view to putting him in jail. I could exploit this apparent animosity between him and Barrett later.

It was time to close the meeting. Sam had only two more goals for that meet. He let Barrett choose a codename. Barrett himself chose the name Wesley. From then on he became known as Special Branch Agent Wesley. He was also given a dedicated Belfast telephone number that he was to use in future to contact his handlers. If anyone found that telephone number on him or saw it on his 'phone bill it could not be traced to the Police. Barrett was impressed. He was told never to contact the CID again directly. I was not so impressed. I could read between the lines. We were being pushed out of the equation within ten days of this man coming forward.

This was extremely unusual in a case where the agent was still insisting on no Special Branch involvement. How on earth could they remove the CID without rocking an already unsteady boat? I could smell a rat, but I had absolutely no idea just how far the Special Branch would go to remove me from the handling of this man. The chances of me getting to prosecute him were fading fast and I didn't like it. I wondered just whose interests the Special Branch was serving. This move was definitely not in the public interest, at any rate.

I only asked that one question that night about the murder of Pat Finucane. It had nothing at all to do with my pursuit of Barrett. Johnny Adair was already in my sights for a long period of imprisonment. But

Barrett did not know that. I wanted to know which murders Adair was involved in and which ones he had nothing to do with. According to Johnny Adair, he was up to his neck in everything that the UFF did. Everybody on the Shankill Road believed that Adair was actually involved in murder. I would have to watch that one.

Adair's terrorist credentials were in question here. Was he really just an organiser of UFF manpower? Was this new young terrorist godfather simply a director of terrorism? Whatever the truth was, it was an operational policing imperative that we put Adair in jail. Trevor and I intended to do just that. I had not believed some of our less informed UFF sources that Adair was actually never personally involved in the murders he had ordered them to do. Yet Barrett was confirming it and he would know.

It surprised me at the time to hear from Barrett that Adair had nothing whatsoever to do with the Finucane murder. We had long suspected him of being involved in the hijacking of the taxi in the Glencairn Estate that was used by the UFF in the murder.

In fairness to Sam, apart from that sharp jab to my knee he did not make a song-and-dance about my blatant breach of our agreement not to mention the Finucane murder. That surprised me.

What I did not know was that the Special Branch were working well ahead of me. They thought that they had just pulled a stroke of genius on us. Sam believed that he had just gained all that the Special Branch needed to keep them right in relation to any future enquiry into the Finucane murder and he knew that I had missed it. I was not thinking about the prospect of any later enquiry into the murder of Pat Finucane at that time. I was in that car in pursuit of the murderers of Pat Finucane on behalf of the RUC. I was not there to keep anyone right.

But then, I had nothing to fear from such an enquiry. Obviously the Special Branch or some of their associates had something to fear. It was fortunate for me that what they had just done would in fact lead to their own downfall and not to mine as they had intended. Unknown to me Thursday, 10 October 1991 would be a date that would become very important to me in later years. It was the date on which the Special Branch had for once outwitted itself.

At the time, 10 October 1991 had come and gone just like any other day for me. The fact that we had been allowed to meet Barrett again as a potential informant had surprised me. Surprised is not a strong enough word. It astonished me. I knew that by meeting him again we had substantially ruined any later attempts to bring him to book for the murder of the solicitor Pat Finucane. I was not happy about that. I was being forced to abandon everything that I was sworn to do. I sought out a senior Police officer whom I knew I could trust with my life. We sat in my car twenty miles from Castlereagh, well away from the prying eyes and ears of the RUC Special Branch.

He listened intently as I related to him the events of 1, 3 and 10 October 1991. When I had finished briefing him, he sat there shaking his head. I waited for his analysis of the situation and for his advice.

"Them boys will have their own reasons for not going after Barrett just yet," he said. "There had to be a good reason not to move, Jonty," he added.

"But what about our old adage of 'strike while the iron is hot'?" I asked.

"Without having all of the facts, it's hard to say what they are playing at," he said.

I had to agree. I wasn't happy with it but I had to agree. The other side of this coin was that a monster like Barrett would remain free to murder again. He would remain at large to terrorise the community. The irony of it all was that now Barrett would interpret our deliberate failure to pursue him as clear approval of all that he had done. I wanted to be no part of that. I fully intended to distance myself from that. It sickened me to the core.

"So what can we do?" I asked.

"Go with the flow, Jonty. There is nothing else you can do," he said.

So what was new? What did I expect this man to say? There was no other avenue open. No right of appeal.

We discussed my enthusiasm to pursue Barrett. The senior Police officer agreed with my analysis. We were duty-bound to prosecute Barrett and if he then implicated RUC officers we were duty-bound to go after them too. He agreed wholeheartedly with my theory, but his support came with a caveat.

"Be very, very careful, Jonty. The Branch can swat you as if you were a fly," he said. "And from what I have heard over the years, they are just waiting for their chance to remove you from your high horse," he added.

I got out of my car and stood with this man in the rain. I shook his hand firmly. I liked this guy enormously. He epitomised everything that was decent about this kind of copper. The RUC was made up of many fine men just like him. The problem was, he genuinely felt that he could do nothing about these apparently perverse decisions made by our "friends" in the Special Branch. Decisions that we all knew were gradually bringing the whole of our Constabulary into disrepute.

I stood there in the rain and watched as he drove out of the darkness of the car park into the well-lit roadway. The rain was almost torrential. It ran down the back of my neck, sending cold shivers up my spine. I wished it could wash away my feelings of being tainted. Wash away my revulsion at our impotence to do anything about the decision not to go for Barrett. I had so wanted that senior officer to tell me that there was an answer, a simple solution to our problem. That there was something I had missed. But he hadn't. He couldn't.

I got into my car and drove to Carrickfergus to speak to Trevor. During the twenty-minute drive there, it struck me that there was another way to skin this particular cat! Barrett was unaware of my intention to bring him to book for the murder of Pat Finucane. In fact, I was now in a favoured position with him. My mind drifted back to his account of the young getaway driver whom he alleged was from Rathcoole.

According to Barrett, the Finucane murder was this young man's "first job" for the UFF. He had panicked. Barrett himself had conceded that the driver was unaware that the UFF mission he had volunteered for was a murder. Barrett had also said that he had taken immediate steps to make sure that it was the lad's "last job" for the UFF. These were allegations which if true would mean that that young driver fitted well into the new criteria for becoming a "converted terrorist" or CT. The potential witness should be a terrorist only recently involved in terrorism. He should have operated within his terrorist group on the periphery only. It would be to our advantage if the potential CT had little or no criminal record. Barrett's description of the getaway driver intrigued me. If he was telling us the truth, we had a potential CT on our hands.

But first we would have to identify him. Only Barrett could help us do that. Once he was identified, I intended to arrest him and interview him in Castlereagh. I also intended to explain the options open to him. In effect I was going to make him an offer that he could not refuse. If this young man chose to tell us the truth and clean his slate, we would then convict him. With the full weight of the Crown and the system behind him, I would then bring him out of jail and spin him against Barrett and the others involved. But how on earth would I get his name from Barrett? He was already aware of the danger of us catching up on the driver. On the tape of 3 October 1991, he had twigged my intention right away. This wasn't going to be easy but there was no other way to advance our cause. If this worked we could still clear up the murder of Pat Finucane. If Barrett's own candid and boastful confession to the murder was not enough to breathe fresh life into that cold case, perhaps the evidence of the young getaway driver might swing the odds in our favour.

According to my record, it was not until Tuesday, 22 October 1991 that the Special Branch pulled a stroke on us that should have alerted me to the fact that the source-handling of Ken Barrett was going to be different to any source-handling that I had ever experienced. Trevor and I were busy interviewing the UFF Brigadier Jim at the Police Office in Castlereagh when Barrett rang in, looking for a meet. He must have been short of cash for gambling on the dogs: he was a frequent visitor to the dog track at Dunmore Stadium.

We agreed that Sam could go alone to meet Barrett with some of his colleagues covering him. We had no other choice. Barrett might very well have information that could save a life. Sam was to waste no time exploiting our absence.

It was Barrett himself who brought the Special Branch antics to our attention. From those very first days of handling this murderer, the Special Branch had moved behind the scenes to frustrate us in any way that they could. We just did not know it. But by 22 October 1991, they had obviously decided to "up the ante".

According to the record, Barrett complained to us on Thursday, 24 October 1991 that he had turned up to meet us (CID) on Tuesday, 22 October 1991 and found that Sam was accompanied by another Police officer. Barrett was furious. He said that Sam had "boasted" to him that he was a Special Branch officer. He said Sam had threatened him. If he would not work solely for the Special Branch, they (the Special Branch) would make sure the UFF knew that he worked for the CID. Sam had referred to the CID as "clowns" and "dickheads".

Sam told Barrett that his bosses in Special Branch had decided that there would no more joint CID and Special Branch meets. Barrett said that Sam was intimidating. I listened with embarrassment as this cold-blooded murderer complained of alleged "dirty tricks" by the

Special Branch. I listened as he spoke about the Special Branch in the lowest possible terms. What could I say? He now knew that I had told him lies.

I had told him that Sam was a CID man because I had been ordered to. But the first chance he got, Sam had told Barrett that he was a Special Branch officer. This was against an agreed CID/Special Branch policy. Sam had believed that Barrett would be impressed. The fool had not believed me when I had made it clear that Barrett hated the Special Branch. Barrett's final complaint angered me.

"Sam says the CID can't get me money. He says you are a nobody, Jonty. You interview people in Castlereagh and the important people, like him, don't interview in Castlereagh. You and Trevor got me £100 but Sam gave me £500. What's the f****n' score, Jonty?" he asked.

Sam was right about the money. The Special Branch could get their hands on tens of thousands of pounds if it was necessary. To give a moron like Barrett £500 for nothing was against all the rules that we had to adhere to in the CID. This was a fact of life for us. Source handling and intelligence gathering was the primary function of the Special Branch. But it was a very minor part of the day-to-day duties of a detective in the CID. There was no way that we could compete with the Special Branch on a financial score. Our CID source reward budget was tight and by late October 1991 we were already half way through the financial year for 1991/92.

Again I had to bite my lip.

"Can you get me cash, Jonty?" Barrett asked again.

I decided to wing it.

"Of course I can," I lied.

"Well, listen to me, you told me that Sam is a decent fella. You told me I could trust him. Well, I'm telling you that you can't trust him. Now get him out of the f****n' car!" he said.

None of this surprised me. Sam had always made it clear that he saw no role for CID in the area of source-handling. His contempt for the CID in general and for me in particular was evident. I knew exactly what Sam was at. He was attempting to squeeze Trevor and me out of the equation. He was not doing this without the full authority and support of his Special Branch authorities. But why? Why risk alienating Barrett? Why make me out to be the liar?

There had been an element of Sam trying to impress Barrett. That had backfired on him. He had not impressed anyone, least of all

Barrett. These tactics were not uncommon where there was friction in
the joint handling of sources, but what made this stand out from the
norm was the timing. The Special Branch knew that this source was
unpredictable. These were not the first complaints from Barrett about
Sam. But prior to this Barrett had believed that Sam was a CID officer.
Given Barrett's hatred of the Special Branch, it was an odd juncture at
which to try to wrest control of him. It was as if it had been done
deliberately to frighten Barrett off. The Special Branch was at its work.
I intended to stay in with Barrett. I needed to speak to him out of the
presence and hearing of Special Branch officers. I needed the name of
the young man who drove the getaway car in the Finucane murder. If
he really did not know that his two UFF accomplices were going to
commit murder, then it was improbable that he could take us towards
those responsible at the top of the UFF echelons. But it was highly likely
that he could identify Barrett and Millar and some of the others. It
would be up to us then to get the rest of them.

We brought Barrett's complaints to the attention of our CID
authorities. We received no support. Sam and his friends could do
whatever they liked. No-one in the CID was going to question the
absolute authority of the Special Branch.

In the meantime, Barrett was proving to be productive. In those
first few weeks of his contact with us, he had volunteered the names
of several RUC men who, he alleged, were passing information on
Republicans to the UDA/UFF. We also recovered one firearm and
ammunition in the Woodvale Estate. Documents seized led to the
preferring of charges and a term in prison against a notorious UFF
gunman who had previously always evaded detection. But in com-
parison with our other sources, Barrett would have been no better
than our usual "£20-a-week man", a term even he himself used to
describe our "lower" informants. For the fact was that in almost all of
the most serious crimes that Barrett told us about, he was the principal
offender. He was the perpetrator. In this context, his future potential
as an informant was questionable.

Trevor and I were able to engineer a few meetings with Barrett
without the Special Branch. It was not easy but we were able to
manage it. The friction that this caused between the CID and the
Special Branch was unbelievable. The Branch gave us no reason why
it should not happen. They were doing exactly the same thing. Their
protests were completely over the top. Why should we not speak to

Barrett without them? No reasons were forthcoming to our authorities. At least no reason that was to be communicated to us. So in the absence of any good or valid reason, Trevor and I continued to meet Barrett alone on a few more occasions. We always met him in Glencairn Park on the fringe of the Loyalist Forthriver/Glencairn Estate.

Our first-line supervisors had to be aware of everything that we had done. It was not in their interests to turn a blind eye to our activities. Nor did we want them to. Our notebooks and journals were kept meticulously, indicating what we had done and exactly who had authorised it. Checks and balances were in place to keep everyone right and that was the way we liked it. Personally speaking, I would not have liked to operate in any other way. So when we did work with the Special Branch, we turned our back on all of those procedures that could keep us within the law. Therefore, we had to either walk away and turn a blind eye to the activities of the Special Branch, or stay aboard and weather the storm. In the case of Ken Barrett and some others, Trevor and I decided on the latter. It was the only way that we could protect the public interest.

In any case, Barrett was so very different. He was a cold-blooded serial killer. He was small in stature, and very thin and gaunt. He used his wild, staring eyes to reinforce his points. He was perhaps the most evil-looking individual it had ever been my duty to meet. We would park up in an agreed place and at an agreed time and wait for Barrett's arrival. We would never see him first. Suddenly the back door of our car would open and he would jump in behind us.

Trevor and I had dubbed him "Freddy Krueger", after the sinister main character of the "A Nightmare on Elm Street" series of horror movies. I argued that Barrett would frighten the life clean out of Freddy Krueger. When you were in the presence of Ken Barrett you knew that you were in the presence of evil.

It always struck me as odd the way that Barrett would boast openly of his involvement in horrific crimes including murder. It was as if he had done so many times before to other RUC men who had done nothing about it. I had my own suspicions as to exactly which branch of the RUC that was, however I kept them to myself.

We would ask Barrett to name or to help us identify the young driver from Rathcoole. He just laughed at us and came back with his usual remark:

"No way, Jonty. You'll turn that wee bastard against me," he would say.

On one occasion, Barrett became so upset that he threatened to take the young driver "out of the equation". I backed off. Barrett would kill him. There was no question about it. If he posed a risk to Barrett's freedom, Barrett would not hesitate.

I was on duty in Tennent Street CID office on the afternoon of 30 October 1991 when one of Sam's supervisors sought me out. What he proposed next astounded me.

"You will never meet Barrett again on your own. It is not enough to bring Trevor. There will be no more CID only meets," he said.

I didn't answer him. His arrogance irritated me. His tone angered me. I cast my eyes to the sky.

"Give me that in writing and I'll consider it," I said finally.

The atmosphere was tense.

"I don't have to give you anything in writing, Jonty," he replied.

He was right of course. That would never do. Obstruction was never done in writing. It couldn't be. Can you just imagine the paper trail that that would have left?

"Furthermore, you have been discussing the identities of the people that Barrett named for recent murders with your own CID authorities. That will stop from today too," he said.

"Says who?" I asked.

"Says our authorities," he replied.

"I will speak to my own authorities," I said.

"Go ahead. It's been agreed. No more CID only meets," he said.

I let it go. I had to accept it. We had never met Barrett without the approval of our own authorities. If the Special Branch had removed that then we were beaten. Only a fool would meet an agent of Barrett's ilk without the proper authority. I had no intention of falling foul of any of our written instructions.

I had really no idea of the lengths that the Special Branch would go to stop me asking any more questions about the murder of Pat Finucane. Things were about to take a very sinister twist.

Chapter 12
Putting the Mix In

On Saturday, 2 November 1991 I was off duty and at home when I received a telephone call from Ken Barrett. This in itself was very unusual because he had been ringing in on the Special Branch direct line number. He had been told never to ring me at home for any reason. I was surprised to hear his gruff, aggressive tone. The conversation went something like this:

"Hello," I said.

"It's me, Ken," he said. "What the f**k is this about you are going to put me in jail for the murder of Pat Finucane?" his voice rising in anger.

"What? Who said that?" I asked. "Ken, it's only a mix. They are trying to put the mix in between us. Sam knows that you can't stand the Special Branch. He's trying to make you more comfortable with his presence by turning you against the CID," I said.

Barrett went quiet. That short silence seemed interminable. I waited and let him speak first.

"Sam's not that smart," Barrett replied.

"No, maybe not, but his bosses are. They are trying to turn you against the CID and it's working," I said.

I thought I had swung things in my favour. Thanks to Sam's antics, Barrett was well aware of the friction that we had with the Special Branch. I waited for his reply.

"You are always asking me about that murder, Jonty," he said.

I couldn't deny it. I played for more time.

"I only asked you about the driver from Rathcoole, Ken," I said.

There was silence. That was good. At least he had stopped screaming down the telephone at me.

"I want to see you, Jonty. I want to look into them big brown eyes of yours. I'll know if you're lying and see if you are, I'll put two in your face!" he said.

"No problem, what time, Ken?" I asked.

Barrett gave me a time. He would be at the "usual" place waiting to speak to me. I put the phone down and lifted it again to ring Trevor. I hoped that Trevor could go with me. Not to go was not an option. I had to confront Barrett and I had to do it face-to-face. The telephone was not the right medium. Anyway, I was aware that the Special Branch was monitoring all of Barrett's telephone calls. If I wanted to get into counter name-calling and questioning credibility with Barrett, the telephone was definitely not the medium to use to do it. Sam had inadvertently warned me weeks ago that they were on "Barrett's blower".

He had been able to quote me chapter and verse of a conversation I had with Barrett where I had made derogatory remarks about the Special Branch. He didn't realise that he had alerted me until I brought it to his attention that the only way he could have known about it was if he had had a "tap" on Barrett's wire. He denied it.

I told Rebecca that I had to go and meet a very, very dangerous informant. I told her that I was concerned that I would not be coming home, that no matter how we died, even if it was apparently a traffic accident, she should have it fully investigated. I wrote out Barrett's name and address and told her to take that to a certain trusted Chief Inspector of Police if anything happened to me. I wasn't being melodramatic. I was not exaggerating the danger that we faced. I just wanted to ensure that if anything untoward did happen, a vigorous and independent investigation would ensue.

The RUC Special Branch had taken a conscious decision to warn a cold-blooded, ruthless Loyalist killer that I was coming after him to put him in jail for the murder of Pat Finucane. They were trying to close all avenues of this enquiry. That sent me a clear signal. They were obviously keen to protect someone. But who, and why?

I reassured Rebecca that both Trevor and I would be armed. We would do our best to make sure that we came home safely. The situation was unbelievable. The Special Branch knew the sort of man Barrett was. They knew that he had stalked the "killing fields" of North Belfast for years, murdering with impunity. He represented everything that was evil about the Troubles. He was the best example of the worst-case scenario and the Special Branch were turning this monster on me. My blood boiled.

Trevor and I were early for the meet with Barrett. We parked in the middle of the car park away from the trees and bushes. We wanted to be able to watch him approach our car in the darkness. We needed to ensure that he was not carrying anything. We sat there for fifteen minutes after the due time, each moment waiting for a burst of automatic gunfire from the darkness of the tree line. It never came. True to form, one of the rear doors of our car opened without warning and Barrett lay down flat on the back seat.

"Drive," he instructed.

Trevor drove off out of the car park to a secluded laneway not a mile from the pick-up point. When we stopped Barrett sat up and got straight to the point, his finger poking at me and his eyes wild and staring.

"Sam says I'm not to speak to you two. He hates you, Jonty. He says you are going to put me in jail for the Finucane murder," he said.

I wasted no time. Two could play at this game. I was determined that if there was going to be a fight for credibility then the CID were going to come out on top. The problem was, I could not exclude Sam in the same manner that he could exclude me. The Walker guidelines were clear and non-negotiable. But yet so often in the past when the Walker recommendations came down on our side, the Special Branch agenda had still taken precedence over important CID operations. On those rare occasions, the Special Branch had successfully argued that the directives of the Walker Report were intended to be mere guidelines. My CID authorities would not have dared to argue with that.

Whatever I was to say in reply it had to keep Sam sweet. We had to keep him in on this if we were to adhere to our written instructions.

"Sam is just putting the mix in, Ken. If we were going to arrest you for the murder of Pat Finucane, we would have done it long ago," I lied.

Barrett stared and stared at me, his wild eyes ablaze. He was searching for as much as a hint of betrayal. He found none. I stared back into those evil eyes and held his gaze.

"Sam wants to turn you against us," I said. "He wants you to relate solely to the Branch and not to the CID. This is the only way he can do it," I argued forcefully.

"Well, he can think again, Jonty. He does hate you. Can you get him out of the car?"

There was no way that I could do that. I decided to try to redeem a situation in which this source was losing confidence in the Special Branch. A situation of their own making. I leaned over the seat to get closer to Barrett.

"It is in the interests of everyone in this car to keep them aboard and that includes you, Ken," I said truthfully.

Barrett was not convinced. It took us the best part of two hours to persuade him to allow Sam to stay with us on the meets. When he was about to leave the car, he stretched out his hand and offered it to me in a handshake. I deliberately dropped a file full of papers from my knee. I bent forward to retrieve them. Barrett was gone from our midst before I sat up again. The atmosphere in the car lifted in an instant. The Special Branch attempt to shut Barrett's mouth had failed miserably. He was obviously more loyal to us than he was to them. This would later prove to be to my personal advantage.

Unknown to me, during my absence from home, Rebecca was on the telephone speaking to our good friend Carrie in Donaghadee when a newsflash came up onto the TV screen to say that two RUC men had been killed in a collision with a bus whilst travelling on the M2. Rebecca started to scream. She thought that Trevor and I had been murdered. Carrie calmed her down. Her husband Arthur, a former RUC detective, said that he would find out if it was Trevor and I and ring her back. For Rebecca it seemed like an age before Arthur rang back to say that it was not Trevor and I who had been killed.

I knew nothing about all of this until I arrived home with Trevor. As I got out of the car, Rebecca rushed over to me and hugged and hugged me. We both had packed more stress, more anxiety into those last few hours than most people would have to cope with in years. I brought Rebecca up to speed with the developments of the day. By the time I had finished relating the story of Barrett to her from start to finish, we were both more than ready for bed. It had been one hell of a stressful day. Was there no end to the treachery of the RUC Special Branch?

My records show that we met Ken Barrett several more times with the Special Branch. The meetings were fraught. We didn't really want Sam there. Barrett definitely didn't want Sam there and Sam didn't want Trevor and me there. It was all so petty. So unnecessary and the very presence of the Special Branch was having a negative effect upon our attempts to get to Barrett or to the truth about the murder of Pat Finucane. It was deliberate obstruction.

On 15 January 1992, Barrett rang me at home to ask me why I hadn't been in touch. Barrett named another man that the UFF had identified as a Special Branch informant. He used this case to illustrate why he did not want to work for them. I told him I would explain the ground rules to him again. I reassured Barrett that I would be in the car with the Special Branch for only as long as he insisted that I remain. Once he was happy with his Special Branch masters, I was away. Barrett was happy to hear that. There was nothing more I could say. I knew that the Special Branch was listening in to every word.

By 18 February 1992, Barrett was so "spooked" by the antics of the Special Branch that he was simply ringing in the information to us. He was also insisting that we "drop" any cash due to him at a pre-arranged spot. The Special Branch was having none of it. They wrongly believed that I had influenced Barrett. Once again, they were judging me by their own standards.

One month later Barrett was complaining again. On Friday, 13 March 1992 he told me that the Special Branch were ringing him at home and putting him under extreme pressure to work for them only. I was sick of it. None of it surprised me. I brought it to the attention of my authorities in the CID. They promised to look into it. By this stage I was merely going through the motions. I had no chance of getting to Barrett or anyone else for that matter in relation to the murder of Pat Finucane, or any other criminal offence that Barrett had confessed to.

Barrett was now Special Branch "Agent Wesley". For the last five months he had been a "protected bird". He now had the full backing of the RUC Special Branch. No-one could touch him. He just did not realise it. He did not trust them. A cold-blooded Loyalist serial killer had joined the ranks of that Special Branch army of agents. They did not care one iota about the blood on his hands. It did not interest them.

I was next due to meet Barrett with Sam at 6.30 pm on the evening of Monday, 16 March 1992. Little did I know it, but that would be the last time that I would meet Barrett in an intelligence-gathering role. Treacherous elements within the RUC Special Branch were just about to excel themselves in their efforts to get me out of the way. Even with all of my long experience of their "dirty tricks", I did not expect what happened next.

According to my record I commenced duty at Tennent Street RUC Station at 8 am on the morning of 16 March 1992. By the time 6 pm came around, I had already been on duty for ten hours. It surprised me when Sam the Branch man did not even make an appearance at Tennent Street to go with me to see Barrett. It wasn't like him. He had many faults but time-keeping was not one of them. I waited until a quarter past six before I rang him at home.

"Hello," Sam answered the phone.

"Hello, Sam, we are due to meet Wesley (Barrett) at 6.30 pm. What's happening? Did he ring in to cancel?" I asked.

"No. No. I forgot all about it," he said in a very matter-of-fact manner.

There was no hint of the usual urgency. I immediately sensed that something was wrong. I started to take notes. Sam broke the silence.

"Go ahead and meet him on your own," he said.

Something was wrong. The Special Branch had always forbidden me to meet this man on my own. My own CID authorities had agreed that we would not meet him alone. Yet here was my most vociferous Special Branch critic inviting me to actually do just that. My alarm bells began to ring. This was unheard of. We always tried to have at least one other CID officer present. We would never go alone. Not without good cause. I bluntly refused.

"Then take Trevor with you," Sam said flippantly.

"Trevor is on duty but he is not available to go with me," I explained.

Sam told me to ring Barrett at home and change the meeting time to 8.30 pm. If Barrett agreed to meet us at that time then he would get some cash and go with me. None of it sounded genuine. I knew that I would have to be very careful here. Was this a precursor to a Special Branch dirty trick? I asked Sam pointedly if there was something that he knew that I did not.

"No," he replied.

I brought it to his attention that Barrett was still complaining that he (Sam) was putting him under pressure to work solely for the Special Branch. Sam denied this on the telephone even though he often admitted it when speaking to me personally. Sam was afraid of his own phone taps! I put the telephone down. My relief Detective Sergeant Ian handed me a cup of tea. He had obviously detected the caution in my tone of voice.

"Is everything alright?" he asked.

No, everything was not all right, I wanted to scream. I wanted to pour my heart out to him. I wanted to tell him what was happening and ask his advice about what I should do next. God knows he was trustworthy enough and straight enough, but I knew better than to say a word.

"Yes, thank you, everything is fine," I replied.

I lifted the telephone in the CID office at around 6.25 pm and rang Barrett's home telephone number. Beverley Quirey answered the phone:

"Hello?"

"Is Ken there?" I asked in reply.

"No, he left here at ten past six to go and meet someone," she said.

I hoped that she had not recognised my voice. I tried to ring Sam back at home but his telephone was continuously engaged. Barrett would be standing there now waiting for us. He might even have vital information that could save a life. I grabbed my enquiry folder, my Police radio telephone and rushed to my car. I would worry about the ramifications of source-handling niceties later. I felt I had no choice but to go alone.

I drove out of Tennent Street and went directly to Glencairn Park. I arrived there at 6.40 pm, ten minutes late for the meet. A small, white, van drove in and out of the car park. There was only one man in it, yet it was very low down on its rear axle, as if it was carrying a lot of weight in the rear. There could well be other men in that van. My instinct told me to be wary. My revolver was sitting just under my right thigh. I wished Trevor was with me.

I noted the name of an engineering company with an address in an industrial estate in Castlereagh emblazoned on the side of the van. I noted the registration number and the unit address on my folder. I was tempted to use my radio telephone to call assistance to check the van, but the last thing I wanted was a car park full of coppers. This would serve only to "spook" Barrett if he did appear.

There was no sign of Barrett. It was raining so heavily that he must have decided to leave when no-one turned up. I waited until 7 pm before driving out of that car park onto the Forthriver Road. I was hungry, so I stopped to buy a meal at a chip shop on the Ballygomartin Road. I switched my Police radio telephone off before I entered the shop.

Unknown to me, Barrett was back at home. He rang my home and asked to speak to me. When he was told I was on duty, he asked Rebecca to contact me and cancel the meet. Rebecca rang the CID office in Tennent Street and spoke to Ian, who tried to get me on the air, but my radio telephone was still switched off. When I had finished my light meal, I drove back into Glencairn Park in my own car. I wanted to see if that van had moved on. The rain had stopped. I arrived back at 7.12 pm. I was surprised to see Barrett walk towards me with a small dog on a lead. He jumped into the front seat beside me and put his little dog in between his legs.

As far as I was aware, Barrett had been expecting a cash meet. He was going to be very disappointed. I got in right away to tell him that the Special Branch had not turned up. There would be no cash. What follows is an account taken from a copy of my RUC journal entry for the day.

"Do you not know what the score is, Jonty?" Barrett asked, his wild eyes staring.

"Know what?" I asked.

"You are in deep shit, Jonty, you are finished. Those bastards hate you," he said.

Barrett said that he knew that Sam would not be there. He stated that Sam had met him with two other men last Thursday night, 12 March 1992, and they had told him not to meet me. He was not allowed to ever agree to meet me again. I was intrigued. I was hanging onto every word. It was such a scene, so out of the norm, that I will never forget it. I wished Trevor was there to support me.

Barrett was not impressed. Not with any of this. Worry and fear were etched across his face. A serial killer was afraid of the Special Branch. This was something to witness. The Special Branch were now terrorising the terrorist.

"It was Sam who told me to phone you and cancel the meet," he said. "I asked him what reason I would give you for cancelling and he said that was my problem. He told me not to speak to you again. He said that you won't be here much longer," he added.

Barrett was studying me, looking for a reaction. He smelt bad. I hadn't noticed that before. The car was also filled with that distinctive musty "wet dog" smell and the dog was shaking the excess water from its back into the floorwell. The small, white van drove back into the car park and parked alongside us. The driver never looked in our direction. That was odd. No eye contact. That was something we were trained to do while we watched the activities of criminals or terrorists. To avoid eye contact at all costs. Was he a Police officer or was he from some other branch of the Security Services? I must have studied him for too long. Barrett noticed him too.

"Who the f**k is that?" asked Barrett. "Is he with you?" he added.

"No," I replied.

The presence of that van parked as closely as it was to us in the large car park where there were no other vehicles about caused me concern. I started the car and drove off out of the car park and up the laneway. I went to the very top of the laneway and turned to go back down again. I pulled my car into a gateway to a field two-thirds of the way down the lane and parked up, leaving ample room for any other cars to pass. I turned off my lights. I was now in a position to see any cars approaching us from a quarter of a mile down that lane. Barrett started again.

"I asked Sam what did he mean, you wouldn't be here, was somebody going to 'whack' (shoot) you," he said.

"And what did he say?" I asked.

I needed all of this. I needed as much as that fool Sam had confided in Barrett. When had all this happened? And where? Was Sam alone with Barrett or did he convey all of this or any of it by telephone? Would the Special Branch have any record of it which my CID authorities could listen to? Would they make it available?

"Sam says they are going to put a serious UFF threat on you and put the mix in with your bosses to get rid of you," he said. "They were arguing in the car in front of me about how a threat on its own wouldn't shift you. They said it would take more than a threat."

Barrett became agitated. He was obviously very worried. I was about to answer him when my attention was drawn to the headlights of a vehicle coming up the laneway towards us. Barrett leaned over to see what had caught my eye. The vehicle sped past us. It was the same small, white van. Just before it came level with us I had turned on my headlights. It was the same man alone in the cab. He did not look at us as he drove past.

"Is that your cover?" Barrett asked.

"No, as far as I know it's not Police," I replied.

"So it could be them other bastards, couldn't it?" he asked.

"I honestly don't know," I replied.

"Are you carrying?" he asked, in a direct reference to my revolver.

"No," I lied. I tried to take the drama out of the situation.

I showed Barrett my folder with the van's registration number and the firm's details written down. He opened his passenger door slightly, causing the interior light to come on. I reached up and turned it off.

"If that van stops behind us or beside us when it comes back down, I'm out of here," he said.

Barrett was judging the suspicious activities of the occupants of the white van by his own standards. He honestly feared that they were assassins. If the van stopped near us, he was not for hanging about. I got the distinct impression that he would leave his little dog and me to our own devices. He had murdered enough people himself to recognise what could well be a preamble to murder.

Within a minute or two, car headlights appeared again as a vehicle travelled down the lane towards us. It could have been anyone. There were several houses at the top of that lane. As it got closer, Barrett dropped the dog's lead into the floorwell of the car and put one foot on the ground outside. If this was the Special Branch and the aim was to "spook" Barrett, it was working.

I never met Barrett, not once, without a fully-loaded revolver under my right thigh. My hand reached for the warm wooden pistol grip of the Ruger .357 Magnum revolver. It was reassuring. Nonetheless, I knew that if these guys were UFF terrorists who had been watching Barrett, it was unlikely that I would ever get a chance to use it. I prayed that the occupants of that van were Police.

The same van drove past us quickly again without stopping. I put my headlights on and checked that I had noted the correct registration number. I had. Barrett put his leg back into the floorwell and closed the car door. I laughed at him and told him to settle down but the truth was that the white van had me worried too.

"Oh yes, they are going to put a serious threat on you and put a 'mix' in with your bosses. They say that will shift you," Barrett continued. "Look what's happening here, Jonty. Them boys are scary bastards. Sam told me that his boss says that from now on, I'm only to meet the Special Branch."

None of this surprised me. The fools, I thought. I let him go on.

"Sam wants me to meet a new fella with him. He says the CID are clowns and he says you are f*****g them about," he added.

I sat there in the darkness in that secluded laneway listening to a killer tell me of how Sam and two other Special Branch officers were conspiring to transfer me out of the Belfast region. Why was it so important that they stop me talking to Barrett about the murder of Pat Finucane? Something was wrong. They had told Barrett the Thursday before that as long as the CID was in the car there would be no more money. If he agreed to meet two Special Branch officers, they would pay him hundreds of pounds on each meet.

Barrett went on to say that when he did not agree to work for them, Sam told him that he had no choice. When Barrett disagreed with that, they threatened him. In an obvious bid to impress Barrett, Sam told him that they could transfer me at any time. Far from impressing his agent, however, Sam had actually demonstrated to his source the depths of treachery that he would stoop to get rid of me. He had only succeeded in alienating him. Barrett had not stopped contacting me. In fact he was now sitting beside me warning me of Special Branch betrayal. Barrett was annoyed at the Special Branch. He did not believe that I would go after him for the murder of Pat Finucane. He could not know that the only people who had saved him from a life sentence were the very men he was now complaining about. It was a funny old world, this dark place that the Special Branch worked in. They obviously had their reasons for helping Barrett. But whatever those reasons might be, I could not see the logic of it. In fact there was more than a little chance that what they were doing was totally illegal. I had no wish to be any part of that.

Now even I was afraid. It wasn't because I had done anything wrong. You didn't have to do anything wrong. The Special Branch would use their usual spin, their nods and winks and innuendos. There were so many senior Police officers out there who were professionally jealous of our achievements. Most of them would be only too willing to embrace any allegations that might be made against me. They would try to make it fit. I thought it ironic when I heard Barrett question my judgement.

"You told me that Sam is a decent fella. You said he could be trusted and I believed you. Now he's even going to Judas you, Jonty, so how can I trust him?" he asked.

That was a fair question but it was no longer my problem. I had realised from the extremely sinister turn of events that the Special Branch would go to any lengths to keep me away from Barrett. They were monitoring his telephone so they knew that he had cancelled this meeting with me. He had told me that earlier. He had walked here with his dog in case I did not get his message. I was so glad that he did show up. This killer did not realise just how important his warning was to me. He was concerned only about the ramifications of all of this for himself.

If that white van had nothing to do with the Special Branch, then they would not know that I had spoken to him at all. Not until it was too late. It was not often that CID officers got a warning in advance of Special Branch's intent to pull one of their dirty tricks. Thanks to Sam's stupidity, I got my advance warning from an evil Loyalist killer. Barrett went on:

"Sam asked me have I ever been to your house, Jonty. Why would he ask me that?" Barrett said.

"I have no idea," I replied.

I knew exactly why Sam had asked Barrett that. One of the golden rules of source-handling is that you do not become too familiar with your informants. To take an informant home is taboo. But those rules are fine for London or Birmingham or Manchester. Here in Northern Ireland, CID officers could not take our CID sources into RUC Stations. To do so would have been to risk the exposure and compromise of the source. You could not be sure that a Police officer sympathetic to one side of the paramilitaries or the other would not see the source and report him to his paramilitary cronies. This was a very real risk. So, yes, I did take some of my informants to my home. There were conditions that I won't go into here. There were checks and balances. There had to be. For instance, senior CID officers were made fully aware of whom we brought there and why it was necessary to do so. I do not recall one objection. But Barrett or evil individuals like Barrett were never invited to my home.

The Special Branch were being mischievous. They were looking for failings; even minor breaches of procedures or protocol would do. The knives were out and the Special Branch believed that they were about to gut me. No-one would be able to stop them. Barrett went on:

"Sam asked me how I got your home telephone number, Jonty. I told him I got it from Tennent Street, but he insisted that you gave it to me. I didn't let you down," Barrett said.

These boys were scraping the barrel but they were right this time. I did give Barrett my home telephone number. They had complained to my CID authorities about the same thing very early on in the handling of Barrett. I had told the truth.

I gave dozens of our well-placed informants my home telephone number. Some of them even knew my address. It wasn't to exchange Christmas cards. It was simply to ensure the quick flow of vital information that could save a life. The informants needed to be able to contact me immediately at any time of the day or night. It did not benefit me personally. In fact, it cost me financially because on many occasions our informants contacted us from telephone boxes. We would ring them back. If I was to face a disciplinary charge, I could argue my case.

"Sam asked me if I know where you live and I said no. Sam wasn't too happy about that," Barrett continued.

I bet he wasn't, I thought.

"Then he asked me did I know that Johnny Adair and Jim Spence know where you live, Jonty," he said. "I told Sam that that's f**k all. The UFF wouldn't touch you. They respect you because you are fair to everybody," Barrett added. "Then Sam comes up with this shit that the UFF know where your ma lives. Aye, that's right but so what?"

I listened intently to what Barrett was saying. I could see exactly where the Special Branch were going with all of this. Taking informants home. Giving them my home telephone number. They could make the allegation that these two senior UFF men, Adair and Spence, were targeting both me and my very elderly mother. Johnny Adair himself had made me aware of a contact he had in Holywood who had told him my mother's address. I had reported that officially when I received it from Adair. The Special Branch were building this into a very serious threat.

My authorities would certainly take these threats and my alleged failings very seriously. How were they to know the "threat" was being devised by the Special Branch in the presence of a UFF killer with the sole intent of removing me from the equation? It would be laughable if it weren't so serious.

Barrett was getting nervous. He had been in my car for too long. He was obviously very frightened.

"Don't tell them boys I have warned you about this, Jonty. Get them out of the car," he said.

I explained that it was not unusual to have in-fighting when you are dealing with Special Branch officers of Sam's sort. But it had not ever been as sinister as this at any time before in my service. Where would it all end? How far would these people go? It was lucky for Sam that Barrett was not very clever. He had not realised that his telephone calls were being monitored. I had warned him before on several occasions that we had become aware that all of the paramilitary groups tapped the telephones of their volunteers who they suspected of being inform-ants. He didn't believe me. That was his prerogative.

But now it was vitally important to me that Barrett did not inadvertently alert Sam to the fact that he had warned me. I told him to watch what he said on his telephone for the next few days. Barrett made to leave the car. He said he would walk home from where we were parked. He wanted to.

"Sam says he will burn me if I don't work for them. What the f**k does "burn" mean, Jonty?" he asked.

"It means that he will tell the UFF that you are working for the Special Branch," I replied.

Barrett was taken aback. He glared at me in that menacing manner of his.

"See what I mean. I know how them boys work. You got me into this, Jonty. You brought them boys in. Get me out of this. I'm not working for them. I've always said that," he added.

That was very true: Barrett had always made clear his reservations about getting involved with the Special Branch. He just didn't get it though. He still thought that there was something I could do to help him. That I could wave some magic wand and make the Special Branch disappear. But there was nothing I could do for him now. He was trapped. He was in the iron grip of a body of men who could be just as ruthless as he was.

In many respects Barrett was good sauce for it. I felt no pity for him. I certainly couldn't help him. I had intended to put him in jail for life. That is where killers belong. But now *I* was at the centre of the Special Branch's attention, not Ken Barrett. They identified not with a fellow Police officer, but with this killer. They had decided to "go for me". They would obviously do whatever it took to obtain their goal, without any regard for the consequences for me personally or for my family. I had pushed them too far. I had obviously taken our CID case too far.

Barrett would have been far better off doing his time for the murder of Pat Finucane. At least he would have been safe. But Barrett now had a new master. He would no longer answer to his UFF Brigadier, Jim. He was no longer a player. He was now a mere pawn in a deadly spying game. He would answer only to the Special Branch. They would be much more demanding masters. While he worked for them, they would protect him from people like me. But Barrett would earn every penny that the Special Branch put into his grubby hands. He was setting off "into the Dark" where only the Special Branch have control—and they guard it jealously.

Barrett's parting words to me were something about not wanting to end up in a body bag. He was going to need every ounce of his street-wise guile just to stay alive. I would have to look after my own backside. I wondered if Sam would really be so stupid as to submit a concocted threat from the UFF against my mother and I. Surely not? Surely it was just a ploy to frighten Barrett?

Barrett had known of their foul little plan since Thursday, 12 March 1992 and it was now 16 March. No alleged threat from terrorists or any expected "mix" had been communicated to me by my authorities. Perhaps Sam and his cronies were having second thoughts. I didn't need this. No-one needed this. I was under enough pressure from both Republican and Loyalist terrorists. I did not need this pointless harassment from fellow Police officers. What on earth was it that they were so keen to hide?

I drove back to Tennent Street RUC Station and made copious notes in my diary. I was furious. Every fibre of my being told me to ring Sam back at his home and ask him what he was playing at. But that would serve only to warn him of Barrett's unexpected loyalty to me. Sam would more than likely allege that it was only a ploy to frighten Barrett. I would not be in a position to argue with him. I resisted that temptation. I wanted answers to Sam's sinister antics but I knew I would have to wait.

The next day was St Patrick's Day, a public holiday for Police officers too. Sam and his colleagues would be on leave. So would I. Wednesday 18 March would tell a tale. I would have to wait until then and see. I drove to Greencastle RUC Station to update Trevor. Things had taken a very sinister twist. I was now fighting on a third front against fellow members of the RUC. Trevor listened to my account of Barrett's allegations. If they were true, at least I was now one step ahead of the Special Branch. That was a very enviable position to be in.

Needless to say, I did not enjoy St Patrick's Day 1992 with my family. My head was spinning with the enormity of the treachery of the Special Branch. Rebecca and I had moved home too many times because of real threats from terrorists. Our two young boys were settling in well in Willcroft Meadows in Ballyrobert, near Ballyclare. Adam loved the local primary school and Simon had just joined his brother there too. Our daughter Lisa had gone to four primary schools and two secondary schools. We did not want the boys to have to go through the same fiasco.

To have to move home because of a genuine terrorist threat was one thing, but to move home at the behest of a concocted "terrorist threat" was an entirely different matter.

Wednesday, 18 March 1992 started off just like any other day. I busied myself in the CID office preparing for cases at the High Court and at Belfast Crown Court later that day. Trevor was busy too, over at Castlereagh. He rang me at lunchtime in an excited state.

"It's here, it's started," Trevor said. "All the Branch men from the North office are keeping me going about a massive threat on you from the UFF!"

I wondered why the alleged threat had not as yet been communicated to me. If it was going to be, I would have Sam the Branch man exactly where I wanted him. I intended to show him up for the fool that he was.

At 3.45 pm that afternoon, I was summoned to the Detective Inspector's office in Tennent Street. He officially informed me that a serious threat from UFF terrorists had been made against me. He had been informed of this by the Sub Divisional Commander (SDC) for Tennent Street. He told me that the matter had first been raised this morning at the ACC Belfast briefing by a Detective Chief Superintendent of the RUC Special Branch. Our Divisional Commander had been present and he had passed it on to our SDC. The threat allegedly included the fact that the UFF were aware of my home address and my mother's home address.

These senior Divisional Police officers were now afraid for my safety. The wheels of the security machinery which existed to protect vulnerable or threatened officers would be set in motion. Security Branch would now ask for the usual threat assessment from the Special Branch. I had absolutely no doubt that their assessment of their own concocted "threat" would be worded in such strong terms that it would ensure my quick removal from the Belfast region.

It was also likely that the Special Branch "mix" that would follow the threat would ensure that I would be returned to uniform duties. Barrett could not have made all of this up. He had told me the truth. Sam's sordid little plan was now a stark reality. He knew it would cause my family and me grief. He didn't care. He was far too busy concentrating on protecting a serial killer. I was asking too many questions. I was standing on too many toes.

It wasn't as if there would be any disciplinary or criminal charges made against me. Not at all, it would be just enough of a "mix" to give the CID authorities an excuse to get me out of the Belfast region and out of the CID. This was unbelievable! How many other unfortunate detectives had they performed this same little number on? I knew of a few. But Sam was in for a shock. I had joined the Police to deal with bullies, not to shy away from them. And Sam and his conspirators were just that—bullies. Barrett's unexpected loyalty to me as a CID officer had given me the edge. I intended to use it to show my CID authorities the sort of people we were dealing with.

The record shows that I attended North Queen Street RUC Station at 8.30 am for a meeting with my Detective Superintendent and my Detective Chief Inspector. We were sitting there discussing Barrett's allegations when the telephone rang. It was the Regional Head of the CID in Belfast. My Superintendent put his finger to his lips, indicating that I should be quiet. The call was obviously about me. I only heard one side of the conversation from the Detective Superintendent.

"Jonty has been dropping the names of Special Branch informants on the Shankill Road, Sir? Is that what they (Special Branch) are saying?" he asked.

There was the "mix". Well, I had nothing to fear from that. It was so reminiscent of old and similar allegations which had been made before. Those had not been investigated either. They couldn't be. I would have been vindicated in a fair and independent enquiry. That would never do: it was much better for the Special Branch to have question marks hanging over me. Much better indeed. My Detective Superintendent turned to me:

"The Special Branch want a meeting at Castlereagh at 2 pm today to discuss your alleged betrayal, Jonty. They say you are dropping the names of their informants on the Shankill Road," he said.

The Special Branch thought they were very clever. My Regional Head of CID was not impressed with me and now my Divisional Head was also looking at me with suspicion. There was an excuse for the Regional Head, but the man seated opposite had just had the benefit of a full briefing. I glared at him.

"The 'mix', Sir. Barrett said that Sam would put the 'mix' in with my bosses. There's your 'mix' and personally speaking, I'm sick of it."

The Detective Superintendent agreed. He would go to Castlereagh and brief the Regional Head before the meeting with the Special Branch. He asked me to be in his office in North Queen Street from 1.30 pm to be available in case he needed to speak to me. When the meeting was over, he would return to his office in North Queen Street and brief me. I recorded all of these events as they happened. He conceded that he knew that the Special Branch would not miss an opportunity to embarrass me.

By 1.30 pm I was back in the Detective Superintendent's office to await his call. About half an hour later, I received a call from Regional Head of CID.

"Tommy has fully briefed me, Jonty. This is disgraceful conduct by the Special Branch. Tell me what is it you want?" he asked.

"What I want is simple, Sir. I want to remain in Tennent Street CID. I do not want to be removed from there or from my position within the CID at the whim of some Special Branch minion," I replied.

"That is OK, Jonty. Consider that agreed, but this thing about Barrett, the Special Branch have me over a barrel there with the Walker Report," he said.

"I don't care about Barrett, Sir. I'll do whatever has to be done," I said.

"OK, Jonty, I will speak to you soon," he said.

The telephone went dead and I set down the handset. At least my position within the CID was secure. My post as an operational detective sergeant in Tennent Street was secure. There would be no need to move house now and no need for all the stress and anxiety that such an upheaval might cause my family and myself.

I so wished that I could have been a fly on the wall of the Regional Head's office. I would have given a lot to see the faces of those very senior Special Branch officers who believed they had the means to remove me from their hair once and for all. They were in for a shock. They were not going to be too enamoured with Sam and his cohorts, who had been so blinded by hate in their efforts to remove me from Barrett that they had actually sat in a Police car and discussed it in front of him. If the Special Branch were so keen to uncover failings or improprieties committed by a Police officer, there were plenty of them there. But I had more than a sneaking suspicion that there would be absolutely nothing done about any of that. Sam and his kind considered themselves unaccountable, untouchable, and every time that the authorities within the CID let them away with such untoward conduct, it served to strengthen that myth.

It was near to 4 pm before my Detective Superintendent arrived back at his office. He said that the Regional Head of Special Branch had arrived with an entourage of senior Special Branch officers at the office of our Regional Head of CID. They had started to make allegations about me "dropping the name" of one of their sources to the UFF on the Shankill Road. Our Regional Head had stopped them dead in their tracks. He told them that I had been warned that these allegations had been concocted. He informed them that none other than Ken Barrett had warned me that this would happen as long ago as 12 March 1992.

The Special Branch were stumped, but quickly concluded that there had obviously been "a clash of personalities at a junior level". They said that they would remove Sam from their agent if the CID would remove me. They would send in two new men to approach Barrett cold. They were confident that they could get their men in with Barrett in a short time. So that was it: I was off the Barrett case officially, and all it had taken was a simple request. So why had they tried to set me up? It just did not make sense.

I asked the Detective Superintendent what I was to do if their agent rang me at home to complain about them, as he was prone to do. That was OK. I could speak to him but I must tell him what the new score was. The CID no longer had any role to play in the handling of this killer. The notes in my RUC diary cover much more than this, but it is sufficient to say that no-one was interested in going after Sam for his treachery. It was made clear to me that if I wanted to question what the Special Branch were doing, I would be on my own.

Following these sinister developments, I contacted a very astute solicitor in Belfast. He was not in his offices. I met him at Belfast Magistrates Court. It was an ideal venue: there would be nothing odd about seeing me in deep conversation with this man there. He greeted me with a hearty handshake and a cheerful smile. I explained to him what had happened. He listened intently as I related the story of how

Barrett had confessed to murdering the solicitor Pat Finucane and how the Special Branch had reacted to it. I explained how the Special Branch had tried to set me up for a transfer out of Belfast over the last few days.

The solicitor gave me clear advice about the importance of keeping proper records. Allegations from me about abuse from the Special Branch were not new to this man. I had regularly called upon his advice throughout my service on the same subject. He had always afforded very good advice, for which I will always be grateful. We agreed that if the Special Branch ever made a move against me, he would represent me.

It wasn't until Friday, 20 March 1992 that Trevor asked me if I had checked out the registration number of the white van with our Central Vehicle Index (CVI). I had forgotten all about it with all the drama. I rang CVI and gave them the registration number. The female operator keyed the details into her terminal. She came back to me right away:

"That vehicle registration mark (VRM) has not yet been issued to anyone," she said.

I was intrigued. I could check that again. Sometimes it takes a few weeks before a new vehicle is actually put onto the computer system. This was a dead end.

"What's the name of the firm on that van?" Trevor asked.

I glanced down at my clipboard. It was in East Belfast! I handed it to Trevor. He studied it and suggested we check it out.

We got into a Police car and drove across to East Belfast. We found the industrial estate in question: it was not far from Lisnasharragh RUC Station. We drove into the complex. The firm was not listed on the board at the gate. The unit numbers went up in to the teens. They ended at the number just before the unit number that had been displayed on the side of the white van.

"Someone is being very clever, Trevor," I said.

It was likely that the white van was connected to some wing of the Security Services, but there was no way that we would ever know. The plot thickened, but it was over for me, as far as I was concerned.

The Special Branch had sent me a very clear signal that if I did not back off, I would suffer personally and so would Rebecca and our children. Trevor and I discussed our options. We both agreed that without the support of our authorities there was nothing more that we could do about Barrett. We had done our best. The chance to put away a serial killer had been squandered by those in authority in the RUC at that time.

My removal from Barrett's handling was in the interests of the Special Branch only. Sam and his Special Branch cohorts obviously did not want me prying into the circumstances of Barrett's involvement in the murder of Pat Finucane. In fairness to Sam, he had always made that clear. But why did he enjoy the full support of his own authorities? Why did the CID authorities refuse to support me?

There had to be answers. Someone in authority was keen to make sure that Trevor and I were stopped dead in our tracks. They didn't care how far they had to go to do so. There was no point in going on. Trevor and I very reluctantly backed off.

From my records, I can say that it wasn't until 6 pm on Saturday, 21 March 1992 that I next heard from Barrett. I was at home when he rang me. I recorded some of what he said. Sam had not made him aware of the new arrangements.

"Sam rang me at home all weekend, Jonty, but I never answered him," Barrett started. "What's the score now anyway?"

I knew that the Special Branch was listening in to every word. I would have to be very careful but there were a lot of points that I wanted to get across on that wire tap.

"They put in that serious threat from the UFF against me and my mother, just like they told you they would," I said. "They also put that 'mix' in with my bosses, just like you said they would," I added.

Barrett went quiet. Then he went on:

"I'm not happy, Jonty. They can't make me work for them. You have to help me here," he said.

"I can't," I replied.

Barrett didn't like this. He was being railroaded into working for the Special Branch and that had never been his intention.

"OK, Jonty, so what happens now?" he asked.

"You will be approached by two new Special Branch officers or you may be introduced to them by Sam," I said.

"F**k Sam," Barrett replied. "I don't want to speak to that treacherous bastard," he added.

Barrett offered to give me a firearm. I politely refused. That was not on: he could give it to the Special Branch. I told him to ring me if he was put under any pressure. I honestly didn't expect to hear from him again.

At 7 pm, only one hour later, Barrett rang in again.

"Sam rang me, Jonty. Were you speaking to him?" he asked.

"Not since last Monday night," I replied.

"Well, he knows that I spoke to you earlier," he said.

That didn't surprise me. The girls in the "hen house" (listening posts) at RUC Headquarters had wasted no time letting Sam and his bosses know about my contact with Barrett. How slow was this moron? Did he not realise how Sam had come to know that we had been in contact?

"Sam told me to meet him tomorrow (Sunday, 22 March 1992) but I refused," he said. "He said things about you, Jonty," he added.

"What sort of things?" I asked.

"He asked me why I was insisting on you being there and I told him that I trust you," he said.

"Is that all?" I asked.

"I told him straight that I don't trust the Special Branch," he added.

"What did Sam say?" I asked.

"He told me that your head is going and you've started dropping the names of informants all around the Shankill. He says you are not well and you can't be trusted," he added. "Sam asked me if I was afraid of you dropping my name. I told him that I was more afraid of him dropping it," he said.

The Special Branch were wasting no time. They were determined to break the trust that Barrett had in me. They could say whatever they liked to this killer to shift his loyalty away from me, and there was not a thing I could do about it. They wanted to slam that door in my face. If it took a bit of character-bashing to swing it, that was fine with them. Barrett went on:

"Sam must think I'm stupid. He told me he was going to put the 'mix' in with your bosses and when that didn't work he's putting the 'mix' in with me," he said.

Barrett was not happy. He said he would cool it for a while and get back to me.

On Monday, 23 March 1992 I attended the office of a senior CID officer and complained bitterly about Sam's slanderous attack upon my character. Was it really so necessary? It was getting ever more sinister and vindictive. I told the senior CID officer that if the current barrage did not stop, I would seek legal advice. I feared disastrous consequences for myself if the Special Branch did not stop targeting me. I had not finished complaining when the senior CID officer came straight back at me. There was no support, no condemnation of the Special Branch. Instead he told me that a senior Special Branch officer had already been on to him to complain that I had rung Barrett and told him not to work for the Special Branch. They had alleged that I had told him to ring me in six months' time.

This was not true. Barrett had contacted me on that first occasion and had asked me to ring him back. On the second occasion I had not rung him back. At no time did I tell Barrett that he was not to work for the Special Branch. I wished I could but I knew better. The tapes from the "hen house" would prove that I was telling the truth but there was no way the Special Branch would let us hear them. I did tell Barrett to ring me in six months' time if he was still refusing to meet with the Special Branch. This had been agreed with my own authorities. I was sick of it all.

The senior CID officer advised me to be very cautious. He agreed that Barrett could contact me by phone if he wished but I should encourage him to work with the Special Branch. I agreed to do so. This would stick in my throat because I still had Barrett in my sights for a sentence of life imprisonment. But I had no choice. The Special Branch were not taking no for an answer.

The days passed without any more calls from Barrett. It was not until 4.10 pm on Saturday, 4 April 1992 that I next heard from him. I was at home and off duty when he rang me from a call box. He was learning. He stated that the Special Branch were putting him under extreme pressure to work for them. He updated me.

"I've met two of them boys, Jonty, and Sam was not one of them," he said. "Can you get me out of this?" he asked.

I explained to him as best as I could that I was not permitted to meet him or help him.

"I'm scared of them boys, Jonty," he said.

That was a bit rich! A serial killer was afraid of Police officers. I had no sympathy for him. I just wanted to keep the contact open. Perhaps some day Barrett might feel forced again to run in our direction. I wanted to make sure that he would choose to run to me. Someday I would use the trust that Barrett had in me to bang him up for life for murder. That's what we should have been doing. All of this other dalliance was just an unfortunate and, I hoped, temporary diversion.

On Thursday, 9 April 1992, three days later, I had occasion to be in contact with a Special Branch detective sergeant from the North office. I was passing him an intelligence report from a high-grade Loyalist source which contained an imminent threat to the life of a notable UVF man. I took the opportunity to seek his view on the conduct of Sam and others who had tried to have me transferred out of Belfast. I made notes of our conversation. His view on the matter beggared belief.

"You should not believe Wesley (Barrett)," he said.

I brought it to his attention that it had been obvious that Barrett had told the truth. He had been vindicated when the threat and the mix did transpire. The officer was undeterred:

"You must remember, Jonty, Wesley is now an agent and the powers that be decide who runs an agent," he said. "Sources do not dictate any terms," he added.

I agreed wholeheartedly, but did that really justify the Special Branch turning on me? I had asked the question but I did not really expect this man to answer me. He could have walked away. He chose not to. In fact, his tone suggested that he was pleased with the absolute power of the Special Branch. He went on:

"If you insist on sticking your nose into areas of Police work that do not concern you, you cannot complain if you get it bitten off."

I was furious. This Police officer saw no distinction between Barrett and myself. Exactly what areas of Police work did not concern me? Why did they not concern me? I had gone after a serial killer and they had obstructed me. It was the Special Branch who were operating outside their own policing principles, not me. Since when was it not my business to pursue a killer? I told him pointedly that I did not expect Policemen to turn on me in that manner. His answer shocked me. He turned to me and pointed his finger into my chest.

"A decision to turn on you in that manner is not made by me or Sam. It is not made at our level. It is made by the powers that be. We do as we are told. It is as simple as that," he said.

Those "powers that be" certainly had a lot to answer for. Those nameless, faceless, gutless Special Branch senior officers were making perverse decisions that were adversely affecting the reputation of the Royal Ulster Constabulary. Why could they not see it? I let it go. There was no point arguing with the likes of this particular man.

On Thursday, 14 May 1992 at 4.10 pm I bumped into a senior Special Branch officer at Tennent Street RUC Station. I was photocopying a file in the corridor when he began to make fun of me in the presence of junior Police officers. The banter came round to the thorny topic of "Agent Wesley". He denied any involvement in the Special Branch plot to transfer me. He alleged that everything was going along fine now with "Wesley". I decided to bring him back down to earth.

"So why is he ringing me complaining, then?" I asked. "If everything is going so well, why does Wesley still ring me?" I added.

His face was a picture. It went red. He was finding it hard to contain his rage. I recorded his reply.

"If Wesley is still ringing you, that is a recipe for disaster for both you and for Wesley, Jonty," he said.

I was sure that he would do all in his power to stop Wesley ringing me again. It was a surprise then when I got a further telephone call from Barrett on Saturday, 16 May 1992. He was absolutely frantic. Only the day before, he had given the Special Branch back one of the SA80 assault rifles that he had stolen from Malone UDR Barracks. Sam had promised him thousands of pounds, to be paid within one hour of the RUC recovering the weapon.

Wesley was complaining that no-one had contacted him since the rifle had been seized. Sam was off on leave and could not be contacted. Wesley wanted me to help him. I rang my senior CID officer. He told me to tell Wesley it was a matter between himself and the Special Branch. He ordered me to change my home telephone number immediately. I readily agreed to do that. I rang Wesley at home and told him that he should refer his complaint to the RUC Special Branch.

Barrett complained to me of a sell-out by the CID. He still did not realise just how lucky he had been. He complained about being blackmailed by the Special Branch. He alleged that his new handlers had made threats to his life, and named the two Special Branch officers who had done so. The names were of no surprise to me.

Barrett would come under pressure now from his own kind in the UFF. Heads would roll because of the loss of that prized SA80 assault rifle. The UFF would be looking for a scapegoat and Barrett would be the prime suspect. Few UFF men knew of the whereabouts of that particular "bed" (arms hide). Barrett was going to have to be careful. I could see the logic in not immediately advancing him the cash. He would have been down at the dog track flashing it about. He couldn't do that. I had to agree with the Special Branch on that one. Barrett was also being taught exactly who was calling the shots.

On Tuesday, 19 May 1992, I contacted British Telecom and requested a change of telephone number. It took five or six days to actually change the number and it was done at my own expense. This is not to mention the inconvenience to my friends and family. But I could not complain. It was me who had given it to Barrett. I would do exactly the same again given the same circumstances. Speed of communication between our sources and us was vital to the saving of life. I would never deliberately cut off that very necessary lifeline. Not ever.

I reported my compliance to the order to change my telephone number to senior CID officers. Barrett was no longer able to contact me at home. I expected that that was the last I would hear from him. We had not long to wait until the UFF scapegoat for the loss of that rifle was made to pay. I was not due to start at Tennent Street CID office until 4 pm on Thursday, 21 May 1992. I was contacted at home and asked to report for duty at 9.30 am to assist in the criminal investigation into the attempted murder of a UDA man called William Alfred Stobie.

He had been shot the evening before by the UFF at the rear of a house in Upper Charleville Street, Belfast. Stobie had been very, very lucky. The UFF had claimed that they had shot him. They alleged that Stobie was an RUC Special Branch informant. They were right. Barrett had mentioned that fact on the first night that Trevor and I had gone to see him. We had passed the information on to the Special Branch. Had they warned him? If they had, there would be a record of it.

I visited Stobie in hospital. I found him to be respectful and courteous. He alleged that Johnny Adair had shot him, but he would not make a statement to that effect. He was terrified of further UFF reprisals. Stobie had paid dearly for the loss of the SA80 assault rifle and he had absolutely nothing to do with it. I harboured more than a suspicion that it was Barrett who had pointed the finger at Stobie, to direct suspicion away from himself. I couldn't prove it, but I was convinced that it was the case. Without Stobie's full co-operation we were unable to bring his would-be killer to book.

I was on duty early one afternoon when I received a further and final telephone call from Barrett. He rang in to the Tennent Street CID office at 2 pm from the Heather Street UDA Club in the Woodvale Estate. Once again, he was fuming. I recorded what he said.

"Jonty, I know that this has f**k all to do with you, but I have this gun in the boot of my car to give to them other boys and they haven't shown up. They were supposed to be here two hours ago. I'm driving up and down the f****n' Shankill Road past all these Police patrols. Can you see what you can do?" he asked.

This was no problem. These things happened. There could be dozens of reasons why his Special Branch handlers had not turned up. I lifted the 'phone and rang the Special Branch North (Belfast) office.

"Hello," came the reply.

I explained how Barrett had rung in. He was waiting for his handlers to meet as agreed but for some reason they were two hours late. I was absolutely stunned and disgusted by the reply.

The officer on the other end of the line named the detective inspector on duty. "He's a 'wanker'. The lads are waiting until 4 pm when he goes off duty." He named the officer who would take over the next shift. "*He's* a great fella, if you know what I mean," he said.

I didn't answer. I couldn't answer. I had absolutely no idea what he meant. I was expecting some pressing operational reason for their failure to turn up. This was incredible! The Special Branch officer was not even embarrassed. He saw nothing difficult or untoward about the unenviable position in which he had placed Barrett. This was so wrong. It was also extremely unprofessional. It was just short of 2.20 pm and Barrett had already waited for over two hours. The reason? Special Branch internal politics! The wrong detective inspector was on duty at the Special Branch North office.

I knew the first detective inspector well. He was a very decent man. Perhaps that is why his face did not fit. He was not one of their favourite men. He was not seen to be a "team player". I had heard young Special Branch officers complain that he questioned odd or irregular conduct. So that made him a "wanker". Personalities were dictating the pace of recovery of a UFF weapon. This childish behaviour was placing their agent at risk of detection by other Police. He could as easily have been compromised by the UFF. Was this how the "experts" worked? God help us, I thought.

Barrett rang back to the CID office at around 2.30 pm. I explained that the meet would not take place until after 4 pm for operational reasons. He wasn't too pleased but he raised no real objections. That was my last contact with Barrett until three years later when he was in jail charged with racketeering. He asked to see me at that stage. His friends in the Special Branch had abandoned him. He wanted me to arrange his release. Needless to say, he stayed in jail.

Chapter 13

"Are you telling me that the Special Branch have sold me a pup?"

It wasn't until March 1999 that I next thought of Barrett. By that time, I was a Detective Sergeant in charge of Unit 4 of the Belfast Regional Crime Squad based in Castlereagh RUC Station. Unit 4 was the only dedicated CID source-handling unit in the Royal Ulster Constabulary. The setting up of such a unit was acknowledgement in itself of the successes of our source-handling endeavours. We were proud of our results. We had just completed "Operation Carrier," a CID operation that had stretched over a number of months.

The focus of the operation was the investigation of ten murders along the North Down coast. A UVF suspect, Thomas David Maginnis, from Newtownards in Co. Down had recently admitted his part in a number of the murders. This had prompted the operation. We had charged Maginnis with two of those brutal murders that we believed could be proved against him. The Director of Public Prosecutions later charged him with five more. The additional five cases had been "cold cases" dating back to the seventies.

I had always found it very professionally gratifying to clear up cold cases. It sent a clear signal to those responsible that we would never give up on our pursuit of them. It also proved to the still-grieving relatives that we did care about what had happened to the deceased. That we would leave no stone unturned in our efforts to bring the perpetrators of such crimes to justice.

Our Chief Constable Sir Ronnie Flanagan was under extreme pressure to re-open the case of the murder of Pat Finucane. Many of the murders we had just cleared were older than the Finucane case. Maginnis had sat in a Police car and had admitted his involvement in those murders in exactly the same unguarded manner as Barrett had done in 1991. I could see how we could use the same procedure we had just used to bring Maginnis to book to get at Ken Barrett. I took the view that even at this late stage the Royal Ulster Constabulary should bring Barrett to justice.

I was fully aware that Sir John Stevens had been recalled to Northern Ireland to open the murder enquiry into the Finucane case. But he had been here twice before and he had been obstructed twice before. I had no real faith in the ability of English Policemen to get to grips with such cases. They would have difficulties getting around the complex network set up by the RUC Special Branch to protect murderers who were their agents from arrest or imprisonment. I knew that we could get Barrett if only we could get the necessary clearance from the Special Branch.

We still had the Crime Squad Vauxhall Astra car we had used in "Operation Carrier". It was wired for sound and vision. It had worked well in the case of Maginnis. He had boasted openly of his personal involvement in the other murders. We could trap Ken Barrett in that same manner using the same car. It would also be possible for us to do so before Sir John Stevens touched down at Belfast Airport.

I decided to confide what I knew about the murder of Pat Finucane and Ken Barrett to Detective Chief Superintendent Brian McVicker. He was the Regional Head of the CID in Belfast at the time, and one of the most respected senior CID officers in the Force. He was hated by some of the more sinister elements of the Special Branch in Belfast: he could see right through them and they did not like it. If he agreed with me, we could make the murder of Pat Finucane the eleventh to have been cleared by the Crime Squad in Belfast in the first three months of 1999. These were astonishing clearance rates by any standards.

According to my records it was at 10.30 am on Thursday, 18 March 1999 when I broached the subject of the Finucane murder with Brian McVicker in his office in Castlereagh RUC Station. I had just finished an intelligence meeting with him and three other senior Police officers. I broke away from the rest of the team in the hallway outside. I went back to the office again. Here was a man I knew I could trust. I knocked his door.

McVicker was surprised to see me again so quickly. He greeted me with a warm smile and a hearty handshake.

"What is it now, Jonty? What's on your mind?" he asked.

"How would you like to clear another murder, Sir?" I asked.

"Another one? Great! Which murder do you have in mind?" he asked.

"The murder of the solicitor Patrick Finucane, Sir," I said.

Brian was not easily rattled. He was no fool either. He knew exactly how politically explosive my proposal was. He studied me. He could see that I was deadly serious.

"How can we do that, Jonty? We have no idea who shot him," he said.

"But we do, Sir. In fact the murderer admitted it to me in a Police car in the presence of three Police officers on 3 October 1991 and the confession was recorded," I said.

"You're not serious?" he said.

"I'm very serious. The man who confessed to us was Ken Barrett and he would confess again if we could get authority to put him into that wired squad car," I said.

Brian studied me.

"And this confession, do you have any reference to it in your note-books or diaries of the day?" he asked.

"Yes, Sir, I do," I replied.

"What exactly did you do about it, Jonty?" he asked.

"Do about it, Sir? There was nothing that I could do. The Special Branch moved to stop me," I replied.

"Your CID authorities of the day, what did they do?" he asked.

"Nothing, Sir. They felt that there was nothing they could do except go with the decision to recruit Barrett as a Special Branch agent," I said.

"There is no way that we will get authority to go on this, Jonty. Sir John Stevens is on the way here to investigate that murder. He'll be here in a few days. I don't believe this. I'll have to inform Headquarters," he said.

Even as Brian lifted that telephone, I knew in my heart that he was right. It was more than likely that the matter would be left to Sir John

Stevens. And yet I felt a wave of relief flood over me. I felt as if I had been cleansed. I had carried the guilt of that particular subject for far too long. I shouldn't have felt guilty, but I did. For at least twenty minutes after my initial briefing to Brian it seemed that everything was happening in slow motion. Every movement, every smell, every image seemed exaggerated and unreal. I had pushed a button and there was no going back.

Far from clearing another murder, this was the beginning of the end for me. In an honest bid to add to our successes, I had inadvertently "blown the whistle". But I had no regrets. I still have no regrets. That is how it all started. It was as simple as that. I didn't hear who Brian was talking to. I didn't care. The euphoria of the success of "Operation Carrier" disappeared in an instant. I knew that the enquiry which would follow would examine what all of us had done. It would examine what the Special Branch had done. It was patently obvious to me that the RUC would not come out of it without severe criticism.

On top of all of that, the Special Branch were not going to take this lying down. They would move to protect their men. I knew I was on my own once again. It wasn't that Brian did not want to help me. He couldn't. No-one could. Even Trevor would be dragged into all of this again. He was on leave at this time and was suffering from the effects of a complete nervous breakdown. He certainly did not need this.

I knew that Brian was right. RUC Headquarters had already commissioned a third Stevens Enquiry and its remit was to investigate the murder of the solicitor Patrick Finucane. There was no way that we could contemplate putting Barrett into that wired squad car. Any information that I had about the confession to the murder of Pat Finucane on 12 February 1989 would have to be given to the new Stevens 3 investigation team. My allegations were damning. It goes without saying that my allegations were viewed by everyone in authority with deep suspicion. It was brought to my attention within a day or two of making the allegations that RUC Headquarters had only had sight of photocopies of my original journals. Someone in authority in Crime Branch was questioning the authenticity of the more damning entries in my diaries.

One very senior CID officer had actually mooted that, bearing in mind the history of my in-fighting with Special Branch officers, it was not beyond the bounds of possibility that I had sat for hours writing out false entries into a new diary or diaries and had then photocopied the entries and destroyed the original fake diaries.

On Friday, 23 April 1999 I was ordered to produce all of my original journals for the period 1 January 1986 to 19 January 1993. I produced the original diaries in question. This did not please those senior CID officers who had sought to question my integrity. Not only were those journals in existence, their authenticity was unquestionable. Senior CID officers who had read their contents at the time had countersigned many of the more damning entries. It was no secret that I had no time for some Special Branch officers. The authentication of diaries was routine in the CID from the late 1980s. I had good reason to be grateful for that particular regulation. Any Special Branch sycophant within our CID hierarchy was going to have to do better than question the authenticity of my written records. I also handed in eleven RUC pocket notebooks. These notebooks were dated from 23 February 1991 to 9 December 1992. The four diaries and eleven notebooks were to be handed over to the Stevens 3 Enquiry team. My authorities told me that the Stevens team would interview me and they would investigate my allegations.

On Tuesday, 27 April 1999 I was summoned to Seapark RUC complex at Carrickfergus, Co. Antrim, to be interviewed by the Stevens 3 team in relation to my allegation that Ken Barrett had confessed to the murder of Pat Finucane on 3 October 1991. This had never been my intention. I had always taken the view, and still do, that it was the responsibility of the Northern Ireland CID to investigate that murder. I had absolutely no faith in passing that responsibility to a team of English detectives, no matter how professional or how impartial they might be. The track record of such teams to get to grips with cases allegedly involving members of the Special Branch was one of failure. As I walked from my car to the main building, I thought of the personal ramifications for my family and myself. I knew that if Barrett was arrested and interviewed under caution he would laugh at these detectives. Barrett was fully aware of the fact that "silence is golden". Such an arrest scenario would serve only to alert this serial killer to the fact that Trevor and I had done our best in 1991 and 1992 to put him in jail for life for the murder of Pat Finucane.

Ken Barrett had warned me in the most graphic manner of exactly what would happen to me if he were ever arrested, charged or convicted of any of the offences he had admitted to us in that Special Branch car in October 1991. Barrett's personal capacity for murder was legendary. I knew that he would be coming after *me* if he were ever arrested. It was crucial that no-one moved against him to use that tape recording of 3 October 1991 until they had agreed on an investigative strategy with the Director of Public Prosecutions (DPP). They would need the full support of the entire prosecution machinery behind them. To go ahead without that would serve only to educate Barrett as to who was giving evidence against him.

Barrett would then be aware of who to eliminate to ensure that any such investigation would fail. To ensure a successful investigation, these detectives would need the full co-operation of myself, Trevor and Sam, the Special Branch man. I knew that I could count on Trevor but Sam was a different kettle of fish entirely. He had always let me know that the Special Branch had no interest in pursuing Barrett for any crime, never mind the murder of Pat Finucane. Would he now co-operate with these detectives in a manner that he had denied me? Or would he dare to treat them with the same contempt as his own CID colleagues? That was yet to be seen. I had a notion that Sam would just do what Sam had always done well—his masters' bidding.

Sam's problem was that some six and a half years had passed since Barrett had made that confession. Times had changed. Those people now in charge of both the Special Branch and CID had changed. I believed that Sam would no longer enjoy the same support that he had in 1991. The only constant was that Barrett was still a serial killer. A murderer who had confessed to one of the most controversial murders of the Troubles, and we had squandered our chance to catch him. Sam was about to get one more chance to join me in this bid to jail Barrett. It was surely time to bury the hatchet and work together in the public interest to jail Barrett, even if we were now six and a half years late in doing so.

I entered the lift and got out on the floor that housed this third Stevens Enquiry team. When the door of the lift opened, I followed the signs indicating the whereabouts of their offices. I turned right out of the lift and walked down the dark wooden-panelled corridor towards their suite. Within a few seconds I was standing outside a heavily-framed and richly-panelled, solid wood door bearing the sign "Stevens Team".

I knew in my heart that once I went in through that door to assist these English Police officers nothing would be the same again. That was unfair. I was only there only to make a statement about Barrett's graphic confession to a murder that it was no longer our responsibility to investigate. It was my clear duty to assist these men. I was not there to give evidence to them about any Police officer in the RUC, not even in the Special Branch. Yet I had an overwhelming feeling of guilt.

I could not have cared less what Sam or his Special Branch faction thought of me. But I did genuinely fear for the awful political and corporate damage that would be caused to the Royal Ulster Constabulary if any of these allegations came to the knowledge of the general public. But it was too late for recriminations. It was too late to worry about what might happen. My authorities had passed responsibility for the investigation of the Finucane murder to the Stevens 3 team and I had a clear duty to assist them. I knocked on that heavy wooden door.

I stepped into the large office now being used to house an incident room staffed by at least six or eight men who were busy at their desks in a manner that any detective would identify with. Computer terminals were switched on, the screens filled with the familiar images of action sheets and message forms. Few of these busy detectives cast more than a glance in my direction.

"I'll just let the governor know you're here," the man who had greeted me at the door said.

He walked off to my right towards a closed office door at the far end of the main office. I stood there for a few minutes enjoying the view from the window. I was thinking of Trevor and his illness and how it had adversely affected his parents, Beth and Arthur McIlwrath. Trevor knew that I was going forward to help the Stevens 3 team. He supported me. He wanted to help too, but he was not well enough to be interviewed. I was brought out of my near-trance by the sudden arrival of two men to my right. I turned round to see an arm outstretched in my direction. It was Vincent McFadden, a tall, broad former English Detective Chief Superintendent. I knew Vincent from his original role as deputy to John Stevens on the Stevens 1 team in 1989. I had interviewed top UFF man Eric McKee with Vincent and Trevor McIlwrath in those final UFF lifts by the Stevens team in 1990.

McKee had been charged and later convicted of possessing information likely to be of use to terrorists at the Crown Court in Crumlin Road Courthouse. I was glad to see Vincent McFadden. The last time we had spoken was when Brian Nelson "broke" during interviews with Vincent's detectives. Nelson had alleged during interviews that he was working for the Security Forces. He appeared to believe that this fact would save him from prosecution. He was talking to the wrong detectives.

Nelson had confessed that weekend and Vincent needed to contact senior RUC personnel at RUC Headquarters simply to inform them of this very important development. He asked me for the home telephone number of the most senior RUC officer on call that weekend. I gave him the number. I was aware that Brian Nelson's admissions would put the cat amongst the pigeons. Back in 1990 the Stevens 1 team had cut through the UDA and the UFF like a knife through butter. It was heart-warming to see these former godfathers of Loyalism "fold" one after another to those determined detectives. With their protection removed, it was easy to bring them to book. The truth is they should never have been protected in the first place. Some of those detained were the architects of much of the grief caused by the UFF over the years. They were the driving force behind those minions who had actually committed the murders.

Vincent McFadden and his men had served the Northern Ireland public impartially and very well during that first investigation. It augured well for everyone that he was back again for Stevens 3. As detectives go, Vincent stands out as perhaps one of the most capable of his day. His tenacity and his prowess as a detective are mentioned in a book on Criminal Profiling by the ground-breaking criminal profiler, David Canter.

During those initial few minutes Vincent asked me about the well-being of my ex-CID partner Trevor McIlwrath. He must have been sorry he asked, because I explained how badly Trevor and his family had been treated by the RUC. Vincent asked me to give Trevor his regards.

John Stevens, the head of the Stevens Enquiry, joined us. Vincent McFadden introduced me to him and gave him the benefit of his insight into our previous assistance to the Stevens 1 Enquiry team. With the usual pleasantries exchanged, it was now time to get down to business. I was introduced to the two members of the team who would interview me and record my witness statement about Ken Barrett and his self-confessed role in the murder of Pat Finucane.

Detective Sergeant Peter Jenkins and Detective Constable Derek Sharman escorted me to an office to my left at the end of the incident room. Despite the use of this suite of offices by these detectives, I could smell the distinct stale smell of decay. These offices which had once swarmed with the hustle and bustle of competitive industry were now almost unused. The musty smell of rooms seldom used or aired permeated the entire building.

I had attended Seapark voluntarily and without a solicitor. I was there to do all I could to put a thrust behind the investigation and to breathe new life into this cold case. To revive the same impetus that could have and should have been seized upon some six and a half years before.

Before I had gone to Seapark several decent and well-meaning senior CID officers who were fully aware of all the circumstances surrounding the case had strongly advised me not to attend without a solicitor. I felt that I had nothing to fear from an impartial team of detectives.

The seating in the interview room was formal. The two detectives were courteous and polite. The atmosphere was cordial. They did everything they could do to put me at ease. I sat in the sweltering heat of that office, going over and over my account of how Ken Barrett had come forward to offer his services as an agent on 1 October 1991. How he had admitted the murder of Pat Finucane so graphically on 3 October 1991 and how the Special Branch constable, Sam, had recorded it all on an audiotape.

The interview lasted for some time before we had to bring it to a close for lunch. I was asked politely not to contact Trevor McIlwrath or discuss anything we had spoken about. I refused to comply. I brought it to the attention of the two detectives that almost every other CID officer had turned their back on Trevor because they had totally misunderstood what had happened. I had not turned my back on him and I had no intention of doing so. I had every intention of co-operating fully with the Stevens team but I must support Trevor. He was in a terrible mental state, agonising over this very subject. I had already promised that I would call at his house for lunch. I had no wish to break that promise. In fairness to the two detectives, once I had explained this, they removed their objection to me visiting Trevor. In any case, the inference had been that Trevor and I would conspire to do our best to embarrass the poor Special Branch. This was not the case. What had been done in 1991 could not be changed. Not by anything that Trevor and I could do or say. The truth cannot be changed . . . or so I thought. I forgot about the unseen hand of the Special Branch. It was about to slap me across the face.

Lunch with Trevor was very intense. My heart went out to him. He was now in such a state of mental distress that he was not thinking straight. I assured him that we both had absolutely nothing to fear from any enquiry. As far as I was concerned, we both had done our best in the circumstances. The Special Branch dictated the pace and the direction of all CID investigations in those days. I had logged and recorded many instances of that.

I returned to the Stevens 3 team suite at Seapark after lunch. The two detectives questioned me, obviously looking for some failing. The atmosphere had shifted from cordial to formal from time to time but I never felt under any undue pressure. I had used the same ploy often to get a suspect to drop his guard while I allowed him to talk himself into knots. These two English detectives were good at their job. The interview lasted for two hours as we pored over my notebooks and diaries. I left Seapark at 4 pm, drained.

I returned at 9 am the next day, Wednesday, 28 April 1999. The interview recommenced with the same two detectives. The atmosphere was once again cordial. They had obviously heard enough of my protests and examples of Special Branch "dirty tricks" yesterday. This time it was straight down to business. Within half an hour they had commenced to record my witness statement. It seemed to take an age before they had completed it.

It contained no allegations of Special Branch impropriety. There were no references to Sam's treachery. No reference to Sam's blatant attempts to obstruct us. The statement was a full and factual account of Ken Barrett's confession to the murder of Pat Finucane. The evidence contained in the statement was directed at the criminal liability of Ken Barrett only. Any dirty washing or allegations of foul play by the Special Branch could be put forward later if necessary.

It was enough for me to make the detectives aware of this in case it became necessary later to refer to such issues in the Crown Court. The detectives were focused on their own narrow remit: to bring the UFF men responsible for the murder of Pat Finucane to justice. Any obstruction by the Special Branch in the past was neither here nor there to them. They assured me that *no-one* would interfere with or obstruct them on this occasion. I felt like laughing in their faces. They appeared to have absolutely no perception of what they were up against, despite the fact that I had spent hours trying to warn them.

When I had completed the witness statement they read it aloud to me. I agreed with it in its entirety. They asked me to sign it. I reached over to sign, but the Welsh Detective Sergeant Peter Jenkins stopped me. He told me to read the statement certificate aloud. I did so. As I was reciting its contents I saw the pair exchange glances and nod to each other. They were smiling to themselves. I thought I was imagining things.

I read the certificate aloud and once I got to the part which read: "... I make (this statement) knowing that, if it is tendered in evidence, I shall be liable to prosecution if I have wilfully stated anything which I know to be false or do not believe to be true ...", I reached to sign the front page below the certificate. The detective sergeant stopped me once again. The pair cleared the desk, leaving only the statement sitting there between them and me and the atmosphere changed totally.

I was aghast. I was completely taken aback. I knew exactly what this meant. These two very astute detectives had somehow gained exactly what they wanted. My problem was that I was not entirely sure what that was. They were no longer looking at me as a witness. It was clear to me that I was now a criminal suspect and I could not for the life of me understand it. For the first time since I had come forward I was wishing that I had listened to the senior CID officers who had advised me not to go to Seapark without a solicitor.

It was the detective sergeant who broke the silence. I knew it was time to *listen*. I had been doing most of the talking. I knew by the sudden change in the atmosphere from cordial to strictly formal that both of these detectives thought that they had me cornered. But why? What had I said or done that was so wrong?

"Before you sign that, Jonty, I want you to think very carefully. Could you be wrong?" he asked.

"No," I answered.

"Could you be mistaken?" he asked.

"No," I answered.

"Now, think very carefully before you sign that certificate, because once you do sign it there is no going back," he said. "You do understand that, don't you?"

"Yes, of course," I replied.

What on earth is he talking about, I thought.

"If you sign that certificate and what you say is not true, that is perjury. You do understand that, Jonty?" he said.

He swung the statement around and moved it closer to me.

"So you're happy enough to go ahead and sign it?" he asked.

"Absolutely," I replied.

I then signed all six pages of my witness statement.

"Would you not agree that a tape recording of that meeting on 3 October 1991 would be an independent technical audio record of exactly what was discussed in the Special Branch car on 3 October 1991?" he asked.

"Well, yes of course, but be careful. People can do things with audiotapes. They can be altered or changed to suit some other agenda," I replied.

The detective sergeant put his hands onto the desk and leaned across it in my direction to punctuate what he was about to say.

"Yes, Jonty, that's right, they can. But we can tell if an audiotape has been altered or changed in any way and that tape has been to our laboratory in the Met (Metropolitan Police). It has not been altered or changed in any way. But I can tell you now for a fact there is no confession on it from Barrett in relation to the murder of Pat Finucane. So how do you explain that?" he asked.

I sat there speechless. I felt sick. I realised that the Special Branch had pulled a fast one. But how? How could they remove a confession from an audiotape without leaving a forensic trace of having done so?

The detective sergeant told me that Sam had handed over an audiotape marked 3 October 1991 to the Stevens 3 team.

So I was aware that Sam had been given no chance to alter or destroy the tape. But how on earth was there no confession from Barrett on it? I was perplexed. I had no answer to this. I looked up at that Welsh detective sergeant. Fair play to him. He had me cornered.

The fact is that truth is never an issue in criminal investigations. That may sound perverse to a civilian but it is true. Detectives merely gather facts to place before a court. Everyone likes to assume that facts lead to the truth. But that is not always the case. Generally speaking they do, but there are still too many cases of persons wrongly convicted on the facts in issue. There are too many instances of travesties of justice.

I did not know what the Special Branch had done but whatever it was, it was inspired. They had effectively turned the truth upside down. Sam had not acted alone here.

It was my experience that Special Branch officers like Sam were ten a penny. No, this was the work of one of their "architects". Someone had put a lot of thought into this one and whatever he or she had done, no matter how perverse it was, it had worked.

"No confession to the murder of Pat Finucane?" I said. "How can that be? How can the audiotape be different to my written records?"

The Stevens team were not there to answer that question. They were behaving like the cat that had just got the cream. They had caught me out telling lies in a murder investigation. I could be charged. I could face a court and be tried for lying when I knew well that I was simply telling an unpalatable truth, but the truth nonetheless.

I asked to be allowed to listen to the entire tape. Perhaps there was something on it that would jog my memory. The detective sergeant left the interview room and returned with Sir John Stevens. I put my request to him. He pointed to me.

"Allow him to listen to the tape. Give him all the writing paper he needs. Let him make whatever notes he wishes and when he is finished, seize his notes and exhibit them," he said.

I noted more than a little disdain in his voice. Sir John Stevens left the room without another word. He obviously did not believe me either. Why should he?

I was allowed to listen to the recording that the Special Branch alleged was on the tape of 3 October 1991. At first there was only the sound of traffic and then a sound like a car door closing. Next Ken Barrett could be clearly heard speaking to us urgently and excitedly about two murders that had occurred earlier that night in North Belfast. He spoke first about the murder of a man he referred to as "wee Harry Ward". He had been shot dead by Republicans in the Diamond Jubilee Bar. Barrett could then be heard to criticise Johnny Adair and his "C" Company UFF for their tit-for-tat retaliation murder of a Catholic taxi driver in the Ardoyne a few hours later.

I realised immediately that by mentioning these two murders Barrett had inadvertently dated that tape. All I needed to know was the date on which those two murders had occurred. I reached for the telephone on the desk to call our CID Regional Intelligence Unit (RIU) at Castlereagh. They would have the answer on their computer system. My stomach was turning over and over. I felt ill. The detective sergeant reached over the desk and put his hand over mine.

"Who are you going to call?" he asked.

"RIU in Castlereagh," I replied truthfully.

"Are they part of the Special Branch?" he asked.

"No. It is our Regional Intelligence Office. I need the date of two murders that are mentioned on this audiotape. That will date this tape," I replied.

He permitted me to proceed. I gave the names of the two victims to the officer on the other end of the line. There was a pause as he keyed the details into his computer terminal. It was too long a pause. To me it seemed an eternity. But I was confident that the date would not be 3 October 1991. I just knew it could not be.

"Yes, Sergeant, here it is. Henry Fleming Ward. He was shot dead in the Diamond Jubilee Bar on the Shankill Road by the IPLO on 10 October 1991," he said.

I knew it! That was a week later. The Special Branch had deliberately switched the tapes! The relief that flooded over me was indescribable. The date of the tape was now official. It had definitely been recorded on 10 October 1991 and not on 3 October 1991 as the Special Branch had alleged. Barrett could not have known of two murders that had occurred a week later—unless he had a crystal ball!

For reasons known only to themselves, the Special Branch had seen fit to switch the tapes to make a liar out of anyone who alleged that Barrett had confessed to the murder of Pat Finucane. I wrote out the details of the Ward murder on the notepaper provided to me by the Stevens team. I brought the date to the attention of the detective sergeant. He patted me on the back in a reassuring manner. He was obviously as pleased as I was.

The Special Branch had not even checked their tape. They had obviously not bothered to ensure that their elaborate ploy to get rid of Barrett's confession would not backfire on them. But it had almost worked. If Ken Barrett himself had not mentioned those murders, it would have been virtually impossible to date the tape. Now it was back to the Special Branch. Would they now allege that they had made a genuine mistake? But would they produce the missing audiotape for 3 October 1991? I bet that they would not.

I had been very fortunate indeed. I had almost fallen victim once again to their dirty tricks. The atmosphere in the interview room changed back to cordial once again as I went over my diary entry for 10 October 1991. We found two other areas where the audio recording actually corroborated the diary entry.

Detective Sergeant Jenkins left the interview room to report what was for them a very disturbing development to his boss Sir John Stevens. He returned to the interview room with Stevens. This time we met each other's gaze. His previous disdain was gone.

"Are you telling me that the Special Branch have sold me a pup?" he asked.

"Sir, I have fought with these people for the best part of 30 years in the public interest because, believe me, it is certainly not in my interests to fight with them. You are asking me to poke a sleeping bear. To poke at a bear that could jump at me at any time and savage me," I said.

Sir John Stevens did not hesitate. He came straight back at me. "Believe me, Jonty, I intend to pull the teeth out of that bear," he said.

I knew by his tone and by his demeanour that he meant it. I was glad to hear it. I was not used to this sort of support. He turned to some of his staff.

"Get over to RUC Headquarters and get that original tape," he demanded.

You will be lucky, I thought.

But it was me who had been lucky. It was fortunate for me that Barrett had mentioned those two murders. I wondered just how long my luck would last. Sir John Stevens came over to me again and asked me pointedly,

"Just what is it you want out of this, Jonty?" he asked.

I did not have to think about the answer to that one. It was simple.

"I just want you to deliver change, Sir. That is all. I have not long to serve in this Constabulary and I want to be assured that the young detectives who follow me, who step into my shoes and lift the baton so to speak, do not suffer the same obstruction, the same undermining, the maligning I have suffered at the hands of these people. That is exactly what I want," I replied.

Stevens studied me before he answered me. He laughed.

"I thought you were going to ask me for the head of Sam or some of his Special Branch colleagues," he said.

"There are no winners at this game, Sir. The losers are the members of the public who have placed their trust in us. By fighting amongst ourselves we are letting them down," I said.

Stevens waited a moment before he spoke again.

"I have listened to some very senior RUC officers speak ill of you,

Johnston. I listened to them but as far as I can see they are not fit to lace your boots," he said.

This was some accolade coming from a senior Police officer of this man's calibre. I was pleasantly surprised. I could only imagine the poison that had been injected by those very senior RUC officers. He did not name them nor did he offer me any insight into exactly what had been alleged. I didn't care. This man now knew that he was facing the runaround. He could expect no assistance from the RUC Special Branch. If he was to be successful in his endeavours, his team would have to stand alone. But such was his presence that I believed that if anyone could do it, he could. His goal for now was Barrett, but if any Special Branch officers were foolish enough to get in his way, I had no doubt that he would deal with them.

On Tuesday, 11 May 1999 and on subsequent dates I attended Seapark and transcribed the audiotape of 10 October 1991 at the request of the Stevens 3 team. It was while I was doing this that I realised the enormity of the deliberate treachery of the RUC Special Branch.

The tenth of October 1991 was the date of our second meeting with Barrett. It was also the day on which Sam had repeatedly insisted that we should not mention the murder of Pat Finucane. He had said that his authorities had declared that we must not question Barrett any further about that particular murder until a decision was made at RUC Headquarters as to whether we were going to prosecute Barrett for that murder or not. Trevor and I had not questioned that. We had not smelled a rat. We had no real reason to suspect foul play.

Yet as I transcribed the tape, I became aware that someone within the hierarchy of the RUC Special Branch had made a conscious decision not only not to prosecute Ken Barrett, but had actually gone to the other extreme by removing any trace of his boastful confession from the audio record. And they had done so within a week of that confession coming into our domain. The decision to obstruct our investigation had been made on a date between 3 and 10 October 1991 and Trevor and I had missed it. It had been done so subtly that we had had no idea that it had occurred.

So that was the reason we were told to be silent on 10 October 1991! That was why we were not allowed to ask any questions of Barrett about the murder of Pat Finucane on that date. To enable the Special Branch to make a similar tape to the one made on 3 October 1991.

There was to be only one glaring omission. There would be no mention of the Finucane murder on that tape. This effectively rid the Special Branch of Barrett's confession. They simply replaced the original tape of 3 October 1991 with the one from 10 October 1991. It was ingenious and it had almost worked.

My mind drifted back to my visit to Sam's office to transcribe the tape of 3 October 1991. Sam and I both had great difficulty with parts of it where the noise of passing traffic had almost drowned out Barrett's voice. Sam had said that he would never park there again. So why then did he return to exactly the same place a week later on 10 October 1991? It had struck me as extremely odd at the time. Now I had my answer.

Not only did the Special Branch need to have the same three detectives in the car with Barrett. It was vital to their sordid little game plan that they returned to the same layby and parked in exactly the same spot as they had done previously. This ensured that there would be the same sounds of passing traffic as there had been on the third. They needed everything to be the same, except for that confession to the murder of Pat Finucane. But the big question was why would they go to these extreme lengths to do this? Did my own CID authorities know of this? Surely not.

As I sat in the small room adjacent to the Stevens suite, transcribing the audiotape, my blood was boiling. I listened to Ken Barrett confessing openly to the attempted murder of a man called Tommy McCreery. Why any Police officer would move to protect such an evil man was beyond me. It ran contrary to everything that the public in Northern Ireland entrusted us to do. No matter what Pat Finucane's political affiliations or Republican leanings may have been, the Royal Ulster Constabulary had a clear duty to do everything in their power to bring his killers to book.

As for me, life within the RUC/CID was never to be the same again. Following my assistance to the Stevens Enquiry, none of my CID colleagues ever said as much as a word to me by way of criticism for going forward. They did not have to. When I walked into a room they simply walked out. They totally ignored me. They passed me in corridors as if I was not there. It was as if I was invisible. I would have much preferred that they had sat down and discussed with me what I had done and the reasons for it. Generally speaking, the CID officers who gave me this silent treatment were officers of little or no real detective ability. For the first time in their service, these men could look down their noses at me. I was a whistleblower, a rat. I had broken with tradition. I was out of step.

There were notable exceptions. Decent Police officers who supported me knew the facts. They had taken the trouble to ask. They had understood my reasons for going forward and they had no problems with what I had done. They told me of rumours that were being maliciously bandied about of how I had made a number of statements to the Stevens team incriminating the Special Branch and my fellow CID officers. According to those fabricated stories there was no end to my treachery. This was nonsense of course but there was nothing that I could do to redress it. I tried to have my tormentors believe that I could not have cared less. I was tired. I was totally disillusioned with it all. I tried to brave it out, but inside it was eating me up.

On the other hand the Special Branch wasted no time in letting me know that they had nothing to fear from what I had told the Stevens team. They were openly hostile towards me, but that was to be expected. One of their number stopped me in a corridor in Castlereagh.

"We are duck's ass tight on that Finucane murder, Jonty. We don't give a f**k about the Stevens team," he said.

I knew that that particular officer had quite a lot to fear. I have often wondered if the Stevens team were ever able to bring that particular Rottweiler to heel. Another Special Branch officer who had a long history of fighting with me actually threatened to have guns planted in the roof space of my home. He said that he would send in his "ninja" men to recover them. This was his idea of a ploy to totally discredit me. He told me straight that I could not expect to bad-mouth the RUC Special Branch to a team of English detectives and not receive payback. His outburst was so filled with venom that I feared that he would do just what he said.

I had now entered a new and very oppressive phase in my career. I was no longer considered trustworthy. In fact, I was considered extremely dangerous by some of the authorities within the Special Branch. There was no telling how they would come back at me for the Barrett affair. I feared the worst. Now I had to protect my family, not only from terrorists but also from sinister elements within the RUC itself.

I watched with interest how Chris Patten the Tory MP was planning to radically change the make-up of our Force. I made a conscious decision to consider early retirement. My retirement was scheduled to take place on 16 April 2007, some eight years away in 1999. Yet, despite all of the problems, I was still addicted to Police work. I still enjoyed the chase. I missed the buzz of pursuing a cold case.

I knew from experience that the answers to all of the Constabulary's questions lay not inside computers, not in procedures or protocols. These were a very necessary part of Police work, but the real answers were to be found out there on the streets of Northern Ireland. There is a wealth of information to be had from ordinary decent people. All they ask is that a Police officer interact with them with respect and treat them as equals.

Once that is done, respect has been earned and the information flows in. It isn't rocket science. It is just common sense and logic. Respect is the key and respect is not gained by the putting on of a uniform. Respect is earned by the way a Police officer treats every person he interacts with. Trevor McIlwrath and I could not cope with the volume of information that we gleaned from the ordinary decent people we encountered on both sides of the political divide.

Gunmen of Barrett's calibre are definitely not ten a penny. Not by any stretch of the imagination. Barrett stands alone in his personal capacity to commit brutal murder. We had never encountered a murder where the gunman displayed such a hatred for his victim. Barrett is an indescribably evil individual. Why he ever looked upon me as his friend, I will never know. I was not his friend. I needed his trust simply to enable me to get close enough to him to gut him. There are a lot of men who languished in Ulster's prisons for years because they made the mistake of trusting me. Men who were responsible for some of the most heinous crimes in the history of the Troubles. I am proud of that. In many of those cases, I was able to get around Special Branch obstruction to put them exactly where they belonged.

I left the Royal Ulster Constabulary under the provisions of the Patten Report on 6 April 2001 following a Loyalist bomb attack on our home in Ballyclare on 4 October 2000. But there was to be no peaceful retirement for my family or myself. I was still embroiled in the Pat Finucane affair.

I co-operated with John Ware and Eamon Hardy of the BBC "Panorama" documentary "A Licence to Kill". When the programme went out on air, Ken Barrett was seen on national television, boasting once again of his personal involvement in the murder of Pat Finucane. BBC journalists had capitalised upon Barrett's penchant to talk openly about the murder. They wiped the floor with him. He was unaware that his confessions were being covertly video-recorded. Two BBC investigative journalists had done exactly what we in the RUC had failed to do in 1991 and again in 1999.

I have no doubt that the BBC programme prompted Sir John Stevens to move his enquiry up a level. Undercover CID officers set Barrett up in an elaborate sting operation that resulted in him being charged with the murder of Pat Finucane. The operation itself was fraught with quite a number of legal difficulties. It could well have been the subject of intense legal scrutiny at Belfast Crown Court when Barrett was to stand trial. At the end of the day, it was never tested.

On Monday, 13 September 2004 Ken Barrett appeared before Lord Justice Weir at Belfast Crown Court at Laganside in Belfast. He surprised everyone but me when he pleaded guilty to a catalogue of serious terrorist offences, including the murder of Pat Finucane. He was sentenced to 22 years in prison. Barrett did not fear his sentence. He was fully aware that all the offences were committed before the signing of the Good Friday Agreement. He believed that he was entitled to the benefits of that Agreement. His case would simply be referred to the Sentence Review Commission. If he qualifies, he will be released within two years.

Trevor and I stood behind Barrett in Belfast Crown Court to hear him being sentenced. It was the end of a long hard road for me. Within seconds of him being brought into the courtroom, Barrett's evil eyes searched the public gallery behind him. I knew that he was looking for me. When our eyes met, the atmosphere was electric. With a fixed stare he sent me a clear signal that he would come after me. It was no surprise to me. He had always made it clear to us that if ever he was arrested or charged with any of the offences he had admitted to us, he would "put two bullets in my face".

I stood in that brand new courtroom and stared back at him. The day that Police officers cower down to a serial killer such as Barrett will be a sad day for law enforcement. I will be looking over my shoulder for as long as I live for men like Barrett who are intent upon revenge. I know that they have the ability to kill me. It never deterred me while I was in the Police service and now I certainly will not allow it to impinge upon my private life any more than is necessary. My only regret is that I was not supported in my pursuit of this evil serial killer in 1991/1992.

God only knows how many unfortunate Northern Ireland citizens were dispatched to an untimely death by Barrett in the interim. I try not to dwell on that. It was not my doing. Let those Police officers who stood in my way and protected this man from me live with it.

Chapter 14

Loose Talk Saves Lives

It was 6 am on a cold February day in 1991. I had been stationed in Tennent Street for just under a year. The search-and-arrest briefing at the CID office there had taken just 30 minutes. Over 40 uniformed RUC officers from different Mobile Support Units (MSU) from around the Belfast region had attended the briefing. Each of the six search-and-arrest teams had been allocated a house to search and was accompanied by a CID officer to deal with any "finds" and to handle the arrests of the UVF suspects, all of whom had been involved in serious crimes including murder. Our target that day was a UVF gang from the Shankill Road. We were to arrest the suspects and hold them in Castlereagh Police Office.

I grabbed my overcoat and clipboard and followed the uniformed crew downstairs and out into the cold morning air. There were men everywhere. Landrover doors were banging shut as officers crewed up their vehicles and prepared to leave the barracks. The air was filled with the crackling sound of Police radios and the revving of Landrover engines. The thin blanket of snow on the ground was disappearing fast, banished by sheets of falling sleet. The sleet bit into my face as I ran to a jeep to join the uniformed crew.

"Hi, Skipper," a voice shouted.

I looked up to see a tall, thin Police officer standing at the rear of a jeep. It was "Hightower", a well-known character in the MSU.

"Hi!" I replied. "Where's 'Dusty'?" I added, referring to his sergeant.

"He's on a day off today, Skipper. He's probably still in his pit," "Hightower" replied.

We got into our respective jeeps and the vehicles left the barracks one after the other, making an impressive convoy as some went left towards Woodvale and others turned right towards the Shankill Road.

Such search-and-arrest operations were routine for all of us in the CID in those days. Little did I know it, but this particular operation was to bring a welcome new development that would serve us well over the following years. This was a time when the UVF was becoming more vicious, mimicking their enemy the Provisional IRA in the setting up of cells to defeat informants or to at least make them more readily identifiable. The cell system meant that those who were to be involved in an operation would only know at the very last moment where and when it was to be carried out, and each man would have no prior knowledge of or contact with those who were to be his accomplices. We in the CID were doing all in our power to penetrate the UVF in spite of their new modus operandi. Today's operation would give us just such a chance.

We stopped at our target house, a small terraced Housing Executive dwelling, at around 6.25 am and debussed from the jeeps. Other Landrovers sped past us along the dark and deserted streets. I approached the front door of our particular house with Carol, our uniformed WPC. I waited for the signal that officers were in position at the rear of the house before knocking on the white PVC front door. The small garden was strewn with litter that must have blown in from the street, for the garden itself was unusually neat and well-tended.

The lights went on in an upstairs bedroom at the front of the house and then in the hallway behind the front door. The door opened slowly and a petite dark-haired woman stood in front of me in her dressing gown and slippers.

"Well?" she asked.

"We have a warrant to search your house, madam," I replied, holding the search warrant up to the light to allow her to examine it.

"Come in," she said, as she bent down to pick up three bottles of milk from her doorstep.

"Billy!" she shouted upstairs. "Come down here. It's the peelers."

She walked inside and we followed her in. The number of RUC men and the nature of their heavy search gear concerned her. My team was eight strong. My target was her husband Billy (not his real name), a notorious UVF gunman and suspected serial killer.

I heard him thunder downstairs. He passed the uniformed Police officers as if they weren't there. He had pulled a pair of jeans on and stood before me bare-chested. His arms were covered in Loyalist tattoos. Although I had read much about this man, this was the first time I had actually met him. I was surprised at how small and wiry he was. Brushing past me, he reached for his cigarettes and lighter from the mantlepiece. He lit a cigarette and I noticed that he was shaking uncontrollably. I asked him why he was shaking. He glared at me.

"I'm freezing, mate, that's why I'm shaking. Now, what's up?" he asked.

"We have a warrant to search your house under the Emergency Provisions Act," I said.

"Go ahead, there's nothing here," he said, as he took long drags from his cigarette. "Get me a fresh shirt, Sonia (not her real name)," he hissed at his wife.

She left the living room and returned a few moments later with a fresh denim shirt. Billy put it on. His small stature totally threw me. This small man, big gun syndrome was common to both paramilitary camps. The local Provo commander in Ardoyne was also very small but he too had a reputation for his bloodlust. On a one-to-one basis, few people would fear these individuals, but the power that guns give them is phenomenal. Billy reminded me so much of the local PIRA commander and of Johnny Adair, the local UFF leader, who was also small in stature but had a fanatical UDA following because of his ruthless disregard for human life. Adair hated anyone and anything with the even slightest association with Roman Catholicism.

The "weed" that stood before me pulling on his denim shirt had an awesome reputation for violence. (I was still in the habit of thinking of the criminal element as so many unwanted weeds in our garden.) He was also a local UVF commander of considerable standing in a tight-knit UVF unit in North Belfast. I intended to arrest him after the house search and book him into Castlereagh. There we would interview him in relation to his alleged involvement in serious terrorist crimes.

The uniformed search team was going from room to room, carrying out their duties with meticulous professionalism. Still standing in the living room, I noticed some very sentimental valentine cards propped proudly on the fireplace. I began to examine the verses and the personal messages the pair had written to each other. It intrigued me to find that a UVF thug of this man's ilk could actually pen such loving words.

"What do you think you are doing?" exclaimed Sonia.

I was taken aback by her sudden appearance in the living room and the tone of her voice. I had asked Carol, the WPC, to keep Sonia and her children in the kitchen out of sight of the search team. Meanwhile Billy was accompanying the team from room to room to ensure that he would be present if anything sinister were to be found.

I swung around to face Sonia, still holding the valentine card in my hand.

"I'm just reading the verse: it's beautiful," I replied.

"It's none of your business!" she said sharply.

Sonia was right of course, and I nodded and apologised, placing the card back onto the mantelpiece with the others. She was holding a steaming mug of tea. I could see that she was embarrassed by the fact that she only had time to put on a housecoat and a pair of slippers before we had entered her home. She kept fidgeting with the belt of her dressing gown in a bid to ensure that it was closed tightly around her. I had seen the same such nervous fidgeting exhibited by countless women during such house searches. I tried to think of something to say to lighten the atmosphere:

"I was just . . ."

"What's he done this time?" she asked.

We had both spoken at once. Sonia laughed. I hadn't expected that.

"Look, I'm sorry, I can't discuss that with you. That is between me and Billy," I replied.

"He tells me nothing," she said. "He goes off for days on end without as much as a word and comes home as if he has just nipped out for a paper," she added.

The search was only halfway completed, and so far we had found nothing. I could hear the familiar sounds of doors banging and drawers opening and closing as the team carried out the search. Carol, the WPC had moved to the doorway of the kitchen and looked at me, rolling her eyes to the ceiling: the two children, probably about ten or eleven years old, were fighting over who should get what from a variety pack of breakfast cereals. Sonia shouted into them in a non-aggressive murmer, asking them to behave.

"Nice kids," I said in a bid to make light conversation.

"Do you have any children?" she asked.

"Yes, two boys and a girl," I replied.

"What ages?" she asked.

"The boys are six and three. My daughter is fifteen. Why?"

"No reason, you just seem interested in the children," she replied.

I explained that despite our obvious conflict with her husband Billy, it was important that we did not upset the children any more than was absolutely necessary in the circumstances.

"The last time the Police were here on a search, one of them called my boy a wee UVF bastard," Sonia said glumly.

I shook my head. This saddened me but it did not surprise me. What any RUC officer hoped to achieve by deliberately alienating the wife or child of a terrorist suspect was beyond me.

"Did your wife get a card, Sergeant?" she asked.

"Pardon?" I asked.

"A valentine card—did your wife get one?" she asked.

"Yes, yes of course," I replied.

"Are you from Tennent Street?" she asked, "It's just, I've never seen you before."

"No, I only arrived in the CID in Tennent Street in July last year", I replied.

"What's your name?" she asked.

This set alarm bells ringing. Why did she want to know my name? Would she make a complaint about me?

"The Policewoman calls you 'Sergeant'. What is your name?" she asked again.

"My name is Brown, Johnston Brown," I replied.

"Will you be lifting Billy, Sergeant Brown?" she asked.

The answer was simple. I decided it was best to be brutally honest.

"Yes, I will," I replied.

"Where will you be taking him, so's I can let the solicitor know?" she asked.

"Castlereagh," I replied.

The atmosphere became tense. She stood there in front of me, staring at me as if trying to fathom exactly what was going on.

"He will be allowed to see a solicitor, won't he?" she asked.

"Yes, of course," I replied.

She sat down on the settee, cradling her cup of tea in both hands. I guessed she was in her late thirties, maybe early forties, but she looked careworn and much older than her years. I was struck by her pleasant attitude: it was not often that we met someone in such confrontational situations who did not automatically treat us with contempt. Usually by this time, we would have been met with a torrent of abuse. I was at a loss as to what I could do or say to ease her situation. She was now becoming visibly upset. Carol, our WPC, moved to sit on the arm of the settee beside her.

I looked at my watch. It was just short of 7 am and I knew from experience that a proper search of these particular houses could take up to an hour. Sonia had gone quiet. Tears were running down her cheeks. Her young daughter had noticed she was upset and had also joined her on the settee. Something inside me told me to do or say something to ease the atmosphere. A sense of hostility was increasing, and Sonia's son was glaring at me. He no doubt thought that I had said something to upset his mother.

Before I had a chance to say any more, we heard the search team come clambering downstairs. The sergeant in charge entered the living room behind Billy, the suspect. The sergeant looked at me and shook his head: nothing had been found upstairs. He ushered us all into the kitchen so that his team could search the living room. I saw Sonia and Billy exchange glances. They communicated with each other silently but effectively. There was no further exchange of conversation between Sonia and myself. By this time she wasn't in the mood for casual conversation. A uniformed team of Police was searching her home in front of her children.

The kitchen and the back yard were the last areas to be searched. An officer had found a replica firearm in a drawer in the kitchen and was examining it carefully. It was innocent enough where it was, in one sense, but such weapons were increasingly being used in criminal activity. A pension book was found in another drawer: it was not in the name of the householder, but of a pensioner from the Woodvale. We logged it on the search record and I called Billy into the kitchen. He glanced at the pension book.

"It's her ma's," he said.

Sonia ran into the kitchen. "For goodness sake, that is my mum's. She can't lift it, so I get it for her every week and take it to her," she said.

I nodded to the constable holding it. He set it back down on the kitchen table and struck the entry he had made for it from the Form 29 (the search record). Sonia glared at him. The search was finally concluded. The uniformed sergeant in charge asked Billy to sign the

Form 29 to confirm that we had caused no damage during the search, and he did so. The team started clearing up and retrieving their equipment. The sergeant closed his clipboard and nodded at me.

"07.33 hours, Jonty," he said.

This was my cue. I was glad that Sonia was aware of the fact that I would be arresting Billy. I moved over beside him. I formally arrested him and cautioned him. He made no reply. He was handcuffed in the hallway out of view of the children.

"Ring the lawyer," he said to Sonia as he was leaving.

I escorted Billy outside and put him into the rear of an armoured RUC Landrover. There was no fuss. No hate-filled profanities. I got up into the Landrover beside him. He asked if he could smoke and motioned to his coat pocket. I took out his cigarettes and his lighter. I lit his cigarette and placed it in his mouth. He could do the rest himself, handcuffed or not.

I could see fellow RUC men coming and going from the house, carrying their heavy search gear back to the waiting jeeps. Sonia was standing at the front door being comforted by her neighbours. I knew from overhearing radio transmissions that the other six houses had been searched. All of the searches had turned in negative. Three other UVF suspects were on their way to Castlereagh. Four arrests out of six was a good result.

After a flutter of frantic to-ing and fro-ing, we were finally on the move. The Landrover filled up with our men and the doors banged closed with that thunderous metallic clang so peculiar to armoured jeeps. We were just about to leave when the sergeant in charge of the search team ran up to the rear of my jeep. He opened the door and without a word handed me a slip of blue note paper. I was jerked violently forward in my seat as the Landrover sped off up the street in pursuit of the other jeeps. I opened the slip of paper. It read: "Sergeant Brown, please ring me on (*telephone number*) before Billy gets out. Sonia." Fortunately Billy, who was seated right beside me, was busy leaning forward, looking out the driver's windscreen to watch our progress towards East Belfast and Castlereagh Police Office. He was so engrossed that he wasn't taking any notice of me or the note.

"How many were lifted?" he asked.

"Four so far, including you," I replied.

"Who?" he asked.

"Please . . ." I replied.

He smiled: "No harm in asking."

At last we pulled into the front gate of Castlereagh RUC Station behind two other jeeps. A civilian in a red Rover car had just been diverted into the heavily fortified "bombproof" bunker to our left that had been built specifically to deal with "proxy" bombs, i.e. those driven into the Station by civilians acting under duress from terrorists. The traffic light at the pneumatic barrier was red. We were going nowhere. The three RUC men on security duty were busy. Even an RUC Landrover was not in itself a licence to enter the Castlereagh complex. Security was very tight in those days. Following a short delay and a search underneath each Police vehicle with large mirrors on low trolleys, we were allowed to proceed inside. I booked Billy into the Police Office and checked prisoners' details on the board, which listed all those detained in the Police Office. Including our four prisoners from "D" Division, there were now eleven prisoners in total and some more were on their way in. I knew that I would not be taking part in the interviews, as I would be taking part in a trial at the Crown Court at Crumlin Road that day. I waited for the Landrover crew to finish their breakfast in the canteen and to drop me back to Tennent Street.

It was around lunchtime that same day at Belfast Crown Court that I found Sonia's note again. I had been searching in my coat pockets for a pen, and had otherwise forgotten all about the note. I walked into the Police room to use the only Police telephone line available to us. This telephone was primarily for the use of the uniformed staff based there but few of them had any objection to CID officers using it too. I called the number. There was no answer. I waited for an hour and rang back: Sonia answered the telephone almost immediately.

She explained that she was sickened by all of the violence. She had heard the uniformed sergeant call me Jonty, and realised that she had heard of me. She said her husband hated me, and when UVF men visited her home, she had heard often them refer to "that b***** Jonty Brown". She told me that she had always been too afraid to talk to the Police before because her husband would boast of the help the UVF got from some RUC men. She felt, however, that she could trust me. She wanted to help us.

She agreed to meet me later that day. She said she always had a two-hour period in the evening when she was on her own, as her children were either over at the Community Centre or out with their friends. She could see me between 8 and 10 pm and would explain exactly where she was coming from then. She said that she knew things and often heard details of what the UVF were planning. Some of her best friends were women who were living with or were married to senior UVF men. She said she was also very friendly with the wife of a top UFF man close to Johnny Adair and would hear from her what the UFF were planning. Sonia explained that she was too afraid to use her own home telephone because Billy kept saying the Special Branch tapped it. She explained that she had given me her mother's telephone number: her mother was "doting" and wouldn't have a clue what was going on. She suggested that I meet her at her mother's house.

Such approaches to us were not uncommon but this one seemed too good to be true. It was also fraught with difficulty. In the first place, Sonia's gender meant that I could never meet her alone, not under any circumstances. Yet she trusted me because she knew that the UVF hated me: how could I convince her that she would also have to trust one of my RUC colleagues? If she was genuine in her decision to come forward, it was imperative that I didn't do or say anything to spook her. Her gender caused me some concern, but it was not my biggest problem. Her choice of venue for a meeting was taboo in itself. Trevor and I were too well known in the district to be seen coming or going to a house there. Yet I had detected an eagerness to volunteer information, and I intended to do my utmost to take advantage of this development which would no doubt prove to be very much in the public interest. Yes, it was fraught with many difficulties, but if we could meet this lady on a regular basis and in a professional manner, there was no doubt that she had great potential for us.

I thanked Sonia for getting in touch and explained the rules governing the meetings with our sources. I could not ever meet her alone: I would have to be accompanied by a CID colleague at all times. I explained that this would always be the same colleague and someone she could trust implicitly. She went silent for a time. I explained to her that the rules were there as much for her protection as for mine. She asked me to let her think about it. I agreed. I gave her my home telephone number and invited her to ring me there at any time. She was obviously rather taken aback by the rules. I detected a distinct note of indecision. I could not leave things up in the air like that.

"Lives depend on trust, Sonia. We must trust each other—meet me just once and allow me to explain," I asked.

There was a pause. Far too long a pause. I wished that I had just turned up with Trevor and laid our cards on the table then. At last

Sonia's timid but broad Belfast accent broke the long silence: "ok, Jonty, when?" she asked.

I decided to strike while the iron was hot. "No better time than tonight," I said. "Walk along Cambrai Street at 8 pm. We will pick you up in a blue Ford Sierra. It is Trevor's car."

"ok, I'll see you at 8 o'clock," she said.

The phone went dead. I then set about clearing the proposed meeting with my CID authorities, and rang Trevor at his office in Greencastle RUC Station to explain what had happened.

"What do you make of her?" he asked.

"I believe she is genuine, Trevor, and anyway we have nothing to lose," I replied.

We agreed to be at Tennent Street CID offce at 7 pm, an hour before the meet itself, so that we could put our heads together in relation to the overall security issues, both for this new source and ourselves. Cambrai Street would be very dark and it carried little pedestrian or road traffic at that time of night. Murders and attempted murders were so commonplace in that dimly lit part of the Woodvale that it had put paid to anyone travelling there on foot unnecessarily. Trevor and I also came up with a list of the active UVF men who ran with Sonia's husband. Theirs was a vicious UVF team. We intended to test Sonia's knowledge of them and their activities.

At 7.30 pm we drove out of Tennent Street RUC Station in Trevor's blue Ford Sierra. We turned left onto Tennent Street and headed towards the Crumlin Road. We then took first left onto Sidney Street West and left again onto Cambrai Street. There was no-one around. We had come deliberately early to ensure that there were no cars parked up side streets filled with UVF men or anyone standing in the shadowy alleyways to our right. There were no potential threats, as far as we could see.

We drove past Sonia's mother's home and saw a car parked outside the little terraced house. The dwelling was bright and well presented. New double-glazed windows and a brand new mahogany door were evidence of a high standard of maintenance. The light was on in the living room but the blinds were drawn, so we could not see who was inside. Trevor parked at the top of the street.

He switched off his lights and the car engine so that we could sit virtually unnoticed in the darkness. Our presence was further shielded by a row of cars parked by residents. Children and adults walked past without even noticing us. We had been doing this for years. We could see right to the bottom of the street and onto Sonia's mother's front door. It was freezing outside the car. Fortunately we had not long to wait.

At exactly ten past eight we saw the front door of the house open. We could make out Sonia's outline as she left the house and walked towards Cambrai Street. She was alone. Trevor waited until she reached the junction of Cambrai Street and turned right towards the Woodvale Road. We kerb-crawled down to the same junction. We turned right onto Cambrai Street just in time to see Sonia crossing the road from right to left some 100 yards ahead of us. Trevor put his foot down on the accelerator and in seconds we pulled up beside Sonia. I smiled at her and opened the rear passenger door from the inside. She jumped quickly into the back seat. I could see that she was nervous.

We drove to a laneway off the Glencairn Estate and stopped in a large secluded car park. We were the only car there. I turned in my seat to face Sonia and introduced Trevor, explaining that he and I had been working together for the past six years. She began to relax. We set out the rules of our contact with her and also gave details of the various financial rewards that would be available to her if her information proved to be accurate. She made it clear she wasn't interested in the money. That was not her reason for coming forward. Sonia hated the Loyalist paramilitaries: in her book, the UVF and the UDA were no better than the Provisional IRA. We had to agree. Too many innocent people were dying, she said. She merely wanted to help to stop it in any small way that was possible. She just needed to be sure that she could trust us. We both assured her of total anonymity.

Apparently Sonia's marriage to Billy was strained to the limit at that time because of his involvement with the UVF. She was sick of his frequent absences; she hated the UVF and all that it stood for. Her greatest fear was that her son would be sucked into the organisation. She assured us that, putting his involvement in the UVF aside, her husband Billy was a good man, a good father, and when he was at home, a loving husband. Trevor and I sat with Sonia for a very long time in that car, with the engine running to keep us warm. We listened intently to her as she unburdened herself of all her problems. We agreed on a strategy for future meetings. We also agreed on how to contact each other for urgent meetings. Sonia listened intently and absorbed it all without the need for endless questions. Trevor and I explained to her that every gun seized, every bullet recovered from the paramilitaries was another life saved. Terrorists were a cancer in our communities and they had to be removed. Their history, their religion or their political aspirations were of absolutely no interest to us. We would move against them when possible and take them down. Any help that Sonia could afford us would be gratefully received. Trevor and I had over 30 sources from all sections of the different paramilitary groups, Protestant and Catholic alike. One more source was always welcome.

We then took a few minutes to complete a source contact sheet with details of Sonia's true identity, her next-of-kin, her children and her full family tree. This would be vital in the event of her ever being compromised. In such circumstances, we would need to act as quickly as possible to remove her and anyone close to her from the threat of retribution by the UVF. We were also hoping of course that we would never have to take such measures. Sonia had no hang-ups, no misgivings: she was under no illusions as to what she was contemplating. This woman was strong and resolute. Only time would tell if she was going to be of any use to us. I knew that even as "eyes and ears" she was so close to Brigade Staff UVF that her information would doubtless be invaluable. I asked her to develop an interest in what her husband and his UVF friends were discussing. The vehicle registration numbers of the cars of anyone that came to her house to visit Billy or pick him up him were, for example, vital pieces of information. We questioned Sonia extensively about various UVF men. She acquitted herself well. I had a good feeling about this.

It was close to 10 pm when we dropped Sonia back at Cambrai Street in the Woodvale. We shadowed her as she made her way back to her car. We drove past her in time to see her turn on the headlights in her car and set off from the kerb side at the front of her mother's home. We did not acknowledge each other as we drove past her at the junction of Ohio Street and Cambrai Street. We had made sure that she had not been followed, at least not on that particular night.

"What do you think, Trevor?" I asked.

"You wouldn't know yet, it's early days, but she does seem to be genuine and very keen to help," he said.

"Drop me off at Tennent Street, Trevor, so that I can get my car. I'll see you down at Greencastle and we can draft up our notes there," I said.

Twenty minutes later I pulled up in my brown Nissan Laurel out-side Greencastle RUC Station. I had served there for over three years from early 1985 until July 1988 and I was well known to the staff. I heard the loud metallic click as the RUC officer pushed the electronic switch that automatically opened the lock on the small, heavily reinforced metal pedestrian gate. The officer had recognised my car, and signalled to me to join him in the fortified concrete Sanger.

I knew this man well. He ushered me into the Sanger and closed the heavy metal door behind me. The heat inside, generated from a Superser gas heater, was overwhelming. The armoured glass window that overlooked the Shore Road and the front gate of the barracks was lying open, to afford an unrestricted view of the front gate and the approach to the station. A submachine-gun was lying on the shelf at the window. A steaming, white, plastic beaker was sitting alongside it. Music filled the air as the voice of Dean Martin crooned a love ballad from a small portable radio. The officer was a regular RUC man. He was in his early fifties and well known for his inability to stay sober. Tonight was no exception.

He was smiling and giggling.

"Thank goodness he is due to sign off at 11 pm," I found myself thinking.

"Listen, Skipper," he said. "Nice music, warm Sanger and a wee drink—what more could a man ask for?" he continued, still sniggering.

He lifted the plastic beaker and held it up to my nose. The smell startled me as I inhaled the unmistakeable, pungent smell of whiskey. There was evidently very little coffee in that cup. He slapped me on the back.

"All this and I'm being paid overtime too," he said.

I excused myself and left the Sanger. Dean Martin was still croon-ing on that damn radio as I walked down the steps and into the front door of Greencastle RUC Station. I ran up the open-plan staircase towards the first floor. I stopped momentarily in front of the shining, black memorial tablet mounted on the wall in memory of our fallen RUC comrade, Constable Lindsay McCormack. McCormack had been brutally murdered by the Provisional IRA at 2.45 pm on 2 March 1983 outside Ballygolan Primary School on the Serpentine Road. He was a community beat Policeman, had worked that district for over eleven years and was well respected by all sections of the community. At 50 years old, he had unfortunately been no match for the two cowardly young Provos who walked up behind him and shot him in the head five times.

I reflected upon how I had visited Lindsay at the request of a decent Special Branch officer who was very concerned for his safety. He had asked me to try my best to make Lindsay aware of the very real danger he was in. I was stationed in Andersonstown at that time. I counselled Lindsay to take care and asked him to consider moving station. But he would not be told. He argued that he loved working this beat and that the people in his district respected him. He refused to be intimidated by the Provos. He refused to believe that some of the locals would have passed on his details to PIRA, insisting that the people on his beat would not do or wish him harm. He was right. It was in fact a Provisional IRA unit from West Belfast that murdered him. Lindsay paid the ultimate price for his determination not to "kow-tow" to Republicans, a price that so many before him and unfortunately so many after him would pay for simply trying to protect and to serve all sections of our divided community. Lindsay had a wife and a son. When I heard of his death, I felt terrible. Perhaps I not laboured my point enough? Could I have said or done anything more to have made him take greater care? My whole being was shaken to the core.

I had known and respected Lindsay McCormack. For me that plaque on the wall was not only a memorial to an RUC constable who refused to be intimidated: it was also a stark reminder that information was vital to the saving of life. The Special Branch warnings of the extent to which the constable's life was in danger had gone unheeded. That information could and should have saved his life. I was a critic at times of the way in which the Special Branch approached situations, but even I knew better than to disregard information about a death threat coming in from one of their Republican agents. The death of Lindsay McCormack was an example of how things could go so terribly wrong.

Trevor was sitting alone at his desk in the small CID office when I arrived to join him. He was completing a pools coupon and had a mug of coffee on his desk. There was another mug beside the kettle with a tea bag in it. Trevor pointed to it for me and sat down at his desk again. We went over the events of the previous hours and decided on how best to report the recruitment of our new source without revealing her identity to anyone, especially those Special Branch minions we knew would want to compromise her. We decided that if Sonia did prove to be an important source, Special Branch would be given a "front man": the name of another individual who, we would allege, was giving us the information. One too many of our CID sources had been burned by certain unscrupulous Special Branch officers, and I was not going to risk that again in this case. I intended to ensure that Sonia remained safe and anonymous. She must never come under UVF suspicion. No CID source had a licence to commit crime and in this regard, we knew that we were on safe ground with Sonia. She was not involved with the UVF or engaged in any other criminal activity. She would report to us only what she was able to learn from pillow talk with her husband and from overhearing conversations between Billy and the other UVF men who frequently visited her home.

We completed our paperwork just before midnight. Sonia was the latest addition to our list of over 30 regular contacts across the Belfast region. If she proved to be as useful as she appeared, she would be invaluable. The fact that she was not involved in terrorism herself in any way and as such in the normal course of things should never have been privy to any UVF or UFF information was an added bonus. This would throw the Loyalist paramilitaries into a state of disarray, and feed the sense of paranoia which seemed to be a feature of such groups anyway. Anything of this nature, which would have the effect of throwing a paramilitary body off balance and out of action, even if only temporarily, was of profound value to us.

Within a few weeks, Sonia was meeting us regularly and reporting on the activities of Billy and his UVF cronies. Initially, the information she provided was low-key and uncontroversial, and as such she generated very little interest from the RUC Special Branch. They made no application to meet our new source: at that stage Sonia was obviously not a threat to any of their agents. We knew of course that this could change at any time, and that we would have to be ready to answer the kind of probing questions the Special Branch might put to us in relation to this source if and when she did arouse their curiosity.

Loose talk saves lives in a paramilitary war. Our experience had proven this to be true, time and again. Sonia's information helped us a great deal. She was not only reporting on the activities of the UVF, she was also able to get us very valuable information about Johnny Adair and his UFF cohorts from one of her best friends, who was

married to a first lieutenant of Adair. Sonia was able to tell us who was
being targeted for murder by the UVF: invariably we would find that
the intended victims were innocent Catholics from neighbouring
Republican estates, and we were able to warn them successfully and
move them on. Later, Sonia reported to us on the whereabouts of UVF
weapons, and very productive house searches and the arrest of UVF
volunteers followed. With such successes, Special Branch interest in
our new source increased and we soon found ourselves being forced
to bring the front man into the picture. Sonia was obviously starting
to embarrass the Special Branch, or she was endangering their UVF
sources in such a way as to leave them open to arrest by the CID.

Within days of the introduction of our front man to Special
Branch, we became aware from him that certain associates of his
involved in the UVF were consciously avoiding him. Someone had
obviously tipped these men off that our front man was talking, and I
did not have to wonder who had done that. Sonia was lucky: had it not
been for our previous experience, we would have registered her and
left her open to compromise by unscrupulous Special Branch men.

It was Wednesday, 3 February 1993 when Sonia reported a UVF
murder plot targeting an alleged top Provo living in Whiteabbey Village.
She did not know the man's identity and she was unable to ask Billy any
questions. She was, however, able to describe exactly where the intended
murder victim lived. I knew him well: he was indeed a Republican, yes,
but he was most certainly not a member of the PIRA. In any case, when
a life—no matter whose—was threatened, we were sworn to protect it.
We passed our information on in the usual manner to the Special
Branch. I was surprised to find that they were already aware of the death
threat. They had ensured that the intended victim was made aware of
the danger he was in through the usual uniformed Police channels.
Sonia continued to relay information to us about how determined the
UVF were to kill the "Provo". On one particular evening, a UVF team from
"D" Company in the Ballysillan were shadowed leaving the Ballysillan
in a stolen car bearing false plates. They were followed to Whiteabbey
where they were stopped by a Special Branch uniformed patrol within
a quarter of mile of the intended victim's house. We knew that they
were armed, but for reasons best known to themselves, the Special
Branch were content to simply ask them a number of routine questions
before allowing them to proceed back to the Shankill. Thankfully, however, on this occasion at least, their murder bid had been thwarted.

On a second occasion, on Wednesday, 10 February 1993, an armed UVF team set out from the Shankill Road in a stolen red Vauxhall Astra car fitted with "ringer plates", to murder the same man. E4a surveillance teams supported by heavily armed and uniformed Special Support Units (SSU) shadowed them again, the aim being to arrest the murder team if they made any move towards their intended victim. This time the UVF thugs got even closer to their target before they ran into an apparently random SSU road stop. The UVF team became so spooked that they immediately dumped the stolen red Vauxhall Astra car at the rear of the Cloughfern Arms Public House on the Doagh Road. They removed the "ringer plates" from the stolen car and left the original number plates in the back seat of the car. They were followed back to their base without any further disruption.

We had now missed two chances to catch terrorists. I was frustrated by the refusal of the Special Branch to arrest a UVF murder team which was armed and on the move on these two occasions. Although it was unlikely that the UVF would attempt to strike again for a long time, I was afraid that the next time we would not be ahead of them. So why did the Special Branch not move to take the murder team down? It didn't make sense to me. I was now afraid that another UVF unit, one that we could not monitor, would be sent to murder the man. I knew the intended victim well.

On Thursday, 11 February 1993, I rang him and asked him to meet me. We discussed his situation. He said that the local Police had been in touch to warn him that "Loyalists" were planning to kill him, but without specifying which Loyalist group was responsible. I explained that this was more than likely a measure taken by the Police to protect their source. I told him that the murder team were from the UVF on the Shankill and that for some unknown reason, they were determined to kill him. He thanked me for the warning. A few days later, he called me back. He told me that he had gone with some other respected Republicans to the Shankill Road to discuss the UVF threat. Precisely, in fact, what I had warned him not to do. They had been received by the highest-ranking UVF men on the Shankill, who had adamantly denied any involvement in the murder plot. After a flurry of activity and various telephone calls here and there, intended to impress the delegation, the "helpful" UVF men finally volunteered that it was more than likely a UDA/UFF plot spawned by Johnny Adair's notorious UDA "C" Company. The UVF men assured them of their "good faith" and even volunteered to carry out their own enquiries to get to the bottom of the whole thing.

The target had been impressed by this apparently genuine response from the UVF. But shortly after this episode, he noticed an unusual increase in the number of strange cars and pedestrians in the vicinity of his home. He was then contacted again by Police who warned him that the Loyalist threat was still very real. I reminded him of the well-known duplicity of the UVF: that they were no different from any other paramilitary group when it came to protecting their public image, so to speak. I told him that I was not asking which group was threatening to take his life: I knew it was the UVF and not the UDA. He believed me. Yet he trusted no-one, not even me. I could live with that. However, the last thing I wanted was for the intended target to drop his guard. Thanks to Sonia, I knew that his life was still in serious danger.

I was on night duty in Tennent Street and in the CID office alone on Tuesday, 16 February 1993, when I got an urgent call from Sonia just after midnight. She was in a very excited state. She was at her mother's house and she urgently wanted to show me a garage just off the Ballysillan Road in Belfast. She asked me to meet her on the Ballysillan Road in ten minutes: she had very little time to spare. As Sonia would be driving herself both to and from the meet, I did not need to bring another officer with me on this occasion. I left the Police station alone and within minutes I pulled the CID car up alongside Sonia's Nissan. Indicating that I should follow her, she turned off the Ballysillan Road and into a small laneway, where she stopped. She pointed to some nearby garages.

"There is a stolen Ford Escort in one of those garages," she said, "It's in the one that isn't locked. That car will be used tomorrow night. They are going back for that Provo down in Whiteabbey," she concluded.

It was a very still night and my footsteps echoed with each footfall on that concrete pathway as I made my way as quietly as possible towards the garage doors. The area where I was standing was bathed in light from huge spotlights around the perimeter of the industrial complex. I tried one of the garage doors. It was locked. The next garage door gave way as I pushed the handle down. I didn't open it fully: I didn't have to. There inside was a white Ford Escort with a red bonnet. I noted the registration number and closed the garage door again as quickly and as quietly as I could. I knew that we would have to leave the area promptly if we were not to draw any unwanted attention to our presence. I walked back to Sonia's car and thanked her for the information. There was no time for idle chat or the exchanging of pleasantries. We both knew that we would have to act quickly if we were to put a stop to the UVF murder plot.

Sonia drove out onto the Ballysillan Road and turned left towards the Crumlin Road. I drove on down the Crumlin Road and turned right at the traffic lights into Tennent Street. Once back at my desk in the CID office, I rang Trevor at home to update him, as was our custom by that stage. The fact that it was well after 1 am in the morning would not bother Trevor. When it came to saving lives, we knew that it was imperative to move as quickly as possible. I asked a CID colleague to check the registration number of the Ford Escort car with our Central Vehicle Index (CVI). I was pouring myself a cup of coffee when he came off the telephone with CVI.

"It's a stolen car, Skipper," my colleague reported back straight away. "It was taken from Milewater Way in New Mossley Estate in Glengormley yesterday," he added.

Yes! I thought, as I sat down to pen a synopsis of the facts known to me and sketch a diagram of the garage complex that housed the stolen car. I also noted the fact that the car was to be used in a UVF murder bid that we had been monitoring with the Special Branch for some time. I posted the note below the door of the Special Branch office. It was in a sealed envelope addressed to my Special Branch counterpart, an officer that I felt I could trust. In the grand scheme of things, he was no more able than I was to argue with his Special Branch masters, but he was a genuine person and new to his post.

The following evening, 16 February 1993, a UVF unit appeared at the garages. There were a number of UVF cars there. They were totally unaware that they were under surveillance by Special Branch under-cover units. The stolen Ford Escort car was removed from the garage. It now bore a different registration number and the red bonnet was painted white: the UVF had been busy in their preparations for this particular mission. Three of their volunteers got into the Escort and drove off towards Newtownabbey, shadowed by E4a operatives. The vehicle was closely monitored as it made several stops in the Newtownabbey area before travelling towards Whiteabbey village. Sonia had alerted us to the fact that the UVF would be using radio frequency scanners, but this did not concern us overly because all of our Special Branch communications were on a highly secure radio net, which could not be accessed by amateurs. We also knew that the murder team would be in direct radio contact with a convoy of other UVF men travelling alongside them. This was a major UVF operation. A great deal of effort was being expended in the bid to murder the man they had so vehemently denied targeting. So much for the genuine concern which had been expressed by the UVF hierarchy.

Trevor and I were listening on our ordinary RUC secure radio net, waiting for confirmation of the arrests which should follow if the Special Branch authorities gave their authorisation. As the murder team approached Whiteabbey village from the Old Shore Road, the uniformed Special Branch support units were already preparing for a "hard stop" (ramming) of their car.

We waited with bated breath as a Special Branch contact allowed us to listen to the drama unfolding on a Special Branch radio in their Operations room in Castlereagh RUC Station. At 6.47 pm the Ford Escort had entered Whiteabbey village and was making its way towards the Shore Road and their intended target. Suddenly, in a flurry of excitement, the SSU vehicles rammed the suspects' car before it reached the Shore Road.

Thirty-five-year-old Gary Davis, the driver of the stolen vehicle, panicked and threw a pair of gloves out of the partially open driver's window. He was removed from the vehicle and arrested. A second man, 33-year-old Stuart McDowell, jumped from the rear seat of the stolen car and attempted to flee from the Police. He was pursued and arrested a short distance away. He attempted to throw away a pair of black woollen gloves just before his arrest, but Police immediately retrieved them. The front seat passenger in the stolen car, 34-year-old Stephen Pitman, attempted to jump out of it quickly, but he was immediately arrested and put to the ground. He was still wearing a pair of black woollen gloves, and he had a red and black cap in his trouser pocket. All three suspected UVF men had offered no resistance and had been put to the floor within seconds by our SSU units.

The stolen car was searched and two heavy-calibre handguns, a loaded Smith and Wesson 59 semi-automatic pistol and a fully loaded .357 Magnum revolver, were recovered. A radio transmitter and scanner were found lying on the back seat, along with gloves and baseball caps which had been hastily discarded. All three UVF suspects were conveyed to Castlereagh Police Office for interview.

Forensic ballistic examination of the Smith and Wesson pistol determined that it had been used previously in three punishment shootings, which had taken place in the North Belfast area between July and October 1992. All three attacks were attributable to the UVF. The Ruger revolver had been stolen from the home of an RUC constable in Carrickfergus on 24 March 1991. One of our own weapons was in safe hands again at least.

When the dust settled, there was the inevitable post-mortem. First and foremost, a life had been saved. The target had been made aware of the threat on a number of occasions previously, but this had been nothing more than an "ass-covering" exercise by the Police in case anything went wrong. We had moved quickly and professionally to save the man's life, and this case in itself was a clear example if any was needed of how much could be achieved when the CID and the Special Branch could work as a team. We had recovered a stolen car, not from the hands of criminals, but from a ruthless UVF active service unit intent on committing murder. We had retrieved two heavy-duty UVF firearms, which would never again be used to maim or murder anyone. Finally, we had arrested the three cowardly UVF men who had volunteered to carry out the murder. Our courts were sick of such people. Previous such cases of teams of gunmen arrested on the move had resulted in sentences of between ten and sixteen years' imprisonment for the perpetrators. It would be a long time before these particular UVF members would get a chance to become involved in a murder plot again.

It was also very interesting to note that all three men arrested were members of the UVF's 1st Battalion "D" Company from the Ballysillan. Fortunately their commander always boasted about what his men were planning to do. He was a good friend of Sonia's husband Billy. I was to be very grateful for Billy's ability to draw information from such people like that and Sonia's willingness to share the details with us, which enabled us to monitor their deadly plans and take preventative action. In this dirty little war of ours in Northern Ireland, loose talk such as this saved many innocent lives.

Chapter 15
Fighting Back

P unishment beatings and kneecappings were commonplace throughout the Province in the early 1990s. Many of the victims would simply turn up by prior arrangement in an alleyway or on waste ground to be brutally beaten or shot in the arms or legs for some alleged misdemeanour. Few of these criminal assaults were ever solved or even properly investigated because the victims were loathe to even make statements, let alone come forward to identify the thugs responsible. This was regrettable but entirely understandable, given the fact that each of the victims had to continue to live in their communities alongside the very people who had inflicted the horrific injuries they had sustained.

It never did sit easy with me to allow any of the paramilitary thugs responsible for such attacks to get off scot-free. I treated every such case that came my way as a major crime incident. I was always looking out for an instance when they would make a mistake and leave me a clue, thereby enabling us to move against them and make an example of them—no matter what religious or political persuasion they would claim to be affiliated to. The kidnap and unlawful imprisonment of adults in order to punish them was bad enough, but it was the cases where brutal so-called punishments were meted out to children which I found truly abhorrent.

It was a beautiful summer's day on Saturday, 8 May 1992 when a two-man UVF punishment team grabbed a 15-year-old boy from a group of his friends in Ligoniel. They dragged him screaming and kicking into the grounds of the nearby St Mark's Parish Church, to a garden at the rear of the rectory on the Ligoniel Road. It was there in that quiet churchyard that these two UVF thugs carried out their brutal "punishment" attack. One of the two held the boy down and made him stretch out his left arm. The other thug then threw a large heavy rock with jagged edges down onto his left hand. The blow actually severed the boy's thumb and at the same time broke every bone in his hand. The UVF man holding out the child's arm yelled:

"F**k, you've took his thumb right off, Geordie."

"F**k him," came the reply. The man wielding the rock couldn't have cared less about the damage he had inflicted.

The pair of cowards then ran from the scene and made good their escape, leaving their victim maimed and bleeding and entirely alone in the church grounds. These "brave" UVF volunteers, allegedly the defenders of Unionism and of the Protestant people, had surely done themselves proud this time, savagely setting upon an innocent member of their own community for some alleged misdemeanour. A child who had no chance of escape from their grip. A child who offered no resistance and was given no chance to protest his innocence. The good men of the original Ulster Volunteer Force, the men of the 36th Ulster Division, Protestant and Catholic alike, who had died in their thousands at the Somme to secure the freedom of their fellow countrymen, would have turned in their graves on discovering that acts of such sickening cowardice were being carried out in their name. The two UVF thugs who attacked that boy in the churchyard that day were nothing more than bullies, plain and simple. I truly relished the prospect of being able to put such men behind bars.

Accompanied by fellow officers, I visited the scene of the crime to commence inquiries. There was very little blood in evidence, considering the seriousness of the assault. I summoned as per usual the services of a Scenes of Crime officer (SOCO), a photographer and a mapper. We held the scene open for hours. My blood was boiling. The UVF were not going to get away with this. This was bullying at its worst. If these men were not brought to book for this crime and quickly, who would be next—a ten year old, or a six year old? I decided that I would do all in my power to stop the two thugs responsible for this crime in their tracks.

Initial enquiries suggested that the punishment beating was a fully sanctioned UVF attack, yet the reasons for such a decision were vague and non-specific. It smacked of the usual ineptitude of 1st Battalion's "D" Company. I contacted Sonia and explained what had happened. I knew that she had absolutely no time for this or any other type of UVF activity. Since her husband Billy was a good friend of the local commander of "D" Company in the Ballysillan, it was just possible that with a little female persuasion he would be willing to disclose the names of the two UVF men responsible. Sonia had been livid with anger when she had learned the details of the incident. She said she would do her level best to help us, and I knew from the tone of her voice that she would do just that.

When I got back to Tennent Street RUC Station, I contacted the Ulster Hospital in Dundonald to enquire about the child's condition. I was keen to speak to him. His condition was serious: he was still in shock and suffering a great deal of pain, and as such was deemed to be unfit to be interviewed by the doctor in charge. In any case, I could not interview him unless his parents were present. I badly needed to ask him if he knew who was responsible for the assault. His friends were too afraid to even speak to my detectives. I was hoping that the victim himself would be more forthcoming when he was fit for interview.

Sonia proved yet again to be as good as her word. I received a request over our secure radio net to contact my "sister". I knew what that meant and I knew exactly where to contact Sonia. She answered her mother's telephone right away. She was able to tell me that it was Geordie Waters Jnr who had thrown the rock down on the boy's hand and that Geordie's mate Charlie "Popeye" Davidson had held the victim down. Both of these men were well known to me. Sonia was also able to confirm that the UVF had sanctioned the beating, but that no-one could say why. Apparently the UVF themselves were still trying to pin down the reasons for the brutality of the attack. Sonia had spoken without pausing for a breath. As soon as she had finished, she put the phone down. There had been no idle chat. No requests for recompense. No complications. Sonia epitomised everything that a good informant could be. She had no criminal record and a hatred for all paramilitaries, from whichever side of the divide. We had come such a long way since she had first made contact with me by means of that little note. In a sense, Sonia's motivation for coming forward was no concern of mine. She was passionately committed to helping us, that much was clear, and I was just so glad that she was there. Informants in the field of ordinary crime were ten a penny. Informants of Sonia's calibre, who were able to help us actively combat terrorism, were few and far between.

I was determined that Sonia was one source that the Special Branch would never "burn". They had no idea who she was, and I intended to keep it that way. The public interest would definitely not be served by disclosing her identity: quite the contrary, in fact. According to Sonia herself, the commander of the UVF's "D" Company was mouthing off to a lot more people than her Billy, and so it was likely that the Special Branch were already aware of what was going on in this case, and of exactly who was responsible for the attack on the boy. They had, however, no intention of sharing their information with us in the CID. Especially if doing so would result in the arrest or, worse still, the conviction and incarceration of one of their informants.

Armed with this new and vital information from Sonia, I decided to contact the boy's parents. Perhaps I could talk them into trusting me. From enquiries locally, I knew that the UVF and their supporters were in general sickened by the viciousness of the attack on the boy. This conflict over the issue was something that I might be able to use to our benefit. I called to see the boy's parents at their home in Ligoniel. Decent and law-abiding people, they were horrified at this unprovoked attack on their child. They had absolutely no idea who was responsible and their son wasn't telling them either. In fact, they had actually been told by local people in the area who were loyal to the UVF not to co-operate with the Police. I spent a long time explaining to them that unless I caught the two UVF thugs, no child in their district would be safe from a similar attack, and that as such I needed their full co-operation. As much as they agreed with everything that I had said, they feared for their child's life. I detected a barrier, a lack of trust, but I knew that if I could convince them to stand up to the local UVF, then I could progress this enquiry to a whole new level. I asked them if they knew of an RUC man whose word they would trust. They mentioned an old neighbour of theirs, a man they respected and admired. His name was Tony and they had heard that he was an RUC motorbike cop. They had, however, lost contact with him since he had moved house.

I knew Tony: he was stationed in Carrickfergus RUC Station in Co. Antrim. I asked them if I could contact him on their behalf and ask

him to speak to them. I made it clear that I knew exactly who had
assaulted and grievously injured their child, but that I needed to hear
it from him. That we had to stand up and confront those two men;
that there was no justification whatsoever for thugs like that to beat
any person. We knew that even the UVF thought that the punishment
meted out to the boy was completely over the top, even by their
standards. The fact that the UVF had not armed the pair of attackers
spoke volumes as to their expectations. Unfortunately, the choice of
volunteers to carry out the beating left a lot to be desired. George
Waters was well known locally for his vicious streak, and yet his
commander made the decision to send him in the child's direction. I
knew that there were differing opinions within the UVF: I sensed there
was a storm brewing and I was not going to miss the chance to exploit
any such friction between the different UVF factions to our advantage.

I contacted Tony, the family's friend from the Police. I explained to
him exactly what I was contemplating: I needed the family beside me,
with me, if I was to deal properly and effectively with the two UVF
thugs. I did not attempt to lessen the enormity of what lay ahead for
the family. Both Tony and I knew that the UVF could so very easily
turn on them. Tony agreed to do his best to convince the family to co-
operate. In the meantime, I went off to canvas the support of the
parents of the children who had been with the boy when he had been
abducted. The more statements we had from witnesses, the greater
our chances of securing convictions against Waters and Davidson.

I had however underestimated the UVF. Their "D" Company
commander ensured that a story about the injured party's alleged
involvement in local crime was released to a Sunday newspaper. It was
nonsense, of course, but the story was enough to ensure that the
young victim lost a lot of sympathy and support from the public.
Locals were warned again not to co-operate with the Police.

The loss of any of the fingers is traumatic and troublesome. The
loss of a thumb, however, renders a hand almost useless, and is
considered to be a major disability. You lose your capacity to grip anything. The young victim went through painful surgery in order to try
to maintain as much movement in his left hand as possible. But
despite several such attempts to help him, he was left permanently
disabled. Subjected as they now were to severe intimidation on an
ongoing basis, the parents of the child found their resolve weakening.
They now had a very real fear of UVF retaliation if their son made a

statement naming the two offenders. I was incensed at this development. I needed the boy's statement urgently if I was to commence a
prosecution against these two thugs.

On Tuesday, 11 May 1992, I moved the stakes up a little. What if we
were able, I suggested to the family, to get them re-housed out of the
area, miles away from Ligoniel before any action was taken against
Waters and Davidson? Would they then allow their son to make a
statement of the facts, naming the pair who had so grievously
wounded him? The parents needed time to think about this, and
asked for some space. The decision was theirs. It was, after all, too late
for their son. But if the UVF got away with this, they would have a
licence to murder or maim any other child in the area who crossed
them. I decided to back off for a while: I had done my level best. I
thanked the boy's parents for their support, making it clear to them
that I was fully aware of the enormity of the possible consequences for
the family if they came forward to give evidence against the UVF. They
knew where to find me if they decided that they wanted to go ahead
anyway.

Sonia had heard that Waters was not in the least bit concerned
about the Police enquiry: apparently he thought that the injury to the
boy was greatly amusing. The passage of time without any Police
action against the culprits had made the UVF feel safe in the knowledge
that their use of intimidation and the iron grip of fear they had on
their own community had once again proven a real barrier to the
Police. It saddened me, but I had to concede that it was fine for me as
an RUC man to sermonise on the moral rectitude of coming forward,
but that at the end of the day, I myself didn't have to live 24/7 in those
paramilitary-infested neighbourhoods.

On Tuesday, 18 May 1992, ten days after the brutal assault on the
boy, I called at a house on the Flush Road in Ligoniel where I knew I
would be welcomed with a cup of tea. It was a routine "tea stop" for
Trevor and I. The householder there, a motor mechanic and a very
decent man, allowed other mechanics to use his sheds to work on cars
on a daily basis. In fact, this man would regularly collect our cars from
the barracks and get them ready for MOT testing for us. There would
normally be anything from three to ten local men congregating there
for tea. Most of the visitors to this man's house were harmless locals
with absolutely no connections to Loyalist paramilitary groups.
Decent men who would tolerate our impromptu visits with little or

no criticism. The banter was generally good. Unfortunately, some other visitors who would also arrive unannounced were from various local Loyalist camps. They would say very little to us in that environment, barely tolerating us rather than welcoming our presence. Johnny Adair, the commander of the UDA's "C" Company, would call in there from time to time on one errand or another.

When we called in on this occasion, I was not particularly surprised then to find the military commander of the UVF's "D" Company in Ballysillan and his first lieutenant sipping on cups of tea. Although I had heard a lot about this particular "weed", it was in fact the first time that I had actually met him. Trevor and I were accompanied that day by a Special Branch officer who was new to Tennent Street, but we had no intention of enlightening those present to his Special Branch status. As far as the men gathered in that kitchen were concerned, he was just another CID officer.

I pulled the local UVF commander about the brutal nature of the punishment attack and its dire consequences for the 15-year-old victim. He said very little, but did make it plain that he knew that I was receiving absolutely no co-operation from the injured party and his parents. There was a smug smile all over his sun-tanned face as he spoke which really got to me: he was obviously revelling in the fact that fear of UVF reprisals was hampering our investigation. Trevor saw that I was getting rattled, and he pulled me by the arm, handing me a mug of hot, strong tea. His back to the senior UVF man, Trevor winked at me and shook his head in the negative, smiling broadly. Trevor lived for moments like this: he knew what was going to happen. That UVF braggart had wound me up no end and he was just about to get a lashing from my tongue. I turned to him, not a foot away from his face, and leaned in further towards him.

"Look," I said, "I'll tell you what I'll do. You send me the UVF man who threw that rock down on the child's hand and I'll just do him for straightforward GBH with intent. One down from attempted murder. We'll forget about the other guy: he was only minimally involved. We won't mention kidnapping, unlawful imprisonment or that fact that the whole episode was an evil UVF-inspired punishment beating. But if you mess me about, I'll be back up here for both of them and I'll throw the book at them."

I knew by the expression on his face that the "weed" was none too pleased. He was not used to threats, not of any kind. He puffed himself up like a hot air balloon. His face became red and twisted. When he did speak, his voice was a shrill scream.

"Who the hell do you think you are?" he exclaimed. "Are you threatening me?"

"Me?" I replied, "I have absolutely no illusions as to who I am. I'm just an ordinary copper doing my job, as I see it. Your problem is that I'm damn good at it. I'm not threatening anybody. I'm just telling you exactly what I'll do. So send your bullyboy down to me to take what he has coming to him, or I'll be up here in a couple of weeks' time to get both of them. The choice is yours and it's that simple."

It took the "weed" a short time to take in exactly what I had said, and when he did, he lost it. Suddenly and without warning, he was there, back in my face, his right hand moulded into the shape of a gun.

"You see, you two bastards," he said, pointing the imaginary gun at Trevor and myself, "I'll see you bastards get one in the head."

"Yeah, yeah," I replied, "Your only problem is we are not fifteen years old and we don't scare easily either. So tell your bullyboy to get down to Tennent Street to see me before I have to come up here for him," I added.

He just stood there and gaped at us, looking around the kitchen for support. But no-one was interested. Those present knew that Trevor and I talked straight, and this type of confrontation was nothing new to them. Any difficulty there was between the UVF commander and us was our problem: they just wished that we would keep it out of their environment. These men could have kicked Trevor and I around that kitchen if the notion had taken them. They knew that. We knew that. It just never happened. I suppose they saw that place as common ground of sorts, a place where we could talk about anything but politics or paramilitaries. Trevor and I had many such "tea stops". One of our favourite stops, and the one which was to cause us the most grief later, was the home of Johnny Adair—but that is another story.

The UVF leader looked around the room in embarrassment before he stormed out of the kitchen and drove out of the drive. I never spoke to him again, in fact. I continued to stalk him unobtrusively and did my level best to put him back in jail where he belonged. He will never know just how lucky he was on more than one occasion.

Almost a month later, on the morning of Tuesday, 15 June 1992, I was in the CID office at Tennent Street when I received an unexpected visit from the injured boy and his parents. The couple now wanted their son to co-operate fully with the Police. They had only one stipulation: that we did not move against the UVF until they had been moved out of Ligoniel. We were only too happy to agree to this. I recorded a witness statement from a very brave 15-year-old boy in which he named his assailants, both of whom, as it turned out, he knew well. It was a case of definite recognition of his attackers, and not merely a tenuous identification.

Our case against George Waters Jnr and Charlie "Popeye" Davidson was almost in the bag. The sooner we could move to arrest them, the better, but we would now have to wait until the family under threat were relocated. Their decision to co-operate with us was a very courageous move for them all, and I intended to fully support them. They had obviously agonised for many days over what to do. Tony the motorcycle cop's advice to come forward had convinced them that it was the right thing to do.

Both of the assailants, George Waters Jnr and Charlie "Popeye" Davidson, later appeared at Belfast Crown Court, Crumlin Road and pleaded guilty to the brutal assault on the 15-year-old boy they had maimed. The pleas of guilty meant that it was not necessary to call any child to the witness box, which was a blessing. This at least was one cowardly attack that the UVF did not get away with. As for George Waters Jnr, the charges he faced in relation to this particular attack were the least of his problems. He faced far more serious allegations when he appeared at Belfast Crown Court later that same day. Charges for offences so serious, in fact, as to reflect the true nature of the beast responsible for assaulting the 15-year-old boy in the church grounds that day.

For me, at least, this was a good result, but there was no happy ending for the injured party or his family. Within a short time of relocating, the father died in a tragic accident, far away from the Troubles in Belfast and completely unrelated to the attack on his son, or to the UVF. And so the boy had to deal with the death of his father as well as the severe disability which, dished out in a moment of madness by two UVF thugs, would be with him for the rest of his life.

Yet at least in this instance, we in the Royal Ulster Constabulary could close the books on the case with a sense of pride, in the knowledge that we had done our level best for the child and his family. Over and above this, we had also taught the UVF's 1st Battalion "D"

Company that we would not tolerate such criminal activity, that when and where possible we would continue to identify weaknesses in their armour and exploit them. Victims of such "punishment" attacks now or in the future would do well to follow this example of courage on the part of an ordinary family. A family who came forward even in the face of the most severe intimidation in order to get justice for their boy.

Chapter 16

Protecting All of the People

During the investigation into the brutal punishment beating of the 15-year-old, Trevor and I had been spending far too much time in the Ligoniel area. We had become very partial to the culinary delights of one particular fish and chip shop at the bottom of the Ligoniel Road. We could not have known it at the time, but despite our best efforts to maintain a low profile, our presence in the area on an almost daily basis had not gone unnoticed by the local Provisional IRA. To them we were the enemy, the unacceptable face of a despised Police Force.

The Special Branch contacted me in my office to warn me that a local Provo suspect, Kevin (not his real name), from the Ligoniel Estate, was actively targeting Trevor and I for murder on behalf of the Provisional IRA in Ardoyne, who had already identified a pattern, a routine that we had unknowingly established. We were well aware that in those days having a routine could be deadly. We were advised to stay out of the Ligoniel Estate or risk losing our lives. This timely advice from the Special Branch was welcome and we had no intention of ignoring it. I knew Kevin well and I also knew exactly which ruthless Provo team he was working for. Their thirst for blood was legendary.

Trevor and I did not waste any time. We immediately scaled down the frequency of our visits to Ligoniel. By this stage, I had obtained the witness statement from the 15-year-old naming the two UVF men responsible for assaulting him, but we still had a lot of work to do to convince the parents of the other children to come forward in support of their friend. All of this was taking time and so we still had reason to go in and out of the Ligoniel area far too often. Yet no matter what the risks to our own personal safety might be, we had no intention of letting up on the pursuit of the boy's two attackers at this stage.

Meanwhile, Sonia was warning us that her husband Billy and his cohorts were less than happy at our ongoing efforts to canvas for local witnesses in relation to the UVF assault. She was able to tell us too that Billy and his cronies had been seeking sanction to attack us from the highest authority in the UVF. She advised us to be very careful and promised to keep us informed of any further developments. She told us that her husband was going on holiday to Spain with six or seven other UVF men soon. The Provos had recently opened fire on the homes of several well-known UVF and UDA men, and Sonia confirmed that Billy was leaving to get offside for his own safety. Sonia was glad that he was going: it meant that he would be out of the Provos' reach for a week at least. She also told us that Billy had mentioned a forth-coming UVF operation to hit back at the IRA, but that unfortunately she was having trouble getting any further details about it from him. I had witnessed at first hand too many tragic results of UVF attempts at retaliation against the IRA. Generally speaking, such efforts were aimed at the neighbouring Catholic population as a whole, and the majority of the victims were innocent people who had simply been in the wrong place at the wrong time. I appealed to Sonia to do her best to find out who the unfortunate target was to be in this instance.

Just before midnight on Tuesday, 22 June 1993, I was at home alone with my two young sons when I received a call from Sonia. She was extremely agitated. She had all the information we needed. Apparently her husband had left that very day for his foreign break with his UVF mates. She had been out for a drive with him the day before and as they went through the Nationalist Ligoniel Estate on the way back to the Shankill from Antrim, Billy had told her all about a Provo who was being targeted for murder by the UVF. She needed to speak to us urgently, but didn't want to talk on the phone. I explained to her that I could not get away immediately, but agreed to ring her back later and let her know a time that would suit us all. We decided that Trevor and I would meet her at a place not far from the Shankill, but well away from the prying eyes of the UVF: a safe place where she had met us often before. My wife Rebecca had been visiting her cousin in Millisle and was due home at any moment.

I got dressed in the meantime and gathered together the items we would need for note-taking. Within a short time I was ready for the road. All I had to do now was to ring Trevor at his home in Co. Antrim.

Despite the lateness of the hour, Trevor said he would be ready to meet me as soon as possible. It was always the same with him. Day or night, he would turn out without question. Detectives with commitment like his were few and far between. It was a matter of life-and-death for some unfortunate individual: that was all Trevor needed to know. There were no unnecessary questions. No excuses. His sound common sense, coupled with his ability to ensure that he never did or said anything to compromise our sources, made him an invaluable partner. By this stage, we had been working together for over eight years. Our respective strengths and weaknesses were well known to each other. The truth was we were more like brothers than Police partners. We had learned the very necessary art of watching each other's back. The world of informant-handling was fraught with hazards, not only for us but for our sources themselves. Over the years we had developed an almost animal instinct for danger. We arranged our meets at places where we could see the arrival of any strange vehicles or pedestrians. We also chose our times carefully. There were occasions when this was not possible. Times like this, when it was Sonia who was calling the shots. In such cases, all we could do was proceed with extreme caution.

Our interviewing techniques were keenly honed by this time, and we drew success after success, even with the most hardened terrorists. In the interview room at Castlereagh Police Station, we were as effective against the Provisional IRA as we were against Loyalists. In fact, we had nothing to prove to anyone within the CID: our record spoke for itself. We had critics, of course, and there were as many of these within our own CID ranks as there were within the Special Branch. Generally speaking, the common denominator was professional jealousy. No other two detectives in the Belfast region returned results that were even comparable to ours. The fact was that Trevor and I were prepared to turn out at a moment's notice and do whatever was necessary to save the next life.

Rebecca arrived home shortly after my initial conversation with Trevor. I told her that we had to go out, that it could be a matter of life-and-death for someone. She understood, as ever. All she asked was that I leave quietly so as not to waken the boys. A short time later, Trevor arrived in his blue Ford Sierra car. We agreed to go to the meet in Rebecca's car, a green Mitsubishi Galant, which the locals would not recognise as mine. I made a quick cup of coffee and rang Sonia. We set the meeting for 1.45 am.

Trevor and I were deliberately fifteen minutes early for this particular meet. The car park that we had chosen was huge. There was only one way in and out of it. At this time of the morning we could see cars approach us from miles away. We drove around the car park with our full headlights on. There was no-one about. Ours was the only vehicle in the entire complex. We drove back to the entrance to await the arrival of our source. Sonia arrived on time. I flashed our headlights three times in quick succession to indicate our presence. This was an agreed signal to let Sonia know that there were no other vehicles present. She stopped her car alongside us and jumped into the back of our car. I knew immediately from her demeanour and state of agitation that she had something important to say.

"They're planning to murder a Provo called Kevin from Ligoniel," she said, "They're going to do it tomorrow morning when he is taking his wee girl to the nursery on the Ligoniel Road."

I knew exactly who she meant. This was the very same Provo who was currently targeting Trevor and I for murder on behalf of the PIRA! I saw Trevor roll his eyes skywards in disbelief. Talk about a twist of fate!

If the Special Branch had not warned us of this man's intention to set us up for murder, we may have been dead before Sonia had told us of this threat to his life. The irony of it all was certainly not lost on Trevor and I. Sonia told us that her husband had boasted that the Provo would be dead and buried before he even got back from his holiday. She was able to confirm that a UVF gunman called George Waters Jnr had been chosen to carry out the killing. Here was yet another irony: George Waters Jnr was the very same man Trevor and I were seeking to charge for the brutal assault of the 15-year-old boy! Billy had said that Waters knew that Kevin routinely walked to the nearby nursery school with his 4-year-old daughter on his shoulders. The job had been meticulously researched and the UVF were convinced that Kevin would be an easy target. He always walked down a hill towards his daughter's nursery at the same time: between 9.30 am and 9.40 am in the mornings. If we did not take decisive action at once, Kevin and his daughter would be shot dead by the UVF by 9.45 am that very morning!

Sonia said that Waters had been told not to kill the child. The UVF did not want the bad press which would inevitably come with the murder of a child. Nor did they want to even contemplate the possibility of retaliation on their own children by some PIRA madman. Billy had confided in Sonia that Waters was boasting to other UVF men that he fully intended to kill both Kevin and his daughter. His argument was that in fourteen years' time the daughter would be a Sinn Féin voter. Waters was to be armed with a vz58 assault rifle. He had been instructed to use it on single shot only, so as to minimise the chances of hitting the child. But Waters had his own game plan. He was bragging that he would use the rifle on fully-automatic: that way he could claim that he had lost control of it. For he fully intended to ensure that no-one survived the attack. George Waters was, of course, not yet aware that I was about to arrest him for the brutal attack on the 15-year-old lad in St Mark's Parish Church grounds. His plans to carry out these vicious murders were the proof, if any was needed, that it was absolutely imperative for us as Police to act quickly and decisively in relation to such thugs. Psychopaths like Waters, of which Northern Ireland had more than its fair share, had only one agenda in mind: to inflict serious harm or even death upon other unsuspecting members of the public, without so much as a thought for the tragedy and havoc caused.

Sonia's fear was for the young child, but neither did she hold any animosity for the father. She knew that Waters had been involved in the recent brutal assault on one of his own community. She was conscious that he was nothing more than a vicious thug and she hated him for it. In fact, Waters' UVF masters were equally aware of the violent nature of their volunteer. They also knew all about his plan to murder the child, yet they had taken no measures to prevent this from happening. Further evidence of the extent of their duplicity.

"If Geordie Waters gets his way, that Provie and his wee girl will be dead by 9.30 or 10 am this morning and it's after 2 am already!" Sonia concluded breathlessly. She rummaged about in her handbag and then handed me a piece of paper. It was a map of the Ligoniel Road area, including the area of the nursery school. There was also a list of the names of the other UVF men who would assist Waters in carrying out the murders. Trevor and I strained to read it. Some of the names were well known to me—there were certainly no surprises. One thing which caught my attention at once was that the man who had selected Kevin as the intended murder victim, the man who had chosen Waters as the gunman and the man in charge of the munitions to be used in the attack were one and the same: it was none other than the commander of the UVF's 1st Battalion "D" Company. The same individual had also been responsible for the selection of another intended murder victim in Whiteabbey recently: the murder mission which in fact we had been able to successfully abort with Sonia's tip-off and the timely intervention of the Special Branch. Trevor's eyes caught mine as he too noticed this name. He and I would have given anything to take that particular "weed" out by the roots, to rid our community once and for all of his pernicious influence.

Kevin's alleged membership of the Provisional IRA was neither here nor there as far as Trevor and I were concerned: his politics or his Republican leanings were irrelevant. Our only concern was the fact that two lives were under threat. Our duty to protect the lives of our fellow citizens came without qualification. The protection of life was the first principle of Police work. For Trevor and I, the situation was black and white: there were no grey areas. It was imperative that we ensured that the UVF were frustrated in their attempt to murder these people. Our only problem was that by rights, we had to take this information to the Special Branch. Only they were allowed to confront these armed paramilitary groups. What they did with the information was their decision and the outcome would be their responsibility.

We spent the next hour or so driving about North Belfast as Sonia told us the fine detail of the UVF murder plan. She pointed out to us the home of the intended driver: again, a man who was well known to us. We discussed the other individuals who, according to Sonia's information, would also be involved. We repeatedly went over the routes the UVF team would take both to and from the intended murder scene. Sonia was able to tell us that Waters would be in the back seat with the vz58 rifle. Apparently, a second gunman would be in the front passenger seat and he would be covering Waters with a handgun. The driver would most likely be unarmed. Sonia had done her homework well. We now had more than enough facts to allow the

Special Branch to set up an operation to save the two lives under threat. If Special Branch Special Support Units (SSU) moved quickly, there was a very good chance that George Waters and his UVF cohorts would be arrested, the weapons recovered, and two or three UVF gunmen locked up. The truth was that only the Special Branch had the resources to conduct such operations to confront terrorists and take them down.

We in the CID did not have access to the same material resources. It made sense for us to co-operate fully with Special Branch.

It was nearly 3.15 am before I was able to get to a public telephone box on the Crumlin Road. I rang the Police exchange and asked for extension "220", the Special Branch desk at Castlereagh. It seemed an age before someone answered.

"Two-two-zero," the Special Branch officer barked. He was trying his best to sound alert but he had obviously just been dozing.

I explained that I needed to meet urgently with our Special Branch contact, one of his detective sergeants: "Please call him at home and tell him to be in the rear car park of Castlereagh Police Station at the door of the Police Office in 30 minutes," I asked. "And please impress upon your sergeant that this is a matter of life-and-death," I added.

We dropped Sonia off at her car in the car park near the Glencairn Estate, thanking her for her invaluable assistance. The question now was whether there would be enough time to set up an ambush. Trevor and I set off for Castlereagh RUC Station. The landmarks were flying past us as I made my way down the Crumlin Road past the Courthouse and HM Prison Crumlin Road onto Carlisle Circus, down into the deserted city centre, over the Queen's Bridge and into East Belfast. At last we drove into the highly secure Castlereagh RUC Station. No-one challenged us: in those days we would have been in and out of these barracks as many as six or seven times a day, and our faces had become our warrant cards. I parked at the rear of the complex adjacent to our Police Office detention centre, as agreed. Less than five minutes later, I saw our Special Branch contact drive in and park beside us. He looked none too pleased: it was almost 4 am, so I assumed the early call-out had upset him.

"You do know that this will cause all sorts of problems in the morning, don't you, Johnston?" he began.

I assumed he already knew all about what was happening.

"Quickly, Johnston, give me a précis of what you have," he continued.

I briefed him fully. He pointed to one of the six names on the list of UVF men to be involved.

"He is one of ours," he said.

"So you are already aware of what is going on, then?" I asked

"Not at all, he hasn't reported any of this to us," he replied, "He's brought nothing into me." He sounded genuinely disappointed that the source had not thought fit to pass on the details of a scheme of such murderous intent.

"So tell me this, if he's not reporting it in, does he still get protected?" I asked.

I was half-hoping to hear him say that he wouldn't. The Special Branch officer's answer astounded me. He explained that the source in question was not required to report on anything to do with "the military", that his primary function was to mingle with high-level UVF men and to report on the leadership and on any changes in the organisation's political direction or strategy. They did not expect him to report on anything "military": the Special Branch had more than enough services for that. My Special Branch contact related all of this to me without batting an eyelid. It seemed to me that there was something inherently wrong with a system that allowed such an anomaly. Yet Special Branch operatives apparently saw absolutely nothing perverse in the fact that this system would actively protect sources who consistently and habitually denied their handlers access to vital intelligence, information that could save lives. The CID, on the other hand, policed in a black-and-white world. There were no grey areas. A source such as this would be rooted out for the weed that he was. Here we were, only hours away from what could be the loss of two lives, one of them of a child of four, and the Special Branch with all their sources had not the slightest idea it was about to happen! This was vindication, if any was needed, of exactly what I had argued all along: that the CID intelligence input was vital to the proper functioning of the Special Branch, that we could complement their efforts in a very significant way. Put their "lost" ball back into play, so to speak. We had done so on many previous occasions.

It was close to 5.30 am before we finished arguing about the rights and wrongs of source-handling. Eventually, we had to agree to disagree. Our Special Branch contact was a decent man, not long in the Special Branch at this point. He was certainly not yet moulded into their way of thinking. Personally, I hoped that he would never change.

He had a warm personality and a common decency which endeared him to our informants. I knew from bitter experience, however, that these same personal traits would vanish one by one as he sunk deeper into the abyss that was the Special Branch. But that day he was willing to help us, and we would need him to use all his powers of persuasion on our behalf to convince those in authority within the Special Branch that this was a good chance to take down this vicious UVF Active Service Unit (ASU). That if we did not move now, they would go on to kill again and again.

Our Special Branch contact could not have agreed more. He shook our hands firmly and set off upstairs within the Castlereagh complex to consult with his duty officer and those in charge. Could he convince them? Had they time? It would certainly not be an easy task to "crash out" all that Special Branch manpower. They would need to be briefed and armed. When they were ready, they would be more than able to deal with the UVF murder team now preparing to strike.

Our information was very specific. Yet we had to agree that there were so many imponderables and so much was at stake that the authorities within the Special Branch might well go for the easier option: to put an overt RUC presence in place outside the nursery and in the Ligoniel Estate. Such a measure would cause the UVF to abort their mission to murder the pair on this particular occasion, but would not mean, of course, that we would be able to stop them if they decided to target the same victims at a later date. Trevor and I stood there in the car park and watched our Special Branch counterpart run upstairs to fight our corner. All we could do now was wait.

We walked over to the Police Office to use a telephone. I needed to speak to the CID officer on night duty at Tennent Street RUC Station. I was in luck. Detective Constable Joseph Bryson answered the phone. I told him to inform Brian McArthur, the Detective Inspector, when he arrived at work in the morning that I had been on my feet all night and that I was retiring to bed for a few hours. The Detective Inspector should be aware that if the Special Branch decided to go for an arrest operation as opposed to an overt Police presence, they might well have three or four prisoners before 10 am. He would also have a number of crime scenes to deal with, and would as such require extra CID manpower. He should put SOCO/Mapping and Photography on standby, as well as detectives to interview the suspects at the Castlereagh Station if there were any arrests. To be forewarned was to be forearmed in situations like this, and I knew that Brian would be pleased to be ahead of events.

Joe was obviously busy taking notes. There was silence at the other end of the telephone. No questions. No having to repeat myself. Good old solid Joe.

"Oh, and Joe," I added as an afterthought, "Tell him not to ring me at home before 12 noon, please."

Joe laughed. "No problem, Skipper," he said.

Trevor and I left Castlereagh Station to go home. We were exhausted: we had already completed a 16-hour day before that call-out from Sonia. We had done everything it had been possible for us to do. We walked to my car and drove to my home in Ballyrobert, Co. Antrim. The absence of any immediate update from our Special Branch contact was indicative that the powers that be were more than likely opting for the softer of the two possible courses of action: they had probably gone for an abort. They would flood Ligoniel with uni-formed Police to deter the UVF from carrying out the murder bid. We had after all been very late in briefing our Special Branch contact. But such were the difficulties of this area of Police work. I knew that it was not an exact science, but that did not make it any easier to accept that in this case we might not get the chance to bring those thugs in.

When we arrived at my home, Trevor half-fell into his Ford Sierra. He was drained too. The responsibility, the pressure were awesome. What if something went wrong? What if the UVF unit came in from a different direction and didn't see the RUC vehicles? What if Sonia had got the day wrong? It didn't even bear thinking about. My mind was full of all of this as I got undressed and climbed into the shower. The water flowing over me was refreshing, and I stood in the shower longer than usual, trying to let the water wash away my fears of failure. In any other walk of life, failure was acceptable: there was always the opportunity to simply try again. But failure in these life-and-death situations was unthinkable. The fall-out in getting it wrong as a Police officer in Northern Ireland at that time could result in the death of a colleague, a valuable source or an innocent citizen. I climbed into bed. It was by this time close to 7.45 am. Rebecca was already up and was busy getting the boys ready for school.

I was tempted to stay awake and listen to my personal Police pocket phone. I wasn't able to. The moment my head hit the pillow, I fell fast asleep. It seemed as if I was only asleep for a few minutes when

Rebecca woke me up abruptly and handed me the telephone. "It's Detective Inspector McArthur," she said. I put the phone to my ear and heard nothing but an eerie silence.

"Brian?" I ventured.

Suddenly there was animation at the other end of the phone.

"Oh, Jonty, yes, it's you. Look, thanks for your note. That put me well ahead. Your operation was successful," said Detective Inspector McArthur.

The Inspector updated me. Two UVF men in a hijacked Ford Sierra taxi had been arrested when their vehicle had been rammed by the SSU. The two prisoners on their way to Castlereagh were George Waters Jnr and David Reid. Waters had been sitting in the back seat of the hijacked car with a VZ58 automatic rifle straddled across his knees. The weapon was fully loaded with a spare clip taped back-to-back. Reid had been in possession of a .38 revolver. Three more UVF suspects had been arrested for hijacking the taxi. The prisoners were on their way to Castlereagh and searches were ongoing.

The Detective Inspector commended me on a good job well done. He asked me to get into work in Tennent Street CID office as soon as I could. People in high office were asking questions and he didn't know some of the more important answers.

"Oh, and . . ." he added.

"Yes, Sir?" I replied.

"Waters had that rifle on fully-automatic. He would have cut that 4-year-old girl in half in a bid to kill her father," he concluded.

I put the phone down. The adrenalin was flowing again. I didn't feel even the least bit tired any more. It is amazing how resilient the human body can be.

I took a moment to ring Trevor. His wife Barbara answered the phone: Trevor was still asleep.

"When he wakes up, tell him that we have five prisoners in the bag including George Waters," I said.

Fair play to our Special Branch contact: he had done extremely well in a very short space of time. Here was evidence of what could be achieved when our two disciplines co-operated with each other. It was now time to get down to some real business. This would fairly put the cat amongst the pigeons. A ruthless UVF unit was reeling for the second time in just a few months. The streets of North Belfast were a lot safer with terrorists like these in custody and facing long-term prison sentences. Moreover, a clear signal would be sent out to others thinking of getting involved in similar offences. By working together, by co-operating and trusting each other, we could knock these paramilitaries for six. Trevor and I had often proven that we could supply the intelligence; the Special Branch had all the resources necessary to deal with armed terrorists. I dressed and made my way immediately to the Tennent Street Barracks. Our Special Branch contact had seen me arrive at the Station. He was at the top of the stairs outside his office. He greeted me and shook my hand.

"When you get a chance, Johnston, come into our office: there is someone here who would like to meet you," he said.

I didn't fancy another lecture on demarcation from some senior Special Branch officer.

"They are not stationed here," he said, smiling. "Honestly," he added.

I asked him to wait while I reported for duty in the CID office. The office was a hive of activity. There were many hearty congratulations from the majority of my CID colleagues. I knew, however, that there would also be officers who would be less than impressed by this "Proddy bashing". Yet if what we had just achieved amounted to "Proddy bashing", I was happy to be a part of it. Any RUC officer who thought otherwise was in my opinion in dire need of psychological help. I would deal with the problem of disapproval from colleagues if and when it raised its ugly head. Two lives had been saved—how could anyone judge that in a negative light?

I took off my jacket and helped my colleagues mop up the mass of paperwork that our successful operation had generated. I was so busy with this that I had completely forgotten about the request from my Special Branch contact to join him in the Special Branch office. It was only a short time later that he came to the Detective Inspector's office. He indicated that I should join him in the corridor. His colleague had had to leave, he said.

"But he gave me a message for you, Johnston," he said.

What he said next shook me utterly. It put an entirely new twist on the events of the previous 24 hours. It also demonstrated graphically as far as I was concerned that nothing in this murky world of our "dirty war" in which we were engaged was ever what it seemed! Just when I thought I had heard it all, the Special Branch would come up with something even more bizarre. Unfortunately, I cannot disclose what was said to me without endangering the life of one of our Special Branch agents.

George Waters and his UVF cohorts were duly charged and remanded in custody. They were tried and convicted. Waters Jnr received a sixteen-year jail sentence for possession of firearms with intent to endanger life. A six-year sentence for assault on the 15-year-old boy was added to this, to be run consecutively, making a total of 22 years' imprisonment for Waters. It was professionally very gratifying for me to know that he had as such been removed from society as a result of our efforts. He was, however, released under the terms of the Good Friday Agreement after serving only four years.

Chapter 17
A Bridge Too Far

Ever since the conviction of the Loyalist UFF godfather Johnny "Mad Dog" Adair in 1995, Rebecca and I had been living under serious and constant threat of attack by UFF terrorists. The second statement of evidence that I had made to bolster the Crown case had sealed Adair's fate. Adair had read between the lines: he did not want me giving evidence against him at Belfast Crown Court before a packed gallery of UFF men. The same second statement would also alter his perception of my part in his downfall: he now saw my involvement in his case as no longer purely professional, but motivated by some personal agenda.

Adair's tendency to hold a grudge until he could get his own back on his perceived enemy was legendary. So I knew that if he ever got out of jail, he would come after me. But it was 1995, and Adair had just been sentenced to a 16-year prison term. I was due to retire the day before my 57th birthday, on 16 April 2007. I thought I would be long gone and forgotten before he could ever be a threat to me again. How wrong I was.

Adair had read enough into those two statements of mine to realise that I could demonstrate to the court that he had incriminated himself by running off at the mouth so often that he would look like a complete fool. Trevor and I knew that he was not afraid of any other aspect of the evidence presented against him. He realised that by the time I had finished with him, the UFF wouldn't have even given him a job washing dishes. He pleaded guilty to directing terrorism and went happily off to jail for sixteen years. I was not in court. My authorities took the view that my presence in the courtroom would cause a riot. Adair shouted abuse in relation to me from the dock. He left the Police in no doubt that the good men of "C" Company would "deal with me". I was under no illusion as to what exactly he meant by that. Security at our home was reviewed and updated.

I had not bargained on the political framework that was to be put in place by the Government as a result of the Good Friday Agreement. It was a framework which was completely contrary to anything that I understood to be lawful or proper, and resulted in the release of Johnny Adair and hundreds of terrorists like him. Political executive decisions would take the place of considered judicial sentences. Terrorists from both sides of the political divide who had been serving very long sentences were released onto the streets of Northern Ireland in wave after wave in a bid to oil the wheels of the train that was to be called the Good Friday Agreement.

Terrorists from both the Republican and Loyalist camps were to be courted by politicians in a bid to wean them into democratic politics. Democracy and the rule of law were to be turned inside out to facilitate this bizarre process. The expectation of everyone was that this would result in peace. It did not bring peace. It resulted only in ceasefires. There is a vast difference between true peace and a ceasefire. Ask any seasoned soldier. The enemy is at their most dangerous when their guns are silent.

When Adair was released onto the streets in 1999, he immediately set about regrouping his old "C" Company. It is testament to the power of his influence that he just walked out of jail and regained control of "C" Company. But he had no war to go back to. He couldn't use his men to launch attacks upon Catholics in the same way as he had done before his incarceration. So he turned his interests to drug-dealing and prostitution. Sources reported his criminal activities to us on a regular basis. Then he broke the golden rule and started to use the drugs he was peddling. He became paranoid. He trusted no-one. He rounded on his former close friends and associates, and turned them out of the Shankill Road.

I knew that it was only a matter of time before he remembered about me. He was always going to come after me to get back at me for putting him in jail in 1995. Our sources within his group were so well placed that we became aware of his intentions to carry out an attack on my home. But we were not aware of exactly what form the attack would take or when it would occur.

History had shown us only too graphically that if Adair took a personal dislike to anyone he would invariably send one of his cronies to launch a pipebomb or gun attack on them. In one such attack, a pipebomb thrown into a house on the Ormeau Road by the UFF had landed inside beside a cot in which an infant was asleep. That poor family was very lucky: miraculously, they escaped unscathed. An attack like that would be traumatic enough but I was more fortunate than most people living under such a threat because my home was fully armoured and protected. Adair knew that sophisticated security measures were in place at my home. He guessed that they would probably frustrate any attempt by the UFF to get at me in that manner. We knew that he was racking his brain to find a way to get back at me. One very highly placed source reported to a senior Police officer that Adair couldn't get to sleep for trying to think up another scheme against me.

To add to my personal difficulty, the ever-changing political scene in Northern Ireland which had resulted in the release of criminals of Adair's ilk virtually forbade us from arresting and questioning him in relation to our intelligence in a manner that would have been normal prior to the signing of the Good Friday Agreement. It was important that we were not seen to be rocking the boat. To arrest Adair was to risk alienating the UDA. This was and is the largest Loyalist paramilitary body in existence in the Province. It seemed to me that our Police Force was completely powerless. We were to do nothing to upset the apple cart. It wasn't that there were no arrests. It just meant that every application to make an arrest or to conduct a search was examined in minute detail. If there was even the slightest chance that it would have any political ramifications, the answer would invariably be no.

The consideration of political stability far outweighed any little personal difficulty that I might have such as the threat of sudden death at the hands of this moron. We were informed that even the very future of the Constabulary was threatened. Our Government had lost its memory. We were no longer a revered Police Force, no longer held in the highest esteem by the British Government. The RUC was suddenly now a liability. We were to be offered up as a sacrificial lamb to Republicans. We were to be blamed for all of our society's ills. The personal safety of my family or myself was obviously no longer as important as it had once been. We were expendable. If my family were to be protected, then I would have to protect them myself. The only way that I could do that was to keep in touch with our CID sources close to Adair on the ground. Unfortunately, Adair's mistrust of even his closest of associates meant that even the UFF men who would be involved in any attack on my home would not know when it was to take place until half an hour before the attack was due to happen.

There was also the in-fighting. The Special Branch had deliberately withdrawn any assistance their agents could provide to protect me from the UFF. Their sources were telling my sources of Adair's plot to attack me. Yet up to my retirement, no formally documented threats to my life came to me from the Special Branch after my assistance to Sir John Stevens. This saddened me but it was certainly did not surprise me. Due to my co-operation with the Stevens 3 team, the Special Branch were no longer interested in helping me to keep ahead of Adair. In fact, I had good reason to believe that some of their more sinister elements were engaged in winding the UFF in "C" Company up and spinning them in my direction. This was putting my life and the lives of my wife and children in danger.

In January 2000, I had learned from CID sources that Adair had even contemplated sending his cronies to our village in Ballyrobert to seize one of my sons. Adair's intention was to have the child tied to a lamp post, kneecapped and with a placard "Drug Dealer" hanging around his neck. He had told one of his very close associates, "That'll put Jonty's head up his backside."

He was right. In all of my 30 years of Police service, I had never felt as vulnerable as I did when I realised that I would have to watch my children every minute of the waking day. This put an incredible burden on both Rebecca and myself. It also meant that we had to sit our young boys down and explain to them as graphically as was possible that they would have to be on constant alert for strangers on foot or in cars. They were not to open the front door to anyone. Not even to a Policeman or a cleric. Adair's "C" Company men had used both of these ploys to good effect to gain access to the homes of other persons they had targeted. At the time of these threats, Adam was not yet sixteen and Simon was thirteen years old. No child should have to live in the shadow of such terror.

Although Adair was put in prison in September 2000, we knew that this would not stop him from orchestrating an attack using his associates on the outside.

The evening of 4 October 2000 was cold but dry. My father-in-law had called at our home to wish us well on our three-day break to York in England. Our youngest son Simon was staying over at the home of one of his friends for the duration of our absence. Our eldest boy Adam was due to stay alone at our home at Willcroft Meadows, Ballyrobert near Ballyclare in Co. Antrim. He was sixteen years old at that time.

Adam had just left on his motorbike to visit one of his friends who lived only a few miles from our home. He was enjoying his new-found independence on his Yamaha scooter. It had been a real boon: he no longer had to wait for me or his mother to ferry him here or there. Adam had always exhibited a degree of common sense that was rarely found in men many years his senior.

The boys had always lived with the ever-present spectre of terrorism in their lives. They too had adopted a fatalistic attitude to the undeniable threat of death. We had tried to keep Simon, the younger, as much in the dark as was possible. Adam though was always careful and extremely vigilant whilst he was around our home. He was very protective of his mother and brother. For as long as he had lived, he had taken in his stride the fact that we had to live in a virtual fortress. We had bullet-resistant windows and doors. We had alarms that warned us of any approach by persons to our home. These infra-red beams covered the areas to the front and rear of our home. We were unable to open the large windows. We had only two windows in the bungalow that opened to enable us to escape from the house in the event of a fire. Three panic buttons were sited throughout the bungalow. Once they had been triggered, their function was two-fold. Firstly, they would turn on all of the outside security lights and start a very loud screamer. Rats hate noise and light. That applies equally to the human rats which stalked the homes of hundreds of members of the Security Forces just like us. Secondly, the panic buttons were attached to a "Hawkeye" radio alarm that would immediately send an alert directly to local Police vehicles. Each Hawkeye was given a number and linked to a local address. The local Police could respond to it in minutes. This Hawkeye had been in place like the other security measures for over eleven years. It had functioned well on every occasion that it had been tested for those eleven years by sending a signal to Belfast Regional Control and directly to the local District Mobile Patrol car.

The reliability of this particular radio alarm was renowned. Unlike its predecessor, the "Magpie", it did not require a second dedicated telephone. The Magpie was obsolete because terrorists could ring and "jam" it. There had been cases of PIRA terrorists doing just that before they attacked and murdered a member of the Security Forces in his home. So the Hawkeye was perhaps the most reassuring of our security measures.

Rebecca and I were alone at home that evening when we heard the steady "beep" that alerted us immediately to the fact that someone was approaching the house. Had it been an animal, it would have sent a very different intermittent tone. Someone was approaching the bungalow. The lights on the alarm panel indicated to me that whoever it was, they were approaching the front door.

Had my father-in-law forgotten something, I wondered. We knew that it definitely wasn't Adam, because we would have heard the noise of his motorcycle first. Rebecca and I were in our study trying to arrange car hire for collection at Liverpool airport the next morning. Our cases were packed and we were preparing for a three-day stay in Pudsey in West Yorkshire with friends. We intended to commute daily to the races at York racecourse. The computer Internet provider kept crashing just before we could complete the hire transaction by credit card. We were so engrossed in all of this that terrorists or terrorism was the last thing on our mind.

"See who that is," Rebecca said nonchalantly.

The door of the study is only a short distance from the entrance hall. As I walked that short distance, I heard heavy footfalls on the concrete porch. Then someone outside made a determined attempt to open our armoured front door. I stopped dead in my tracks. Everything started to happen then as if in slow motion. The hall curtains were fully closed. I could not see who was there. But equally importantly, they could not see me. Then whoever it was outside made a determined effort to open the letterbox in the door. This was not a friend. My friends and family knew that that letterbox did not open. I felt the hair standing up on the back of my neck. I froze. Rebecca was unaware of the drama that was unfolding in such close proximity to her. I was just a few feet from the front door when I heard a heavy metallic "thud" as the terrorist placed what would later be described as a pipebomb on the concrete porch outside the front door.

"Who is it?" Rebecca's voice brought me back to earth. I backed away from the front door a few feet. Suddenly there was a loud explosion. It was deafening. Heavy ornaments that had been on a display cabinet flew towards me. The air was full of fumes from the explosion. The hall curtains were on fire. I could hear Rebecca screaming behind me. "Don't go outside!" I shouted.

The time delay between the metallic thud and the explosion of the device was so short that there was not a chance of the bomber escaping uninjured. I couldn't move. Something—fear, instinct, a foreboding, call it what you like—but something told me not to go outside. Rebecca handed me the fire extinguisher. "Put the fire out!" she instructed. "Have you pushed the panic button?" she asked.

I didn't answer. I was standing there transfixed, staring at the fire that was engulfing our curtains and carpet at the front door. Ignoring me, Rebecca rushed to the kitchen and hit the Hawkeye panic button which would alert the local Police patrols.

It may have been the sound of the alarms going off. It may have been Rebecca's cool commands, but suddenly I snapped out of the trance I had been in and quickly put out the small fire around the front door. Much of it was simply petrol vapour, although I had no idea of that at the time. I drew back the curtains to see what damage had been caused. The tarmac driveway was on fire. Flames were crackling to the right of the doorway. The armoured door was intact. Neighbours I had lived beside for eleven years were outside the door. There was no dead or injured terrorist, and I was glad. The scene was bad enough without that. I opened the front door and went outside. It was chaotic. Neighbours and well-wishers helped me to extinguish the flames. I realised that sugar or some other sticky substance had been added to the petrol to make it sticky, so that it would adhere to surfaces and burn. This was a devilish device. More than just an ordinary, everyday pipebomb!

It seemed like an age before the Police arrived. When they did, I asked them what had kept them. I didn't know any of them personally. The tall, thin sergeant was a tremendous fellow: he couldn't do enough. It had been a long time, I told him, since Rebecca had hit that Hawkeye panic button. Even the neighbours had commented on how

long it was taking for the Police to arrive. "Hawkeye?" asked the
sergeant. "We didn't get any Hawkeye, Jonty: two members of the
Security Forces rang in to report an explosion. Both of them thought
it came from here. That's why we are here!"

No Hawkeye? That was odd, because the panic button had a three-
fold function. Firstly, to radio a call direct to the local District Mobile
Patrol (DMP) car. Secondly, to turn on all security lights to bathe the
terrorists in light. Lastly, to set off a siren and bells that would practi-
cally deafen any terrorist and draw attention to our predicament!
Functions two and three had worked well and worked immediately.
Why had the Hawkeye not worked? Things weren't adding up.
Something was terribly wrong.

The area was soon flooded with Police. The Ammunitions
Technical Officer (ATO) came to examine the scene. He took his time.
I was intrigued by what his deliberations would find. Who or which
group was responsible for this attack? The UDA/UFF had been targeting
me since early January 2000, and we knew from intelligence reports
that an attack on me or my family was imminent. Then again of
course, the collapse of the criminal proceedings against Thomas
David Maginnis, a self-confessed murderer and UVF/Loyalist
Volunteer Force/Red Hand Commando man the Friday before meant
that the LVF could well be responsible. Maginnis' friend, the notorious
serial killer Frankie "the beast" Curry, had been at the centre of our
criminal investigation into a series of murders along the North Down
coast. Curry would not have hesitated to have my home attacked.

In addition to all of this, a well-known UVF murderer from the
Shore Road—a ruthless bastard if ever there was one—had been seen
down in Willowcroft Meadows only recently. I knew that his friends
in the Special Branch had told him of my intent to catch and jail him.
I had heard that he was intending to kill me and blame it on Johnny
Adair's UDA/UFF 2nd Battalion "C" Company. So there was no shortage
of suspects. The ATO findings would be crucial.

I had not long to wait. The device, the officer told me, was of
typical UDA/UFF origin. It had been designed with small canisters of
petrol filled with sugar. The device was designed so that it could be
"posted" into the letterbox. The explosion would have lit the petrol
and the effect inside the house would have been devastating. In
essence, once the bomb came through my letterbox and detonated,
my heavily fortified doors would have worked against me. A ball of

fire would have burst along the corridors and into the rooms seeking any combustible material. That would of course have included Rebecca and myself! One look at the devastation outside the house and you could just imagine what could have happened if our letter-box had not been sealed in 1995 following the conviction and sentence of Johnny Adair. Someone hadn't done their homework. Yes, the letterbox was there but it was sealed. Deliberately sealed, so as to stop anyone pushing such a device in through it. But why had Hawkeye not worked? That was the only aspect of my security that was controlled by the Special Branch Technical Support Unit (TSU). It had worked every quarter under test and even on two or three occasions over the last eleven years when we had inadvertently pressed it whilst decorating or whatever. This was something I intended to get to the bottom of. I had very good reason to be suspicious.

Someone called the Police dog handlers. One was an enthusiastic WPC. She followed a trail right from the front porch past the integral garage and across the side garden to the fence. She had noted that the barbed wire on top of the posts holding the sheep fence of the nearby field was cut. Her dog led her across to the far side of the field directly in line. She noted again that the top section of barbed wire had been cut. The terrorist had come in by and left by the fields adjacent to the blind side of my home.

So that was why the terrorist had been able to escape unhurt. All he had had to do was light the fuse, take two steps backwards and go right towards the fields. Once around the corner, in a split second he was safe from any shrapnel. There was no car. No getaway driver. Those fields lead to the railway lines that go to Mossley or Whiteabbey. Our attackers were well away!

I stood back and watched fellow RUC officers do all in their power to comfort Rebecca. I was filled with an unexplainable anger and rage. I tried to put on a brave face, but inside I was falling apart. For the first time in my life, I had completely lost control. For the first time in years, I felt completely vulnerable. The realisation that I was unable to protect my family from such an attack hit me like a hammer. Despite the fact that I had lived for years with the threat of something like this, I was shaken to the core when it actually happened.

I had taken great pains to stress to my authorities that my family was in grave danger from Adair and his cohorts in "C" Company since January 2000. They had treated my difficulty seriously but not seriously enough to fully protect my family and myself. I felt alone and abandoned. If it could happen once, it could happen again. I was being targeted because I was successful in putting terrorists away. Yet I felt utterly isolated and alone.

The ATO left the scene at 12.40 am. The other agencies left one after another, until once again Rebecca and I were alone in the house. The silence was eerie and unsettling. I wanted to lift the telephone and ask for a static guard until we could vacate our home. I decided against it. I considered it odd that there was no offer of an RUC guard. This would have been normal in such circumstances. The local Police said that they would pay "passing attention" before they left. I knew from bitter experience exactly what that meant. I was disappointed, to say the least.

It must have been around 2 am before Rebecca and I finally climbed into bed to try to get some sleep. But I could not sleep. I felt so very vulnerable. I got up often and walked around the house, checking that the doors and windows were locked and secure. I still do this to this day. My Ruger revolver was never far from my side.

I remember well standing in the bedroom watching Rebecca deep in a drug-induced sleep. I stared out of the front window for hours. In fairness to the local Police, they did drive into our cul-de-sac during that long night more often than I would have expected. I stood at my bedroom window watching. Watching and waiting for the terrorists to return to finish the job. Adair had told me often that he would send his men back again to finish a job that they had failed to do at the first attempt. I was taking no chances.

It was around 4 am on the morning of 5 October 2000, as I sat there guarding my home, that I made the conscious decision that I would never return to duty in the Royal Ulster Constabulary. My position in the Force post-Stevens was untenable. It was strange, but once I had made that simple decision, I felt unburdened. I climbed back into bed and fell asleep.

I awoke to a steady stream of telephone calls from friends and family enquiring about our welfare. Then, at around 7.30 am, our alarms inside the house sounded once again to alert us to the presence of persons approaching outside. I jumped up, startled by the alert and glanced outside through the louver blinds. It was the Press. I contacted the RUC Press Office at Headquarters and asked them to send a Press Officer to deal with any enquiries that they might have.

I was fortunate enough to speak to a colleague whom I knew and trusted. He enlightened me to the fact that we no longer sent Press Officers to such scenes: I was on my own. I was advised not to mention the fact that I was an RUC officer, or that I suspected that Adair's cohorts had planted the device. My colleague was trying to be helpful. But the earlier RUC Press release had been very short and non-specific, alleging that "the home of a middle-aged couple in the Ballyclare area had been attacked by a pipebomb," and that "the attack was not thought to be connected to the ongoing Loyalist feud". This was probably the standard manner in which the RUC Press Office dealt with all such incidents. My difficulty was that to the uninformed, the effect was to suggest that our home had been attacked for some other, more sinister reason—because, for example, we were drug dealers or paedophiles. I was having none of that. I walked outside and approached a nearby woman reporter.

"Have you any idea why your home should have been attacked in this manner?" she asked.

"I put Johnny Adair in jail for sixteen years in 1995 and last month the RUC put him back where he belongs again. If you ask me, I believe that he has lost his sense of humour altogether," I replied.

"Can I print that?" she asked.

"Most certainly," I replied.

As the day wore on, I answered a stream of other questions from a barrage of reporters. I no longer cared what anyone thought of what I was saying. I no longer cared about anything other than the protection of my family and myself. The days of me being concerned about what the RUC thought were over. Loyalty is a two-way street. I did not see my loyalty over those past 30 years being repaid when I needed it most. It was clear to me that from here on in, I was on my own.

That afternoon, an engineer from TSU arrived at our home to ascertain why the Hawkeye had malfunctioned. My kitchen was full of people there to offer support to us. I escorted the engineer to the garage by way of the utility room and allowed him to examine the device. A short time later, he reappeared in my kitchen. I asked him why the device had not worked. He said it was simple: there was not enough power in the battery to get the signal to the mast. If the signal did not reach the mast, it could not be relayed to the local Police car. With that, the engineer turned on his heels and left.

It was an hour or so later, when Rebecca and I were going over what he had said, that it dawned on us that the Hawkeye was powered by mains electricity. It had a battery attached only as a back-up if the mains failed. The bomb had not caused the power to fail. We were back to square one: why had the Hawkeye failed? We will never know. Within 48 hours of the attack on our home, we were moved to a "safe" house approximately six miles away. We remained in that safe house for six long months before we moved again to a new and heavily-fortified home.

The last three years of my service in the RUC's CID had been fraught with many difficulties for me both as a Police officer and as a husband and father. My involvement in the cases of Ken Barrett and Johnny Adair had left me out on a limb. The case of the brutal murder of Pat Finucane and Barrett's involvement in it has followed me well into my retirement. But the implications of my personal involvement in the Adair case were worse still.

Personally speaking, I was proud that my evidence had been so crucial to Adair's downfall. He was good value for every day that he served. Every day that he was in jail was a good day for the public interest here in Northern Ireland. That is easy for me to say as a former detective sergeant. But speaking as a husband and a father, I am forced to acknowledge that it also cost my family dearly, as we strove to readjust after the shock of those serious and sinister threats. We lost a home that we had lived happily in for thirteen years. It has not been easy for any of us to embrace our new environment. As a family, we are still suffering from the fallout of all the subsequent trauma.

In many respects, my involvement in the prosecution of Johnny "Mad Dog" Adair and the resulting attack on my family was indeed a bridge too far.

Epilogue

I n this book I have attempted to give the reader an insight into what it was like to serve in the Royal Ulster Constabulary from the early 1970s through to 2001. It is not intended to be an exhaustive account of my career. I have instead chosen incidents in which I was personally involved over the years to illustrate the difficulties of policing in such a divided community.

I have tried to illustrate with examples of incidents I experienced at first hand that, far from being the armed wing of Unionism, as it was often portrayed to be, the RUC strove to be an impartial and effective Police Service, and was filled with ordinary and mainly honorable men and women doing their utmost to operate to the best of their ability in the face of extreme adversity. I fully realise that Republicans may choose to focus exclusively on those instances in the book where members of the RUC are shown to have failed to remain impartial. I fully expect such a response: it is something over which I have no control.

However, I want to stress that it was my experience that the vast majority of RUC officers went about their day-to-day duties affording equal respect to all sections of the community. It must never be forgotten that we lost 300 RUC officers to terrorism, and that over 9,000 Policemen and women were injured during the Troubles. Eight Police officers were murdered by Loyalist terror groups. The first RUC officer to die in the Troubles, Constable Victor Arbuckle, was shot dead in October 1969 by a Loyalist assassin. He was a 29-year-old

Protestant. The last RUC officer to die was Constable Frank O'Reilly, a 30-year-old Catholic who was fatally injured in a Loyalist bomb attack upon his Landrover at Drumcree in October 1998. His assassin could not have known that he was a Catholic. Many other RUC officers were grievously injured by Loyalists.

As a CID officer working within the RUC, it was always my function to investigate and pursue criminals from wherever they came. During the three decades covered by this book, thousands of Loyalists were convicted for serious terrorist offences and incarcerated for long sentences in Northern Ireland's prisons. They did not just arrive at the gates of those prisons and give themselves up. They were put there by the efforts and hard work of members of the RUC who then had to live in close proximity to the friends and families of the terrorists they had incarcerated. This took real courage. These considerations and the facts above were all conveniently overlooked by those who strove to depict us as "the armed wing of Unionism".

The recent Stevens 3 Enquiry into the conduct of the Police in Northern Ireland found that there was evidence of institutionalised collusion within the RUC Special Branch. This is undoubtedly true, and much of what I have recounted in this book in relation to the Special Branch supports such an assertion. But it would be ill-advised indeed of the general public to tar the entire Royal Ulster Constabulary with the same brush. While I did encounter some individuals in the other branches of the Force who were less than impartial, there was in my experience no sense in which this was operating at an institutional level. In a Police Service of over 12,000 members, it would follow that some would lean towards one faction or another, but those of us who strove to "police without fear or favour", and that was the vast majority of us, accepted this and strove to work around such individuals.

Undeniably, however, it was my experience that certain RUC Special Branch officers were working against the very principle that they had taken an oath to uphold, namely the protection of life. It saddened me that these officers were supported by like-minded senior Special Branch officers, but that was the reality. When a Police officer starts to qualify the principle of the protection of life and work to save certain lives while sacrificing others, he is in the wrong business. And yet I uncovered evidence that such things did happen.

I realise that there may also be those who will read this narrative and say that during my career as a detective, I was guilty of prejudice of a different kind: namely, as some of my colleagues put it so eloquently at the time, of "Proddy bashing". To those who reach such a conclusion as a result of reading this book, I can only say that, while it may be true that the majority of incidents I have recounted here relate to instances which involved Loyalist paramilitaries, these are only a few examples of the hundreds of cases I dealt with. During the entire length of my service, I was under almost constant death threat from Republican paramilitaries: the very good reason for this was that I tackled Republican terrorists every bit as relentlessly as Loyalist terrorists. There was also the very practical consideration that my "specialist area" throughout my career as a detective was the investigation of Loyalist paramilitary crime: the practice at the time was for detectives to focus on their field of expertise rather than dealing with cases across the board.

Many other of the most controversial cases I dealt with have not been included in this narrative, due to the fact that they are at present still subject to the process of criminal investigation and, as such, the rules of sub judice prevail. Still other cases, such as my pursuit of the Loyalist godfather Johnny Adair, have not been included here simply because of considerations of space. I fully intend to make some of these cases the subject of a further book in the future.